# Curbing
# the Global
# Economic
# Downturn

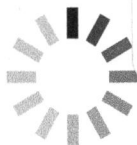

The **Institute of Southeast Asian Studies (ISEAS)** was established as an autonomous organization in 1968. It is a regional centre dedicated to the study of socio-political, security and economic trends and developments in Southeast Asia and its wider geostrategic and economic environment. The Institute's research programmes are the Regional Economic Studies (RES, including ASEAN and APEC), Regional Strategic and Political Studies (RSPS), and Regional Social and Cultural Studies (RSCS).

**ISEAS Publishing**, an established academic press, has issued more than 2,000 books and journals. It is the largest scholarly publisher of research about Southeast Asia from within the region. ISEAS Publishing works with many other academic and trade publishers and distributors to disseminate important research and analyses from and about Southeast Asia to the rest of the world.

# Curbing the Global Economic Downturn

## Southeast Asian Macroeconomic Policy

Edited by
Aekapol Chongvilaivan

LSEAS INSTITUTE OF SOUTHEAST SIAN STUDIES
SINGAPORE

First published in Singapore in 2010 by
ISEAS Publishing
Institute of Southeast Asian Studies
30 Heng Mui Keng Terrace
Pasir Panjang
Singapore 119614

*E-mail*: publish@iseas.edu.sg
*Website*: <http://bookshop.iseas.edu.sg>

*The responsibility for facts and opinions in this publication rests exclusively with the authors and their interpretations do not necessarily reflect the views or the policy of the publisher or its supporters.*

ISEAS Library Cataloguing-in-Publication Data

Curbing the global economic downturn : Southeast Asian macroeconomic policy / edited by Aekapol Chongvilaivan.
  1.  Fiscal policy—Southeast Asia.
  2.  Southeast Asia—Economic policy.
  3.  Southeast Asia—Economic conditions.
  I.  Aekapol Chongvilaivan.
HC441 A24           2010

ISBN 978-981-4279-67-3 (soft cover)
ISBN 978-981-4279-68-0 (E-Book PDF)

Typeset by Superskill Graphics Pte Ltd
Printed in Singapore by Photoplates Private Limited

# CONTENTS

# ACKNOWLEDGEMENTS

Chapter 1: "Macroeconomic Impacts of a Financial Crisis", first appeared as "Measuring Economy-wide Impacts of a Financial Shock", by Iwan J. Azis and Yuri Mansury, *ASEAN Economic Bulletin* 20, no. 2 (2003): 112–27.

Chapter 2: "Capital Inflow Reversals, Current Account Adjustments, and Macroeconomic Performance", first appeared as "Current Account Reversal during a Currency Crisis: The Malaysian Experience", by Gan Wee Beng and Soon Lee Ying, *ASEAN Economic Bulletin* 20, no. 2 (2003): 128–43.

Chapter 3: "Supply-Side Causes of Macroeconomic Fluctuations in a Small Open Economy", first appeared as "Singapore Business Cycles: A Supply-Side Analysis", by Choy Keen Meng, *ASEAN Economic Bulletin* 20, no. 1 (2003): 1–10.

Chapter 4: "Effectiveness of Fiscal Stimuli", first appeared as "The Viability of Fiscal Policy in South Korea, Taiwan, and Thailand", by Tsangyao Chang, Wen Rong Liu, and Henry Thompson, *ASEAN Economic Bulletin* 19, no. 2 (2002): 170–77.

Chapter 5: "Public Debt Sustainability and Its Macroeconomic Impacts", first appeared as "Public Debt Sustainability and Its Macroeconomic Implications in ASEAN-4", by Anthony J. Makin, *ASEAN Economic Bulletin* 22, no. 3 (2005): 284–96.

Chapter 6: "Gains from Intra- and Inter-Regional Trade and Economic Co-operation", first appeared as "Go with the Gang, ASEAN!", by Sasatra

Sudsawasd and Prasopchoke Mongsawad, *ASEAN Economic Bulletin* 24, no. 3 (2007): 339–56.

Chapter 7: "From Economic Reform to Closer Economic Ties: Regional- and National-Level Issues", first appeared as "Closer Trade and Financial Co-operation in ASEAN: Issues at the Regional and National Level with Focus on the Philippines", by Jenny D. Balboa, Erlinda M. Medalla, and Josef T. Yap, *ASEAN Economic Bulletin* 24, no. 1 (2007): 119–37.

Chapter 8: "Macroeconomic Surveillance and Financial Co-operation", first appeared as "The ASEAN Surveillance Process and the East Asian Monetary Fund", by Worapot Manupipatpong, *ASEAN Economic Bulletin* 19, no. 1 (2002): 111–22.

# INTRODUCTION

The global economy has been in the grip of the worst economic downturn since World War II, painting a bleak picture of the global economic outlook around the world. The global economic slump in 2009 witnessed a contraction of the advanced economies by 2 per cent — 2.4 per cent for the United States (US), 1.8 per cent for the European Union (EU), and 5.8 per cent for Japan. While a turnaround in the economic prospects in 2010–11 is expected to be gradual and highly uncertain, the International Monetary Fund (IMF) cautioned that the timing and pace of the recovery hinge critically on strong policy actions to rebalance growth paths.

The impact of the global economic turmoil on the Southeast Asian community, however, is less clear-cut. The Asian Development Bank (ADB) revised downward the major Southeast Asian economies' growth to the worst post-1997 contraction in 2009 — at least 6 per cent for Singapore, 2.7 per cent for Thailand and 0.2 per cent for Malaysia. The rest of the region, in contrast, had yet to feel the ripple effects as the economic growth remained robust — 7 per cent for Vietnam, 4.8 per cent for Cambodia, 4.5 per cent for Indonesia and 3.7 per cent for the Philippines.

The Southeast Asian region as a whole is by no means recession-proof, nevertheless. Recent developments convey a series of caveats and worries about the resilience and sustainability of its economic conditions. The International Labour Organization (ILO), for instance, estimated a spike in unemployment rates across the region from 5.7 per cent in 2008 to 6.2 per cent in 2009. This means 7.2 million more jobless people due to the fallout from the global economic recession.

In fact, among the worst hit regions is Southeast Asia where the emerging economies have long thrived on export-led development and foreign direct investment (FDI). On the one hand, the trade link between Southeast Asia and major industrialized countries is substantial, with the US, the EU and Japan sharing more than 60 per cent of total demand for exports from the region. Undoubtedly, the globally prevailing economic slump saps global demand, cutting back on imports from the region. In the most export-oriented economies like Malaysia, Singapore, and Thailand, export growth was dramatically reduced by some 40 per cent in 2008–09. The gloomy economic fortune around the corner, on the other hand, weakens business confidence and investors' risk appetite. Unceasing capital inflow reversals and sudden capital flight aggravate their real economies vis-à-vis sharp currency depreciation, deferred investment in new plants and machinery, lacklustre durable goods consumption, and impulsive swings in the stock market. ADB estimated that net equity outflows from the region have totalled US$72 billion during the same period.

Southeast Asian policy-makers have eased macroeconomic policy to tackle the looming economic climate — falling industrial orders, shrinking industrial production, slashed export demand and deteriorating labour markets. The attempts at the national level to weather the global economic storm and bolster the economic cycle include the boldest stimulus packages that many governments in the region unilaterally injected into their economies and huge cuts in interest rates that the central banks announced.

Many experts, nonetheless, have argued that those fiscal and monetary expansions are unlikely to actually provide much of a boost to the regional economy. Now that all countries cannot export at the same time, the liquidity of all governments around the world that is poured into their economies is unlikely to help rejuvenate export performance and beef-up employment and production. In addition, the limited multiplier effects of fiscal and monetary stimuli are also attributable to emerging protectionism — a series of hikes in tariff and non-tariff barriers like anti-dumping actions, voluntary export restraints, standards, and labour- and capital-market regulations — that emanated from uncoordinated macroeconomic actions to fight the prolonged economic depression. These misguided government interventions pose serious challenges to the Southeast Asian economic community.

The first quarter of 2009 has seen a wide array of coordinated arrangements at the regional and international levels to jointly unravel emerging trade protection and help bring the economies out of the current recession as soon as possible. The leaders of the Association of Southeast Asian Nations (ASEAN) at the summit meeting made a stand against protectionism and agreed on collective macroeconomic policies, including fiscal stimulus, monetary easing, access to credit and trade financing, and measures to revive buoyant domestic demand. The G20 Summit also concluded that the member countries are now in dire need of fine-tuning resilient packages that are able to get growth back, to create jobs for citizens, and to re-globalize the international community.

Yet "how" to optimally pursue collaborative macroeconomic policy remains unanswered. The ASEAN Summit Meeting did not provide any specific policies or actions that its members can take on. Neither did the G20 Summit reached a consensus on how to solve the global economic turmoil. The quest for regional and global solutions has been hampered critically by the complication of individual economies and the diverse levels of economic and cultural development.

After all, there is no one-size-fit-all panacea for economic ills. The answer to this question lies with the in-depth, region-specific research inquiries into how macroeconomic tools are at work in the Southeast Asian economies. The objective of this book is to examine in-depth region-specific research on how macroeconomic tools are at work in the Southeast Asian countries. The compilation from *ASEAN Economic Bulletin* has provided this and a forum for policy-oriented discussion of contemporary economic interest. The Bulletin is also well-established as a series of original contributions on the ample scope of economic studies, that is, macroeconomics, public economics, international trade and finance, development economics, financial economics, agricultural economics and environmental economics, among many others.

In a nutshell, this book will establish itself as a compendium that provides a timely response to and a key reference for a broad range of readerships — policy-makers, practitioners, academics, and serious researchers who are interested in developments and designs of macroeconomic policy and economic co-operation that potentially help the Southeast Asian economies embark upon the adverse impacts of the global economic downturn.

All said and done, I would like to confer my heartfelt thanks to all *ASEAN Economic Bulletin* contributors whose cutting-edge research paved the way toward the production of this book. In particular, my special thanks are due to Iwan J. Azis, Yuri Mansury, Gan Wee Beng, Soon Lee Ying, Choy Keen Meng, Tsangyao Chang, Wen Rong Liu, Henry Thompson, Anthony J. Makin, Sasatra Sudsawasd, Prasopchoke Mongsawad, Jenny D. Balboa, Erlinda M. Medalla, Josef T. Yap, and Worapot Manupipatpong. I must also gratefully acknowledge Triena Ong for her advices on publication of this book. Last but not least, the book would not have been possible without support and encouragement rendered by Director K. Kesavapany, Denis Hew, and Lee Poh Onn.

*Editor*
*Aekapol Chongvilaivan*
*Fellow and ASEAN Economic Bulletin Co-editor*
*Regional Economic Studies*
*Institute of Southeast Asian Studies*
*April 2009*

# LIST OF CONTRIBUTORS

**Iwan J. Azis** is a Professor in Johnson Graduate School of Management at Cornell University in New York, USA.

**Jenny D. Balboa** is Supervising Research Specialist at the Philippine Institute for Development Studies.

**Tsangyao Chang** is Professor in the Department of Economics at Feng Chia University in Taichung, Taiwan.

**Choy Keen Meng** is a Postdoctoral Fellow in the Department of Economics, National University of Singapore.

**Gan Wee Beng** is Executive Director of CIMB Investment Bank, Kuala Lumpur, Malaysia.

**Wen Rong Liu** is Associate Professor of Co-operative Economics at Feng Chia University, Taichung, Taiwan.

**Anthony J. Makin** is Professor of Economics at Griffith Business School, Griffith University, Australia.

**Yuri Mansury** is currently a Ruth L. Kirschstein post-doctoral research fellow in the Division of Health Sciences and Technology, Massachusetts Institute of Technology in Cambridge, USA.

**Worapot Manupipatpong** is Director of the Bureau of Finance and Surveillance at the ASEAN Secretariat in Jakarta.

**Erlinda M. Medalla** is Senior Research Fellow at the Philippine Institute for Development Studies.

**Prasopchoke Mongsawad** is Assistant Professor of Economics at the School of Development Economics, National Institute of Development Administration, Bangkok, Thailand.

**Soon Lee Ying** is Associate Professor at the Nanyang Business School, Nanyang Technological University, Singapore.

**Sasatra Sudsawasd** is Assistant Professor of Economics at the School of Development Economics, National Institute of Development Administration, Bangkok, Thailand.

**Henry Thompson** is Professor of Economics at Auburn University, Alabama, USA.

**Josef T. Yap** is President of the Philippine Institute for Development Studies.

# PART I

## ECONOMIC FLUCTUATIONS: MACROECONOMIC EFFECTS AND POLICY RESPONSES

# 1

# MACROECONOMIC IMPACTS OF A FINANCIAL CRISIS

## Iwan J. Azis and Yuri Mansury

## I. INTRODUCTION

The onset of the Asian financial shock in the summer of 1997 led to a simultaneous contraction of almost all sectors of production in the crisis-hit country. While the theory of propagation mechanisms from the financial to the real sector in business cycle has been explored (see, for example, Bernanke, Gertler, and Gilchrist 1996), empirical works that aim to identify and measure a shock impact within a general equilibrium framework are rare. This paper attempts to fill the gap.

Using the specific case of Indonesia, Thorbecke (1998) and Azis (1998, 2000*a*) were among the first who attempted to adopt a general equilibrium model for such an analysis. While the former used the Social Accounting Matrix (SAM) multipliers, the latter traced the economy-wide impacts using Structural Path Analysis (SPA) and subsequently employed a price-endogenous CGE model with detailed specifications of the financial sector.[1]

The limitation of previous SAM multipliers and SPA studies was the arbitrary manner with which the shock is introduced to the modelled economic system. Within these studies, the standard practice was to induce an artificial fall in the output of sectors that are known *ex-post* to contract during the crisis. Such an *ad hoc* method of introducing shock into the system does not capture the actual mechanics of the crisis which was triggered by movements in the financial variables (i.e., foreign capital) rather than in production. The problem is that sectoral output can decline because of numerous types of shocks, of which a financial turmoil is only one of them. Simply reducing the sectoral output artificially thus fails to recognize the origin of the crisis and neglects the linkage between financial sector and the rest of the economy.

Another consequence of an *ad hoc* introduction of the shock is that it prohibits us from gauging the magnitude of the contraction if the crisis had been the only shock that occurred, *ceteris paribus*. Instead of determining endogenously the impact of the crisis on production, the decline in production is predetermined exogenously based on actual data as if the decline is all due to the financial crisis. This tacit assumption is likely to bias any study of impact estimation. The sources of the bias are the exclusion of other shocks that had nothing to do with the financial crisis (for example, the El Nino-induced drought that caused agriculture-crop failures, and massive haze problems that led to further decline in the agricultural output).

Using a more sophisticated financial CGE model would be desirable. However, the needed data are often lacking, and capturing the intricate mechanisms of variables in such a model is far from easy. In this paper, we propose an alternative method to transcend the aforementioned limitation of the standard SAM-based approach without having to construct a CGE model. Specifically, we augment the standard SAM by incorporating a fairly detailed financial sector based on the flow-of-funds data, thus allowing financial variables to be the original source of the shock (a standard SAM condenses financial transactions into a single savings/investments account). While the concept of the flow-of-funds matrix is not new, our contribution is in the *explicit* use of such matrix in the SAM system. The construction of the flow-of-funds matrix is described in the Appendix.

## II. METHODOLOGY

The standard inverse of $(I - A_n)$ from the following multiplier $M_a$

$$y_n = A_n y_n + x = (I - A_n)^{-1}x = M_a x, \tag{1}$$

is a useful tool for estimating the impact of an exogenous shock on income of the endogenous accounts. It captures the direct and indirect effects of the shock. However, a multiplier analysis does not reveal the network of paths through which an injection is transmitted (Defourney and Thorbecke 1984). To identify the principal paths of transmission, we employ the SPA method.

The starting point in SPA is to equate the intensity of an "influence" travelling from pole $i$ to pole $j$ as the SAM average propensity $a_{ji}$.[2] Define an *arc* $(i, j)$ as the link between the pole of origin and that of destination. Define a *path* as a sequence of consecutive arcs — the *length* of which is the number of arcs between the origin and destination poles. For example, *arc* $(i, j)$ is a path with unit length, whereas *path* $(i, x, y, j)$ has length equal to three. An *elementary path* is a path that does not pass more than once through the same pole. In contrast, a *circuit* is a path for which the starting pole of an influence is also its destination pole. For example, the *path* $(x, y, z, x)$ is a circuit.

SPA recognizes three types of "influences", namely (1) direct influence *DI*; (2) total influence *TI*; and (3) global influence *GI*. The distinction among these influences will be explored next. But first, Figure 1 illustrates these three types of influences travelling from pole $i$ to pole $j$. Figure 1A illustrates direct influence *DI*, Figure 1B total influence *TI*, and Figure 1C global influence *GI*.

Direct influence $DI_{(i \to j)}$ travels through the elementary path that connects two poles $i$ and $j$. It is defined as the change in income or production of pole $j$ induced by an additional one dollar (or any unit of currency) generated in $i$. A direct influence $DI_{(i \to j)}$ that travels along an *arc* $(i, j)$ is equal to the average expenditure propensity $a_{ji}$:

$$DI_{(i \to j)} = a_{ji}. \qquad (2)$$

But $DI_{(i \to j)}$ can also travel along a *path* $(i, \ldots, j)$ with length greater than one, in which case its magnitude is the product of the intensities of the arcs connecting the path. For example, the direct influence that traverses the *path* $(i, x, y, j)$ has the magnitude $a_{xi} \cdot a_{yx} \cdot a_{jy}$ (see Figure 1A).

In most cases, poles along an elementary path are connected to other poles or paths, forming closed circuits that amplify the direct influences. Total influence $TI_{(i \to j)}$ along the *path* $(i, \ldots, j)$ is defined as $DI_{(i \to j)}$ plus all of the indirect effects of the circuits formed along that path. For example, the direct influence $a_{xi} a_{yx}$ in Figure 1B is transmitted back from $y$ to $x$, creating a circuit with the magnitude $(a_{xi} a_{yx})(a_{xy} + a_{zy} a_{xz})$, which in turn is transmitted back to $y$. Hence, a series of feedback impulses are generated along that circuit, yielding a new set of multipliers:

$$a_{xi} a_{yx} [I - a_{yx}(a_{xy} + a_{zy} a_{xz})]^{-1}. \qquad (3)$$

To compute total influence, the term in Equation 3 has to be multiplied by $a_{jy}$ because an influence has to traverse the *arc* $(y, j)$ before reaching the

## FIGURE 1
### Types of Influences in a Structural Path Analysis

(A) Direct influence on *path*(*i*, *x*, *y*, *j*)

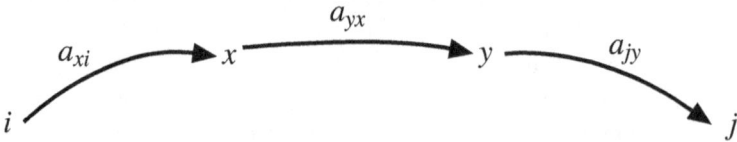

(B) Total influence on *path*(*i*, *x*, *y*, *j*), including adjacent circuits

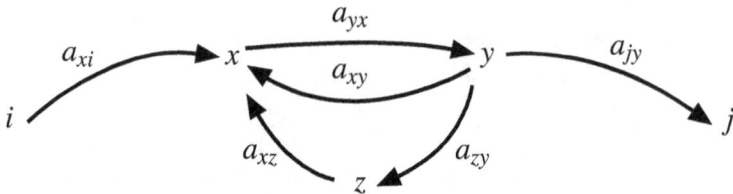

(C) Global influence: All elementary paths and circuits linking
    poles *i* and *j*

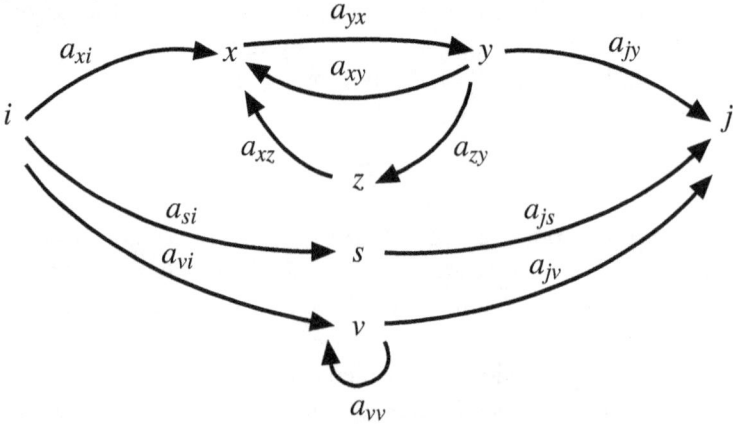

final destination at pole $j$ (see Figure 1B). The resulting total influence $TI_{(i \to j)}$ is therefore:

$$TI_{(i \to j)} = a_{xi} a_{yx} a_{jy} [I - a_{yx}(a_{xy} + a_{zy} a_{xz})]^{-1}. \qquad (4)$$

The sum of all total influences $TI_{(i \to j)}$ between poles $i$ and $j$ constitutes global influence $GI_{(i \to j)}$, which measures the total changes in production or income of pole $j$ due to injecting pole $i$ with one dollar of additional income. In effect, global influence $GI_{(i \to j)}$ encapsulates all the direct as well as the feedback effects generated by the adjacent circuits (see Figure 1C). By construction, the magnitude of $GI_{(i \to j)}$ is equal to the SAM multiplier $M_{aij}$, and hence the matrix of multiplier $M_a$ (see Equation 1) can also be called the matrix of global influence.

In analysing the impact of a crisis, the pertinent question is how the contraction in production due to the shock affects various types of labours and ultimately different household groups.

To see how SPA can be utilized against the backdrop of a financial crisis, consider a hypothetical economy with a single household, two sectors (agriculture and manufacturing), and two factors of production (capital and labour). In such an economy, capital rents and labour wages constitute the total earnings of household. For simplicity, assume also that agriculture exclusively employs labour, while manufacturing employs only capital. However, let us assume that the production of agriculture requires the intermediate input from the manufacturing sector and vice versa.

Suppose that in such a hypothetical economy, foreign investors suddenly decide to withdraw their capital investments (i.e., a financial shock due to the reverse flows of foreign capital). Figure 2 shows the paths through which such an exogenous shock in *Foreign Capital* is transmitted to *Household*. The neoclassical story here is as follows. First, the withdrawal of foreign capital leads to a contraction in real investments, which reduces the sales of both manufacturing and agriculture goods, in turn depressing the production of both. As a result, capital and labour experience a fall in income, which translates into lower household income. Alternatively, the Keynesian story is as follows. An imminent financial crisis due to the flight of foreign capital leads to a general expectation of an economic contraction, and hence falling revenues for business firms. Anticipating a looming depression, firms respond by reducing their inventories *vis-à-vis* lower output, yet in doing so inevitably affect household incomes in an adverse manner.

Consider the elementary path *Foreign Capital → Investments → Manufacturing Sales → Manufacturing Production → Capital → Household.* Component of the shock that travels directly through that elementary path, without detour, represents an instance of the direct influence $DI_{(Foreign\ Capital \to Household)}$.

However, part of the shock travelled from manufacturing production to agriculture sales via an input-output link, then hitting back manufacturing sales via the other input-output link. Such a path contains the circuit *Sales: Manufacturing → Manufacturing Production → Agriculture Sales → Agriculture Production → Manufacturing Sales* (recall that a circuit begins and ends on the same pole). The direct influence and the circuit-feedback effects constitute an instance of the total influence $TI_{(Foreign\ Capital \to Household)}$.

FIGURE 2
SPA of a Hypothetical Economy

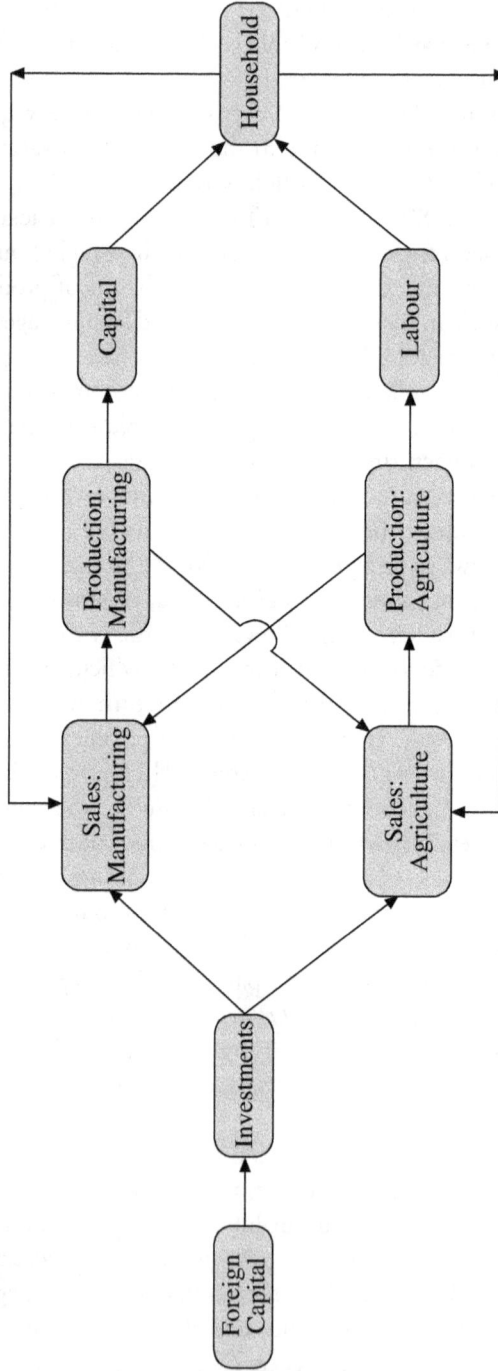

Finally, the cumulative impact of all total influences between foreign capital and household represents the global influence $GI_{(Foreign\ Capital\to\ Household)}$. By construction, the magnitude of the global influence is equal to the multiplier impact on household income due to $1 of foreign capital withdrawal.

## III. MULTIPLIER ANALYSIS

For the multiplier analysis, we endogenize 94 out of 102 accounts from the 1995-SAM. The standard (real sector) SAM is expanded by incorporating the flow-of-funds matrix compiled from various sources.[3]

The following are the stages of simulation:

1. Foreign equity flows (*vis-à-vis* portfolio investments) plunged by 92 per cent between 1995 and 1997.
2. In the same period between 1995 and 1997, time deposits denominated in local currency (rupiah) fell by 75 per cent, while foreign currency deposits rose by 572 per cent.
3. Subsequently, between 1997 and 1998 the flows of foreign private debt fell by 824 per cent. The outflows of private capital, however, were compensated to some extent by the inflows of official foreign debts (mainly IMF debt disbursements). We assume that the inflows of official debts translated into a 150 per cent increase in government spending (both on- and off-budget).
4. During 1997–98 the liquidity credit issued by the Indonesian central bank increased by 690 per cent.
5. Finally, between 1998 and 1999 there was a severe credit crunch such that commercial bank credit plunged by 188 per cent. We assume that in this last stage of the simulation, banks extended no new loans to businesses. That is, extended new credit fell to zero.

A series of tables are generated (available upon request) following the above stages (normalized by setting the base run to unity). On the trend of value-added, at the end of stage 5 the worst performing sectors relative to the base run are, from worst to better, construction, banking and insurance, mining, social services, and trade and storage. The best performing sectors are, in declining order, public administration, textiles, restaurant and hotel, air transportation, and food crops.

The massive decline in service-oriented activities appears due to their close link to the financial sector *vis-à-vis* foreign portfolio investments and commercial bank loans. By contrast, manufacturing sectors performed relatively better because they consist mostly of medium and small-scale enterprises that are less dependent on the banking system. In addition, exports of the manufacturing sector constituted a significant portion of output and thus were less susceptible to a recession in the domestic market.

It is worth noting that the agricultural sector never appears as one of the hardest-hit sectors in any stage of the simulation. This finding shows that the contraction in agricultural sector was not due to the financial crisis, but rather to the fortuitous drought brought about by El Nino and other weather-related factors (Johnson 1998). This sector remains the economy's main generator of employment despite its declining share in output and became even more so during the crisis.[4] The crisis actually had reversed the shift of employment from agriculture to manufacturing. While employment in virtually every other sector contracted, agriculture employment actually rose by 10 per cent. In light of the fall in manufacturing exports, evidently workers had drifted from tradable activities in manufacturing back to agriculture.

On the labour income, at the end of stage 5, the worst-fared factors relative to the base run are, from worst to better, manual paid rural, unpaid urban professionals, manual paid urban, manual unpaid urban, and private capital. While the best performing factors are, in declining order, paid rural professionals, paid urban professionals, clerical paid rural, unpaid agricultural workers, and paid agricultural workers.

The trend of incomes of institutions shows that in stage 1 the flight of foreign equity led to a declining income for all institutions. The hardest-hit households here are rural low (–6.22 per cent), urban low (–5.89 per cent), urban high (–5.31 per cent), small farmers (–5.11 per cent), and medium farmers (–5.10 per cent). In stage 2, the shift from the rupiah time deposits to foreign currency deposits resulted only in a marginal increase of income across all households.

In stage 3, institutions that are most adversely affected are private companies (–157.40 per cent), domestic banks (–45.55 per cent), urban low (–14.77 per cent), urban high (–12.80 per cent), and urban non-labour (–11.26 per cent). At this stage, the five worst-fared institutions relative to the base run are private companies, domestic banks, urban low, urban high, and urban non-labour. It comes as no surprise that private companies and domestic banks suffered the most from the capital outflows. At the same time, however, there is an inflow of official debts (including from the IMF).

It is noteworthy that in contrast to stage 2, at the end of stage 3 urban households become the hardest-hit households replacing their rural counterparts. This reversal of ranking is due to the fact that rural households benefited significantly from increased government spending and, hence, experienced a lower fall in income than did the urban dwellers. Thus, due to higher government expenditures funded by IMF debt disbursements, in stage 3 households that fared the *best* relative to the base run are those headed by agricultural employees, small farmers, rural low, rural high, and large farmers. The relatively shielded income of agricultural workers is consistent with the actual realization.

In stage 4, liquidity injection from the central bank (*Bantuan Likuiditas Bank Indonesia* or BLBI) to the private sector prevented institutions from a collapse, and in some cases they even grew at the following rates: domestic banks (+65.17 per cent), private companies (+7.30 per cent), urban low (+1.73 per cent), rural low (+1.70 per cent), and urban high (+1.51 per cent). As expected, domestic banks and private companies benefited significantly from BI liquidity injection. At this stage, the hardest-hit institutions relative to the base run consists of private companies, urban low, urban high, urban non-labour, and medium farmers.

However, as the largest recipient banks are politically powerful, BLBI created an extreme opportunity for "moral hazard". More seriously, the facility was extended without the central bank being able to exercise any control over the uses that the recipient banks made of it. Within just a few months, the extended BLBI reached Rp100 trillion, much of which was used to buy foreign exchange and shift assets abroad. As a result, and despite the massive liquidity injection, a credit crunch was inevitable, severely curtailing the income of institutions further. The most adversely affected are private companies (−18.65 per cent), urban low (−13.97 per cent), rural low (−13.78 per cent), urban high (−12.25 per cent), and medium farmers (−11.49 per cent). At the end of this stage, the hardest-hit institutions relative to the base run are (from worst to better) private companies, urban low, urban high, rural low, and medium farmers. The best performing households are (in declining order) agricultural workers, small farmers, rural high, large farmers, and urban non-labour.

While generally the above outcomes are consistent with the actual data, the ranking for real incomes in 1995 and 1998 is slightly different, i.e., urban low (−18.9 per cent), rural non-labour (−17.2 per cent), urban non-labour (−16.1 per cent), rural low (−12.9 per cent), and urban high (−10.9 per cent). Two explanations account for the discrepancy. First, our simulation excludes non-financial shocks that also had adverse consequences on the economy (for example, El Nino-induced draught, the political turmoil that brought down the Soeharto government, and the haze problems). In a sense, our model succeeded in establishing the *net* impact of a shock due to the financial crisis alone by holding everything else constant. The other missing element is the effect of changes in relative prices — due to large currency depreciation and liquidity crunch during the crisis — that cannot be captured within an exogenous-price model. A systematic impact analysis of relative-price changes must resort to a price-endogenous CGE model.

Despite the limited disaggregation of household level, our simulation was able to replicate the actual changes in *aggregate* measures of income inequality. An unambiguous comparison of aggregate inequality requires a cardinal measure. We chose to employ measures that satisfy the symmetry, replication invariance, mean independence, and transfer axioms, namely coefficient of variations, Gini coefficient, and Theil entropy index (Sen 1997).

We compute the inequality measures to facilitate comparison of household income distribution based on actual 1995 SUSENAS data with that implied in the last stage of our model simulation. This comparison is thus based on aggregate data rather than household-level data. It is revealed that all measures suggest the distribution of income became less unequal due to the series of events during the crisis. The more egalitarian distribution is consistent with the *actual* reported Gini coefficients, both overall and in urban and rural areas, which had been on a declining trend during the crisis (Irawan and Romdiati 2000).

The robustness of the above finding can be checked through a sensitivity analysis. We found that under a broad range of income elasticities, there is no change in the ranking of hardest-hit sectors, factors, and households due to the multiplier impact of the crisis. Specifically, varying households' income elasticity of consumption between 0.9 and 1.1 result in the same ranking of hardest-hit sectors, factors, and households. Moreover, under no circumstances the multipliers differ from the original by more than 2 per cent. There is a minor rearrangement outside of the top-five most-affected accounts, but our conclusion from the previous section remains unchanged. Hence, even if, as often suggested, the structure of the SAM changed during the crisis, it has little bearing on the results of our impact analysis.

## IV. STRUCTURAL PATH ANALYSIS

To open the "black box", a further step is taken to disentangle the inextricably linked relationship between the financial sector and the real sector and the income block. This is accomplished by using a structural path analysis (SPA), which decomposes the SAM multipliers (or the global influences) into direct and indirect influences.

Decomposing a large-scale SAM is not a trivial task. In the Indonesian case where ninety-four accounts are designated as endogenous, the number of elementary paths between any two poles can be very large.[5] However, we found that in the case of the Indonesian SAM it is extremely rare to find a path of length four or longer transmitting more than 0.1 per cent of the global influence. Below we present the results from applying SPA selectively to the stages in which institutions experienced a decline in income, namely, stages one, three, and five.

Multiplier analysis identifies five institutions that suffered the most from the flight of foreign equity (stage 1), namely, rural low, urban low, urban high, small farmers, and medium farmers. Here we seek to establish the channels through which the shock was transmitted from foreign equity to these households. We shall use the prefixes $P$ and $D$ to abbreviate production activity and domestic commodity, respectively. For example, $PFood$ denotes the activity of producing food crops, whereas $DFood$ designates the commodity (output) from that sector that was sold domestically.

Table 1 shows the application of SPA to the paths that link foreign equity $ForEquity$ to the hardest-hit household groups. In all cases, households suffered due to the fall in investment demand $Invest$ for the output from various sectors. $Construction$ proved to be the dominant channel of transmission: either the first- or the second-largest total influence $TI$ is transmitted via construction. It can also be seen that except for urban high $UrbHigh$, the hardest-hit households suffered primarily because of the loss in income as manual-paid workers $ManPd$ in the construction sector.

In light of the fact that construction was the hardest-hit sector during the crisis, SPA shows how the flight of foreign equity translated into the fall in household income via declining construction activity. However, the extent to which income was affected by the decline in construction is not uniform across different groups. In particular, the low-income non-agricultural households were more susceptible due to heavy reliance on income from their occupation as manual workers in construction. In the case of rural low, the cumulative total influence $TI$ transmitted from foreign equity to construction to manual workers (both paid and unpaid) to rural low constituted 44.6 per cent of the global influence $GI$ originated in foreign equity (case 1, Table 1). For urban low, cumulative total influence from the same paths made of 31.4 per cent of the global influence (case 2, Table 1).

By contrast, the élite urban high and the poor agricultural households of small and medium farmers exhibited more diversified sources of income. In the case of urban high, the shock from foreign equity was transmitted mainly through clerical paid workers $ClerPdUrb$ in the $banking$ sector (6.4 per cent of $GI$), while a close second was the transmission via construction to this category of workers (5.9 per cent of $GI$).

# TABLE 1
## Structural Path Analysis: Foreign Equity as the Pole of Origin

| Case | Origin of Shock (i) | Destination (j) | Global Influence GI | Elementary Path i→j | Direct Influence DI | Path Multiplier $M_p$ | Total Influence TI | TI/GI (%) |
|---|---|---|---|---|---|---|---|---|
| 1 | ForEquity | RurLow | 0.103 | ForEquity→Invest→DConstruct→PConstruct→ManPdRur→RurLow | 0.032 | 1.267 | 0.041 | 39.5 |
| | | | | ForEquity→Invest→DConstruct→PConstruct→ManURur→RurLow | 0.004 | 1.267 | 0.005 | 5.1 |
| | | | | ForEquity→Invest→DNonFood→PNonFood→Land→RurLow | 0.000 | 1.651 | 0.001 | 0.5 |
| | | | | ForEquity→Invest→Dmining→PMining→ManPRur→RurLow | 0.001 | 1.271 | 0.001 | 1.0 |
| | | | | ForEquity→Invest→Dmining→PMining→ManURur→RurLow | 0.001 | 1.270 | 0.001 | 0.6 |
| 2 | ForEquity | UrbLow | 0.138 | ForEquity→Invest→DConstruct→PConstruct→ManPdUrb→UrbLow | 0.028 | 1.313 | 0.037 | 26.7 |
| | | | | ForEquity→Invest→DConstruct→PConstruct→ManUUrb→UrbLow | 0.005 | 1.306 | 0.006 | 4.7 |
| | | | | ForEquity→Invest→DTextile→PTextile→ManPdUrb→UrbLow | 0.002 | 1.680 | 0.003 | 2.4 |
| | | | | ForEquity→Invest→DConstruct→PConstruct→ClerPdUrb→UrbLow | 0.002 | 1.365 | 0.003 | 2.0 |
| | | | | ForEquity→Invest→Dbank→PBank→ClerPdUrb→UrbLow | 0.002 | 1.459 | 0.003 | 2.2 |
| 3 | ForEquity | UrbHigh | 0.141 | ForEquity→Invest→DBank→PBank→ClerPdUrb→UrbHigh | 0.006 | 1.446 | 0.009 | 6.4 |
| | | | | ForEquity→Invest→DConstruct→PConstruct→ClerPdUrb→UrbHigh | 0.006 | 1.357 | 0.008 | 5.9 |
| | | | | ForEquity→Invest→DConstruct→PConstruct→ProfPdUrb→UrbHigh | 0.005 | 1.329 | 0.007 | 5.0 |
| | | | | ForEquity→Invest→DConstruct→PConstruct→OtCapUrb→UrbHigh | 0.004 | 1.357 | 0.005 | 3.8 |
| | | | | ForEquity→Invest→DConstruct→PConstruct→ManPdUrb→UrbHigh | 0.003 | 1.378 | 0.004 | 3.0 |
| 4 | ForEquity | FarmSml | 0.050 | ForEquity→Invest→DConstruct→PConstruct→ManPdRur→FarmSml | 0.004 | 1.278 | 0.005 | 10.1 |
| | | | | ForEquity→Invest→DConstruct→PConstruct→OtCapRur→FarmSml | 0.001 | 1.315 | 0.002 | 3.7 |
| | | | | ForEquity→Invest→DNonFood→PNonFood→AgUnpaid→FarmSml | 0.000 | 1.724 | 0.001 | 1.1 |
| | | | | ForEquity→Invest→DTextile→PTextile→OtCapRur→FarmSml | 0.000 | 1.681 | 0.001 | 1.4 |
| | | | | ForEquity→Invest→Dconstruct→PConstruct→ManPdUrb→FarmSml | 0.001 | 1.303 | 0.001 | 1.4 |
| 5 | ForEquity | FarmMed | 0.027 | ForEquity→Invest→DConstruct→PConstruct→ManPdRur→FarmMed | 0.001 | 1.241 | 0.001 | 4.8 |
| | | | | ForEquity→Invest→DConstruct→PConstruct→OtCapRur→FarmMed | 0.001 | 1.285 | 0.001 | 3.6 |
| | | | | ForEquity→Invest→DNonFood→PNonFood→AgPaid→FarmMed | 0.000 | 1.609 | 0.000 | 0.1 |
| | | | | ForEquity→Invest→DNonFood→PNonFood→AgUnpaid→FarmMed | 0.000 | 1.706 | 0.000 | 1.2 |
| | | | | ForEquity→Invest→DNonFood→PNonFood→ManPRur→FarmMed | 0.000 | 1.611 | 0.000 | 0.0 |

NOTES: These abbreviations are used: For factors of production: Ag = Agricultural, Man = Manual Operator, Cler = Clerical, Pro = Professional, Pd = Paid, U = Unpaid, Rur = Rural, Urb = Urban (e.g. AgPdUrb = Agricultural Paid Urban), OtCapRur = Other (Unincorporated) Rural Capital, OtCapUrb = Other (Unincorporated) Urban Capital, PrivCap = Private Capital. For institutions: Rur = Rural, Urb = Urban. For production: P = Production sector, D = Domestic Commodity.

SOURCE: Authors' simulation using the Indonesian 1995 SAM augmented by the flow of funds.

Figure 3 exhibits the three largest paths (in terms of $TI/GI$) for each of the three households that were hit the hardest in stage 1, namely, rural low, urban low, and urban high. The figure is meant to show the ubiquitous channels through which construction affects the hardest-hit households.

In stage 3, multiplier analysis indicates that private companies, domestic banks, urban low, urban high, and urban non-labour are the institutions that suffered the most when foreign lenders refused to rollover the debts of the private sector. Table 2 shows that the impact on private companies was a direct consequence of the sudden reversal in foreign debt flows (98.5 per cent of $GI$), while other channels were essentially trivial. It is thus through the direct impact of the reversal in foreign debt flows that Indonesian corporations ended up as the most battered institution during the crisis. In the case of domestic banks, *DomBank*, the direct channel was also dominant (33.7 per cent of $GI$), but the indirect impact due to client companies withdrawing their time deposits (23.2 per cent of $GI$) and reducing their equity participation (22.8 per cent) was significant as well. Indeed, the inter-linkages between client firms and banks during the Asian financial crisis based on the balance sheet effect (Krugman 2001) have been identified clearly by some authors. Using the case of Korea, Bae, Kang, and Lim (2002) discussed such inter-linkages through the bank and firm values.

For the three household groups that were hardest hit in this stage, none of the individual paths was significant enough to contribute more than 2 per cent of $GI$.

Figure 4 illustrates the relationships contained in Table 2. To avoid clutter we show only the three largest paths (in terms of $TI/GI$) for each of the five institutions that were hardest hit in stage 1. Figure 4 reveals that, in contrast to stage 1 where the shock from foreign equity was reverberated to households via production activities, here the shock from foreign debt was transmitted either directly or through inter-institution transfers. Further, the role of private companies is pivotal in the circular distribution of the transfers. For example, the shock from foreign debt was partly transmitted via the banking system to companies, which in turn withdrew their time deposits in domestic banks and reduced their dividend payments to urban low, urban high, and urban non-labour.

In the final stage, multiplier analysis shows that credit crunch severely curtailed the income of private companies, urban low, rural low, urban high, and medium farmers. Table 3 shows that here also the construction sector proves to be instrumental in transmitting the shock from the credit crunch to the fall in household income. But the *textile* sector emerges as an important secondary channel, particularly for companies, urban low, and rural low.

FIGURE 3

Paths from a Shock in Foreign Equity: Ubiquitous Channels Through Which Construction Affects Household Incomes

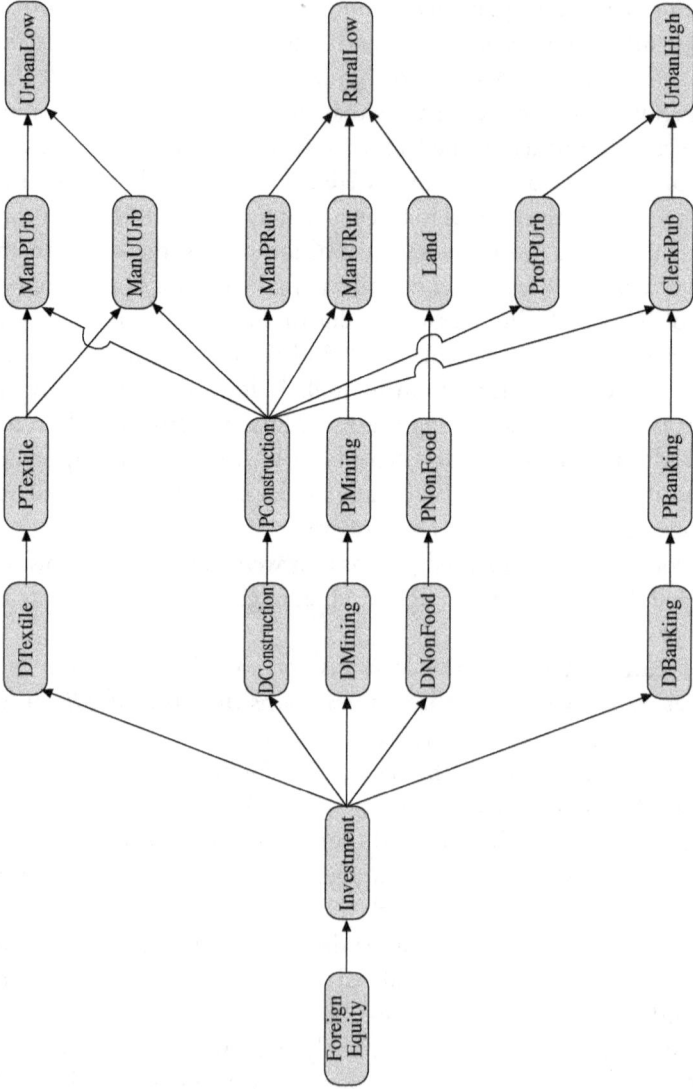

## TABLE 2
### Structural Path Analysis: Foreign Debt as the Pole of Origin

| Case | Origin of Shock (i) | Destination (j) | Global Influence GI | Elementary Path i → j | Direct Influence DI | Path Multiplier $M_p$ | Total Influence TI | TI/GI (%) |
|---|---|---|---|---|---|---|---|---|
| 1 | ForDebt | Company | 0.708 | ForDebt → Company | 0.642 | 1.087 | 0.697 | 98.5 |
| | | | | ForDebt → DomBank → Company | 0.001 | 1.146 | 0.001 | 0.2 |
| | | | | ForDebt → CentralBank → Company | 0.000 | 1.105 | 0.000 | 0.0 |
| | | | | ForDebt → CentralBank → DomBank → Company | 0.000 | 1.146 | 0.000 | 0.0 |
| | | | | ForDebt → ForBank → CentralBank → Company | 0.000 | 1.106 | 0.000 | 0.0 |
| 2 | ForDebt | DomBank | 0.189 | ForDebt → DomBank | 0.059 | 1.081 | 0.064 | 33.7 |
| | | | | ForDebt → Company → TimeDpt → DomBank | 0.038 | 1.146 | 0.044 | 23.2 |
| | | | | ForDebt → Company → DomBank | 0.038 | 1.146 | 0.043 | 22.8 |
| | | | | ForDebt → Company → ForDpt → DomBank | 0.012 | 1.147 | 0.014 | 7.6 |
| | | | | ForDebt → Company → DemandDpt → DomBank | 0.008 | 1.146 | 0.009 | 5.0 |
| 3 | ForDebt | UrbLow | 0.048 | ForDebt → Company → UrbLow | 0.000 | 1.246 | 0.000 | 0.2 |
| | | | | ForDebt → DomBank → Company → UrbLow | 0.000 | 1.303 | 0.000 | 0.0 |
| 4 | ForDebt | UrbHigh | 0.049 | ForDebt → Company → UrbHigh | 0.000 | 1.282 | 0.000 | 0.1 |
| | | | | ForDebt → DomBank → Company → UrbHigh | 0.000 | 1.330 | 0.000 | 0.0 |
| 5 | ForDebt | UrbNonLabour | 0.010 | ForDebt → Company → UrbNonLabour | 0.000 | 1.123 | 0.000 | 1.6 |
| | | | | ForDebt → Company → RurHigh → UrbNonLabour | 0.000 | 1.257 | 0.000 | 0.0 |
| | | | | ForDebt → Company → UrbLow → UrbNonLabour | 0.000 | 1.282 | 0.000 | 0.0 |
| | | | | ForDebt → DomBank → Company → UrbNonLabour | 0.000 | 1.180 | 0.000 | 0.0 |

NOTES: These abbreviations are used: For factors of production: $Ag$ = Agricultural, $Man$ = Manual Operator, $Cler$ = Clerical, $Pro$ = Professional, $Pd$ = Paid, $U$ = Unpaid, $Rur$ = Rural, $Urb$ = Urban (e.g., $AgPdUrb$ = Agricultural Paid Urban), $OtCapRur$ = Other (Unincorporated) Rural Capital, $OtCapUrb$ = Other (Unincorporated) Urban Capital, $PrivCap$ = Private Capital. For institutions: $Rur$ = Rural, $Urb$ = Urban. For production: $P$ = Production sector, $D$ = Domestic Commodity.

SOURCE: Authors' simulation using the Indonesian 1995 SAM augmented by the flow of funds.

**FIGURE 4**
**Paths from a Shock in Foreign Debt: Channels Through Which Corporate and Banking Sectors Affect Household Incomes**

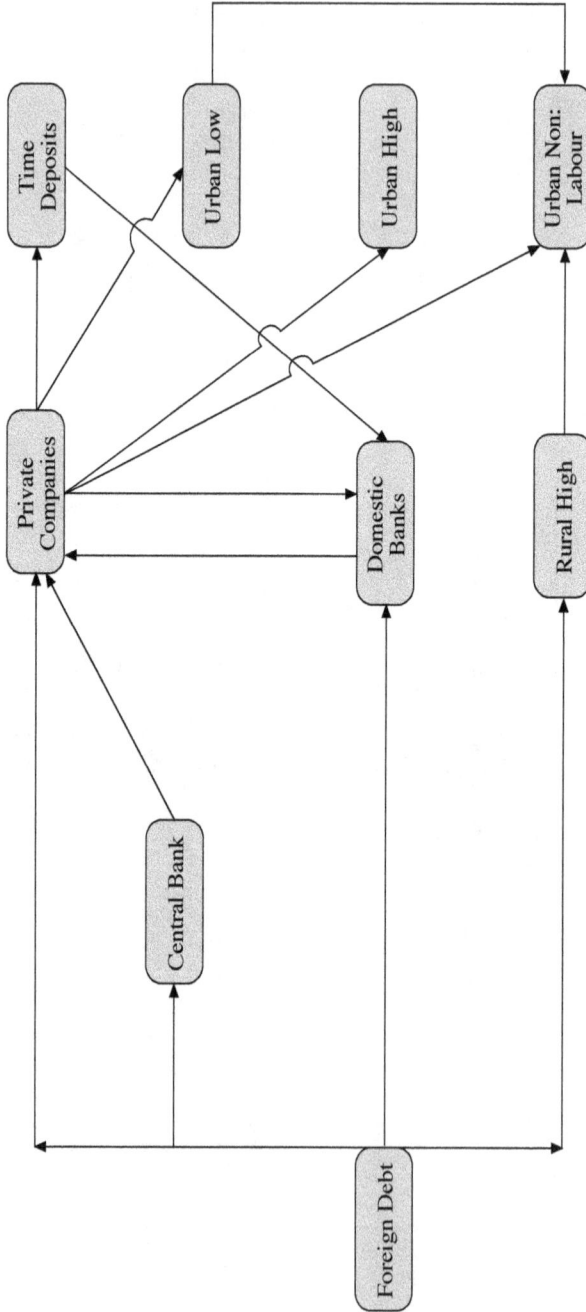

## TABLE 3
## Structural Path Analysis: Credit as the Pole of Origin

| Case | Origin of Shock (i) | Destination (i) | Global Influence GI | Elementary Path i→j | Direct Influence DI | Path Multiplier $M_p$ | Total Influence TI | TI/GI (%) |
|---|---|---|---|---|---|---|---|---|
| 1 | Credit | Company | 0.148 | Credit → Invest → DConstruct → PConstruct → PrivCap → Company | 0.043 | 1.181 | 0.051 | 34.2 |
|  |  |  |  | Credit → Invest → DBank → PBank → PrivCap → Company | 0.008 | 1.281 | 0.010 | 6.6 |
|  |  |  |  | Credit → Invest → DTextile → PTextile → PrivCap → Company | 0.004 | 1.513 | 0.005 | 3.7 |
|  |  |  |  | Credit → Invest → DPaper → PPaper → PrivCap → Company | 0.002 | 1.409 | 0.003 | 1.9 |
|  |  |  |  | Credit → Invest → DConstruct → OtCapUrb → Company | 0.001 | 1.273 | 0.001 | 0.5 |
| 2 | Credit | UrbLow | 0.138 | Credit → Invest → DConstruct → PConstruct → ManPdUrb → UrbLow | 0.028 | 1.313 | 0.037 | 26.7 |
|  |  |  |  | Credit → Invest → DConstruct → PConstruct → ManUUrb → UrbLow | 0.005 | 1.306 | 0.006 | 4.7 |
|  |  |  |  | Credit → Invest → DTextile → PTextile → ManPdUrb → UrbLow | 0.002 | 1.68 | 0.003 | 2.4 |
|  |  |  |  | Credit → Invest → DConstruct → PConstruct → ClerPdUrb → UrbLow | 0.002 | 1.365 | 0.003 | 2.0 |
|  |  |  |  | Credit → Invest → DBank → PBank → ClerPdUrb → UrbLow | 0.002 | 1.459 | 0.003 | 2.2 |
| 3 | Credit | RurLow | 0.103 | Credit → Invest → DConstruct → PConstruct → ManPdRur → RurLow | 0.032 | 1.267 | 0.041 | 39.5 |
|  |  |  |  | Credit → Invest → DConstruct → PConstruct → ManURur → RurLow | 0.004 | 1.267 | 0.005 | 5.1 |
|  |  |  |  | Credit → Invest → DTextile → PTextile → ManPdRur → RurLow | 0.001 | 1.626 | 0.001 | 1.1 |
|  |  |  |  | Credit → Invest → DConstruct → PConstruct → OtCapRur → RurLow | 0.001 | 1.332 | 0.001 | 1.1 |
|  |  |  |  | Credit → Invest → DMining → PMining → ManPdRur → RurLow | 0.001 | 1.271 | 0.001 | 1.0 |
| 4 | Credit | UrbHigh | 0.141 | Credit → Invest → DBank → PBank → ClerPdUrb → UrbHigh | 0.006 | 1.446 | 0.009 | 6.4 |
|  |  |  |  | Credit → Invest → DConstruct → PConstruct → ClerPdUrb → UrbHigh | 0.006 | 1.357 | 0.008 | 5.9 |
|  |  |  |  | Credit → Invest → DConstruct → PConstruct → ProPdUrb → UrbHigh | 0.005 | 1.329 | 0.007 | 5.0 |
|  |  |  |  | Credit → Invest → DConstruct → PConstruct → OtCapUrb → UrbHigh | 0.004 | 1.357 | 0.005 | 3.8 |
|  |  |  |  | Credit → Invest → DConstruct → PConstruct → ManPdUrb → UrbHigh | 0.003 | 1.378 | 0.004 | 3.0 |
| 5 | Credit | FarmMed | 0.027 | Credit → Invest → DConstruct → PConstruct → ManPdRur → FarmMed | 0.001 | 1.241 | 0.001 | 4.8 |
|  |  |  |  | Credit → Invest → DConstruct → PConstruct → OtCapRur → FarmMed | 0.001 | 1.285 | 0.001 | 3.6 |
|  |  |  |  | Credit → Invest → DNonFood → PNonFood → AgPaid → FarmMed | 0.000 | 1.609 | 0.000 | 0.1 |
|  |  |  |  | Credit → Invest → DNonFood → PNonFood → AgUnpaid → FarmMed | 0.000 | 1.706 | 0.000 | 1.2 |
|  |  |  |  | Credit → Invest → DNonFood → PNonFood → ManPdRur → FarmMed | 0.000 | 1.611 | 0.000 | 0.0 |

NOTES: These abbreviations are used: For factors of production: Ag=Agricultural, Man=Manual Operator, Cler=Clerical, Pro=Professional, Pd=Paid, U=Unpaid. Rur=Rural, Urb=Urban (e.g. AgPdUrb=Agricultural Paid Urban), OtCapRur=Other (Unincorporated) Rural Capital, OtCapUrb=Other (Unincorporated) Urban Capital, PrivCap=Private Capital. For institutions: Rur=Rural, Urb=Urban. For production: P=Production sector, D=Domestic Commodity.

SOURCE: Authors' simulation using the Indonesian 1995 SAM augmented by the flow of funds.

Figure 5 illustrates these relationships, but limited to the three largest paths for the top three institutions that were hardest hit in this stage.

There is a held belief that in the absence of a reliable social security system, household transfers in Indonesia rose spontaneously as a substitute. Household transfers flowing through the network of households that are closely connected due to family ties, same ethnic background, location proximity, or just plain desire to assist the poor during a period of hardship. This network is a manifestation of the "Asian value" that encourages the voluntary act of helping the poor neighbours. In effect, transfers serve as a privately-funded social safety net that arose from the altruistic motive of the benevolent, better-off households. Thus, changes in the SAM transfer matrix are of special interest because they may reflect the altruistic motive of households to assist their distressed neighbours.

Here we shall examine the transfers of income among various economic institutions. Inter-institutional transfers, which constitute a redistribution of income, can originate from households (for example, rural parents supporting students in urban areas or urban workers sending remittances to retired parents in rural areas), from companies (for example, dividends), and from the government (for example, direct subsidy to poor households). The term "transfer" refers to the occasion where money changed hands between two parties but not in exchange for goods consumed or services rendered.

If altruism indeed motivated households to assist their low-income and hardest-hit neighbours, then we would expect to see an increasing share of transfers to low-level urban and rural households as well as to small farmers. Based on the 1995 and 1999 data, it is revealed that the percentage of transfers to the low-income and hardest-hit households actually *decreased* virtually across the board.

The decrease in the share of transfers to hardest-hit groups must be offset by an increase somewhere else. In 1999, the majority of households increased their share of transfers mainly to rural non-labour force and rural high households. This finding is unexpected since these two household groups were neither the poorest nor the hardest hit by the crisis. Even more baffling is the fact that a number of households — notably large farmers, rural high, and the poor urban low — significantly increased their share of transfers to the affluent high-level urban households. Although urban high households experienced a sharp percentage decline in real per capita income, their absolute level of income was still comfortably greater than urban low households which, against all conventional wisdom, increased their transfers to urban high by 150 per cent.

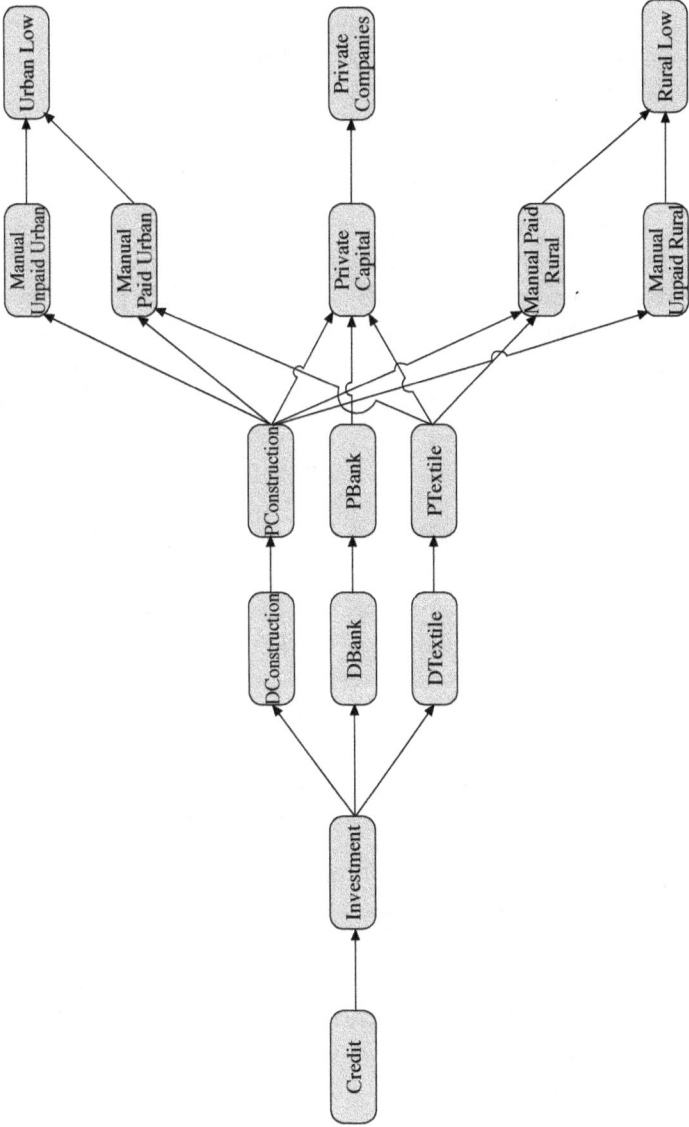

**FIGURE 5**
**Paths from a Shock in Bank Credits: Channels Through Which Financial, Real, and
Construction Sectors Affect Household Incomes**

To summarize, there is no convincing evidence that households acted altruistically to assist their distressed neighbours during the crisis. In addition, it appears that redistribution *vis-à-vis* inter-household transfers has become increasingly more *regressive*. That is, households allocated a lower share of their transfers to the destitute and hardest-hit small farmers and rural low households, while allocating higher shares to the well-off rural high and urban high households.

## IV. CONCLUSIONS

The transmission of financial shock to household income distribution is analysed using the case of Indonesia. It is shown that a general equilibrium approach based on a financial sector-augmented SAM can be used to overcome some of the major limitations of the standard SAM-based approach. By integrating financial and real sector, the model can capture clear inter-linkages among variables, resolving some arbitrary hypotheses. The Asian financial crisis that began with the massive selling of financial assets (currency, stocks, and debts) in anticipation of further exchange rate depreciation, generated a particular pattern of income distribution. Those benefiting from currency depreciation and high interest rate are presumably the high-income groups who held dollar-denominated assets and had a large saving account. However, the same income groups might lose if they were employed in sectors that are highly dependent on imports. As shown in the case of Indonesia, the resulting net impact on the relative income distribution is ambiguous because the movement of financial variables often compensates the effect of real-side variables.

In view of the fact that construction was the hardest-hit sector, the low-income non-agricultural households were more susceptible due to their heavy reliance on manual work in that sector. The construction sector also proves to be instrumental in transmitting the shock from the credit crunch to the fall in household income. To the extent that a formal social safety net is lacking, informal system is expected to mitigate the impact on the poor. It is therefore intriguing that we found no convincing evidence that households acted altruistically to assist their distressed neighbours during the crisis. The redistribution *vis-à-vis* inter-household transfers has in fact become increasingly more *regressive*.

Yet another key finding of our study is the pivotal role of government current expenditures (both on- and off-budget) in protecting the income of rural households. We showed that without an increase in government expenditures, rural households would have ended up as the hardest-hit households. Thus, even despite the absence of formal social safety nets (i.e., direct transfers from the government to low-income households), government expenditures could stimulate production in those sectors that provide the principal source of employment for rural households.

Since SAM is now available in practically all ASEAN countries hit by the crisis, it would be useful to conduct a similar analysis in those countries. While the multiplier analysis provides the direct and indirect effects of the shock (the "what"), SPA is able to capture the mechanism that produce such effects (the "how").

## Appendix

### Construction of the Flow of Funds

Merging the real SAM with the flow of funds guarantees that the base run is equilibrated in two fronts (Robinson 1991). First, the real SAM assures equilibrium in the commodity markets and in the balance of payments. The second equilibrium is in the market for loanable funds, guaranteed by the flow-of-funds matrix *vis-à-vis* the matching of aggregate savings (supply of funds) with total investments (demand for funds). The matrix of flow of funds can be inserted into the real SAM by replacing the column of investments and the row of savings, in effect "zooming into" the saving/investment account. However, the Indonesian statistical bureau (BPS) has yet to publish the flow of funds in a matrix format. The data for the construction of the flow-of-fund matrix thus have to be compiled from various sources. First, savings and investments data are derived from the real SAM, which is necessary to guarantee the consistency between the real economy and the financial sector. The assets and liabilities of commercial banks and the monetary authority (i.e., the central bank) are posted in the website of Bank of Indonesia (http://www.bi.go.id). Foreign portfolio investments, direct investments, and debts are taken from the World Bank publication of *Global Development Finance*. Government's equity participation is proxied by the development expenditures of the central government posted in the website of the Indonesian statistical bureau (http:// www.bps.go.id). Finally, the exchange rate (the average Rp/U.S.$ rate is used to convert transactions denominated in foreign currency) is from the IMF publication of *International Financial Statistics*.

Our starting point is to divide companies, which is recognized as a single institution in the real SAM, into commercial banks and non-bank "companies". The former is broken down further into "domestic banks" and "foreign banks". The government, which was a single entity in the real SAM, is divided into the "central bank" and the "government"; the former regulates the monetary sector, while the latter affects the economy primarily through fiscal policies. The financial actors thus consist of households, production sectors, the central bank, the government, domestic banks, foreign banks, companies, and the rest of the world.

Next, we need to select the different categories of financial instruments. At the top level, we classify financial assets into five types: "foreign non-equity assets", "domestic currency and bank deposits", "equity", "domestic loans", and "interbank instruments". Foreign non-equity assets include those assets issued abroad, such as U.S. T-bills, as well as foreign holding of domestically issued debts, which consist of both long-term and short-term debts of the government and the private sector. Bank deposits comprise those components of broad money $M_2$, namely demand (checking) deposits, time deposits, and deposits denominated in foreign currencies. Equity is subdivided according to whether the owner is domestic or foreign. The last category is the interbank instruments which refer to those at the disposal of the central bank to regulate the banking system, including required reserves and liquidity support.

A proper analysis of the resulting change in income distribution requires a disaggregation of households' flow of funds. Since the breakdown of the flow of funds by household groups is not available, we use the distribution of currency and bank deposits by household groups as in Thorbecke (1992). To guarantee that savings of household group $j$ are consistent with the real SAM figures, we compute household $j$'s change in equity holding as the residual, i.e., by subtracting changes in currency and bank deposits from savings.

## Notes

1.  A similar approach was also used in Azis (2000$b$) to investigate the impact of the downfall of the manufacturing sector on household income.
2.  An "influence" is the metaphor in the literature for an additional flow of income or output, which can be either positive or negative.
3.  The eight exogenous variables are as follows: foreign equity (comprising foreign portfolio and direct investments), foreign non-equity assets (including public and private debt values), time deposits denominated in rupiah, deposits denominated in foreign currency (both checking and saving deposits), commercial bank credits, central bank, the government, and the rest of the world. In our simulation, we replicate the series of shocks according to the actual changes of these exogenous variables between 1995 and 1999.
4.  The agricultural sector accounts for one-third of GDP in the early 1970s, 23 per cent in the early 1980s, and 15 per cent in 1997.
5.  For example, 844 elementary paths were identified in the French input-output table, which was disaggregated into only *six* sectors. See Defourny and Thorbecke (1984, p. 123).

## References

Azis, Iwan J. "Transition from Financial Crisis to Social Crisis". In *Social Implications of the Asian Financial Crisis*. Seoul: UNDP and Korean Development Institute (KDI), 1998.

————. "Simulating Economy-wide Models to Capture the Transition from Financial Crisis to Social Crisis". *The Annals of Regional Science* 34, no. 2 (2000$a$): 251–78.

————. "Non-Linear General Equilibrium Impacts of Financial Crisis and Manufacturing Downfall". *The Developing Economies* 2 (December 2000$b$): 518–46.

Bae, Kee-Hong, Jun-Koo Kang, and Chan-Woo Lim. "The Value of Durable Bank Relationships: Evidence from Korean Banking Shocks". *Journal of Financial Economics* 64 (2002): 181–214.

Bernanke, Ben, Mark Gertler, and Simon Gilchrist. "The Financial Accelerator and the Flight to Quality". *Review of Economics and Statistics* 78 (February 1996): 1–15.

Defourny, Jacques and Erik Thorbecke. "Structural Path Analysis and Multiplier Decomposition within a Social Accounting Matrix Framework". *Economic Journal* 94 (1984): 111–36.

Irawan, P. and H. Romdiati. "The Impacts of Crisis on Poverty and Its Implications for Development Strategies". Paper presented at the National Workshop on Food and Nutrition VII, Jakarta, 10–12 May 2000.

Johnson, Colin. "Survey of Recent Developments". *Bulletin of Indonesian Economic Studies* 34 (1998): 2, 3–57.

Krugman, Paul. "Balance Sheets, the Transfer Problem, and Financial Crises". In *International Finance and Financial Crises, Essays in Honor of Robert P. Flood, Jr.*, edited by P. Isard, A. Razin, and A. Rose. Dordrecht, Kluwer, Boston: Kluwer Academic Publishers, 2001.

Robinson, Sherman. "Macroeconomics, Financial Variables, and Computable General Equilibrium Models". *World Development* 19, no. 11 (1991): 1509–25.

Sen, Amartya. *On Economic Inequality*. Rev. ed. Oxford: Clarendon Press, 1997.

Thorbecke, Erik. *Adjustment and Equity in Indonesia*. Paris: OECD Development Centre, 1992.

Thorbecke, Willem. "The Economic Crisis in Indonesia: Social Costs and Policy Implications". UNDP Office of Development Studies Working Paper No. 7, 1998.

# 2

# CAPITAL INFLOW REVERSALS, CURRENT ACCOUNT ADJUSTMENTS, AND MACROECONOMIC PERFORMANCE

## Gan Wee Beng and Soon Lee Ying

### I. INTRODUCTION

During the 1997–98 East Asian financial crisis, the affected economies experienced a massive outflow of portfolio capital. To effect the transfer of such financial resources, the current account of the balance of payments underwent a dramatic reversal within a relatively compressed time period accompanied by massive reduction in domestic spending, sharp depreciation in the real exchange rate, and upward pressure on the real interest rate. This paper studies Malaysia's experience with current account reversal following the outbreak of the financial crisis. During the period 1997–98, the economy experienced a net short-term capital outflow of RM34.6 billion, representing 6.5 per cent of nominal gross national product (GNP). In response, the current account reversed itself from a deficit that averaged 6.2 per cent of GNP during the period 1990–97 to a surplus of 13.7 per cent in 1998.

The magnitude of the current account reversal in Malaysia was the largest among the four East Asian economies that were most severely affected by the currency crisis. As Table 1 indicates, the current account in Indonesia reversed from an average deficit of 2.5 per cent of nominal gross domestic product

**TABLE 1**
**Current Account and Real GDP Growth for Four East Asian Economies, 1993–2001**
**(In percentage)**

| | Malaysia | | Indonesia | | Thailand | | South Korea | |
|---|---|---|---|---|---|---|---|---|
| | CA | GDP | CA | GDP | CA | GDP | CA | GDP |
| 1993 | -4.6 | 9.9 | -1.5 | 6.5 | -5.1 | 8.3 | 0.3 | 5.5 |
| 1994 | -7.6 | 9.2 | -1.7 | 7.5 | -5.6 | 9.0 | -1.0 | 8.3 |
| 1995 | -9.7 | 9.8 | -3.4 | 8.2 | -8.1 | 9.2 | -1.7 | 8.9 |
| 1996 | -4.7 | 10.0 | -3.4 | 7.8 | -8.1 | 5.9 | -4.4 | 6.8 |
| 1997 | -5.9 | 7.3 | -2.4 | 4.7 | -0.8 | -1.4 | -1.7 | 5.0 |
| 1998 | 13.2 | -7.4 | 4.2 | -13.1 | 12.8 | -10.5 | 12.7 | -6.7 |
| 1999 | 15.9 | 6.1 | 4.1 | 0.8 | 10.1 | 4.4 | 6.0 | 10.9 |
| 2000 | 9.3 | 8.3 | 5.4 | 4.8 | 7.6 | 4.6 | 2.7 | 9.3 |
| 2001 | 8.3 | 0.4 | 4.9 | 3.4 | 5.4 | 1.9 | 1.9 | 3.1 |

NOTES: CA = current account in percentage of nominal GDP; GDP = per cent real annual GDP growth.
SOURCE: IMF (various issues).

(GDP) from 1993–97 to an average surplus of 4.6 per cent from 1998–2000, representing a reversal of 7.1 per cent. For Thailand, the switch-around in the current account amounted to 15.7 per cent of GDP. In contrast, Malaysia's external balance reversal during the same period amounted to 19.3 per cent of GDP. Such a massive turnaround in the current account, however, was accomplished with relatively less severe contraction in domestic demand. In 1998, economic activity in Malaysia contracted by 7.4 per cent compared with 13.1 per cent in Indonesia and 10.5 per cent in Thailand. Malaysia's current account reversal therefore appears to have been less painful in terms of the contraction necessary to achieve the reduction in domestic absorption to effect the transfer of resources abroad.

Malaysia stood out among the crisis-hit countries as the only one that did not follow the conventional restrictive macroeconomic policy to stabilize the exchange rate and bring about improvement in the external balance. Instead the authorities chose to fix the exchange rate and impose capital controls, and pursued a moderate expansionary policy. Malaysia therefore presents an interesting case study of current account reversal, and this paper represents an attempt to provide a better understanding of the events following the outbreak of crisis and the adjustment process during the critical years of recovery.

Section II of the paper analyses the dynamics of the external balance adjustment and how key macroeconomic variables shifted to facilitate the required real transfer employing an event-study approach. To complement the descriptive event-study findings, we estimate a structural vector autogression (SVAR) model in Section III to provide an econometric evaluation on the dynamics of the current account adjustment in response to shocks in relative prices and domestic income. Section IV summarizes the overall findings and draws some implications from the Malaysian experience on how the large current account deficit was reversed within a short period of time.

## II. CURRENT ACCOUNT ADJUSTMENT AND MACROECONOMIC PERFORMANCE

An event-study approach to characterizing the dynamics of current account reversal would require an identification of the period before the external balance turned itself from a deficit to a surplus position and an analysis of the behaviour of the economy during the periods before and after the event.[1] The objective of such an analysis is to appraise the duration and the sustainability of the current account reversal and to evaluate how costly the adjustment process was in terms of macroeconomic performance. Using the criteria set out by Milesti-Ferretti and Razin (1998) for a significant and sustained turnaround in the external balance,[2] we identified the fourth quarter of 1997 as the period before the current account reversed into a surplus position (Figure 1).

Figure 1 shows the path of the current account and the manner in which other macroeconomic variables adjust in conjunction with the movement in the external balance twelve quarters before and twelve quarters after 1997:4 ($t - 12$ to $t + 12$), together with the plus and minus two standard deviations band. Several features of the current account behaviour should be noted. Firstly, the magnitude of the current account deficit was well above 2 per cent of nominal GDP in each of the quarters before 1997:4, with the highest deficit of 14.4 per cent registered in 1995:2. Secondly, the average deficit in the current account over the twelve quarters before the reversal took place amounted to 7.1 per cent of GDP while in twelve quarters surplus following the reversal, the surplus averaged 12.9 per cent of GDP. Thirdly, the current account had continuously remained in a surplus position in each quarter following the reversal, achieving a maximum surplus amounting to 18 per cent of GDP in 1999:3. On the other hand, before the reversal took place, the smallest deficit of 3 per cent of GDP was recorded in 1996:2. In short, the current account reversal experienced by Malaysia during the recent currency crisis satisfies the Milesti-Ferretti and Razin (1998) criteria.

The manner in which the current account adjustment was effected can be seen from the behaviour of the key macroeconomic and financial variables. The modern intertemporal approach to current account focuses on the role of forward-looking saving and investment behaviour, relative to the country intertemporal budget constraint, in determining the path of the external balance (Obstfeld and Rogoff 1995). In an integrated international financial market, capital flows from abroad, which constitute an important component of the intertemporal budget constraint, allows a country to smooth its consumption and investment profiles over time in response to transitory shocks in domestic cash flows (Obstfeld 1994; Ghosh 1995). An important implication of the intertemporal approach to the current account is that a reduction in the net foreign capital inflows, by giving rise to a liquidity constraint situation, makes saving and investment decisions sensitive to a fall in domestic income, thereby bringing about a quick adjustment in the current account.[3]

In Malaysia the current account deficit before 1997:4 was largely due to high investment ratio, financed substantially by capital inflows. The capital outflows following the outbreak of the financial crisis created a severe liquidity constraint situation in the corporate sector. In 1997 the net outflow of debt-creating and equity capital amounted to RM12.9 billion; in 1998 an

**FIGURE 1**
**Current Account Adjustment and Macroeconomic Variables**

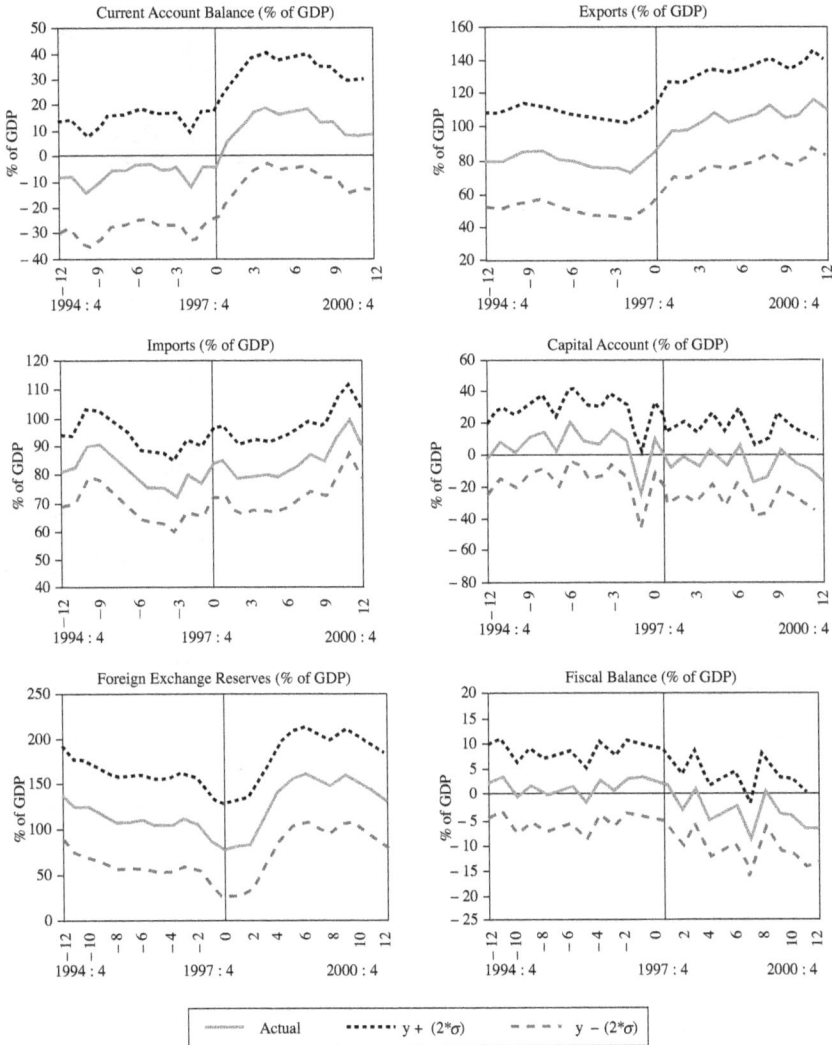

Current Account Balance (% of GDP)

Exports (% of GDP)

Imports (% of GDP)

Capital Account (% of GDP)

Foreign Exchange Reserves (% of GDP)

Fiscal Balance (% of GDP)

Actual          y + (2*σ)          y − (2*σ)

## FIGURE 1 — *continued*

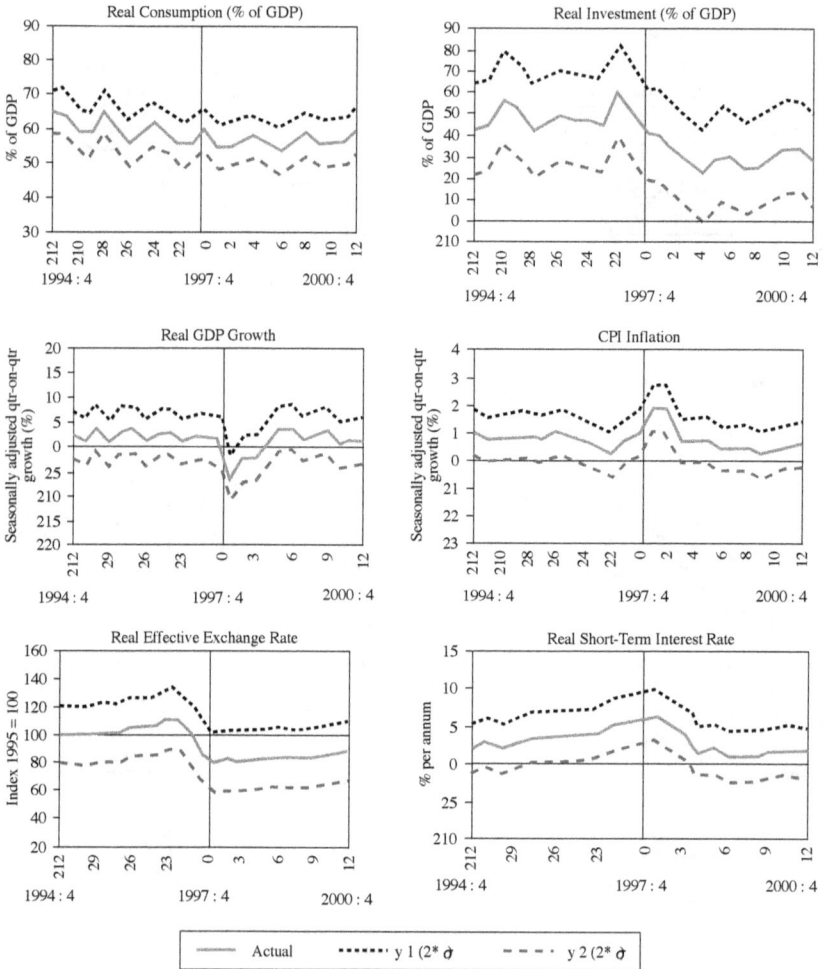

| Actual | ⋯⋯ y 1 (2* σ) | ─ ─ ─ y 2 (2* σ) |

additional outflow of RM21.7 billion was recorded. Stock market capitalization which stood at RM888 billion at the beginning of 1997, declined to RM200 billion in September 1998. The yield of one-year Malaysian government securities rose from an average of 6.5 per cent at the beginning of 1997 to a peak of 10.1 per cent in June 1998. Falling equity prices, high interest rates, together with the depreciation in the exchange rate led to substantial losses among the non-financial corporations, thereby creating further pressure to scale back investment.[4]

In response to these developments, aggregate investment to GDP ratio fell sharply to 30 per cent after 1997:4 compared with an average ratio of 53 per cent before that quarter. The retrenchment in private investment was most severe in the services and construction sectors where large infrastructure projects with high import content were either cancelled or deferred.[5] Investment in the manufacturing sector, which typically accounted for 34 per cent of private investment, contracted by 38 per cent in 1998.

On the other hand, consumption, since it was not supported by capital inflows from abroad, declined moderately. The average consumption to GDP ratio for the twelve quarters after 1997:4 fell to 56.3 per cent compared with an average ratio of 60 per cent the quarter before. The moderate adjustment in the consumption ratio most likely reflected the consumption-smoothing behaviour following the slowdown in income growth.

The adjustment in imports and exports, in the general equilibrium context, mirrored the saving and investment behaviour. Import to GDP ratio continued to decline from 1997:4 until late 1998 while the export ratio started to increase from the fourth quarter of 1997, rising from 86 per cent to a peak of 112 per cent in the last quarter of 1999. For the year 1998, the increase in exports was insufficient to offset the decline in real investment and consumption, resulting in the continuous contraction of real output for three consecutive quarters.

The turnaround in the trade balance to a surplus position in 1998, which amounted to 21 per cent of GDP, was contributed by an increase in the export ratio as well as by a compression in the import ratio arising from the drop in the domestic absorption.[6] By 1999, the trade balance surplus, which increased further to 24 per cent of GDP, was mainly attributed to the buoyant export performance.

The increase in the value of merchandise export in 1998 reflected largely the valuation effect arising from the depreciation of the ringgit. As Table 2 shows, in terms of volume, merchandise exports merely rose by 1 per cent. Merchandise import volume, on the other hand, fell by 20 per cent and this served to offset the increase in local currency price of imports which rose by

**TABLE 2**
**Percentage Change in Price and Volume of Exports and Imports,**
**1998–2000**

|          | 1998  | 1999  | 2000 |
|----------|-------|-------|------|
| *Exports* |       |       |      |
| Volume   | 1.1   | 19.3  | 11.6 |
| Price    | –6.2  | –2.7  | 6.2  |
| *Imports* |       |       |      |
| Volume   | –19.9 | 19.3  | 18.6 |
| Price    | –7.9  | –2.4  | 6.0  |

NOTE: Computed from prices expressed in U.S. dollar.
SOURCE: Bank Negara Malaysia, *Annual Reports* (various issues).

29 per cent, thereby resulting in an overall increase in the value of imports by only 3 per cent. However, from 1999, the volume effect of the real depreciation on exports has been the dominant influence in determining the merchandise trade surplus. Export volume rose by 19 per cent while import volume increased by 15 per cent. The expansion in export volume from 1999 has been the result of increase in manufactured and mineral exports. The manufactured items were electronic goods and electrical products together with wood-based products.

The depreciation of the real exchange rate facilitated the adjustment in the trade balance in two ways. First, the real exchange rate depreciation enhanced the international competitiveness of Malaysian exports while at the same time it made imports, in domestic currency terms, more expensive. Second, the exchange rate depreciation raised the domestic price of tradable goods relative to the price of non-tradable goods produced in the economy, thereby changing the incentive for the production and consumption of these goods. An exchange rate-induced increase in the price of tradable goods made its production more profitable, causing resources to shift out of the non-tradable sector into the tradable sector. At the same time, the shift in the relative price of tradable goods created an incentive in consumption to substitute the consumption of tradable goods for non-tradables. Hence the shift in the domestic resources from the production of non-tradables to tradable goods and the switching of domestic spending from tradables to non-tradables provided another explanation for the improvement in the country's current account.

Table 3 shows two proxies for the relative price of non-tradable goods, namely the price of domestically produced services relative to the price of exportables and housing prices relative to the price of exportables. Both series indicate that the relative price of non-tradable goods declined after 1997 following the depreciation of the ringgit. Supported by favourable supply conditions and growing international demand, the greater profitability of manufactured goods led to rising output and enhanced share of manufacturing value-added in national output (Table 3).

In general, the supply-side capacity of the Malaysian manufacturing sector showed considerable resilience and flexibility, which enabled the sector to take advantage of the enhanced international competitiveness brought about by the real depreciation of the exchange rate. Approximately half of Malaysian manufactured output were produced by majority-owned foreign firms, the balance sheet of which remained relatively unaffected by the financial crisis.[7] By the second half of 1999, manufacturing production rose by 23 per cent, compared with a growth of 3.5 per cent, in the first half.[8] In 2000, in response to rising capacity utilization, large-scale capacity expansion was under way. Import of capital goods for the year rose by 48 per cent compared with a growth of 13 per cent in 1999.

## TABLE 3
## Relative Price of Non-tradable Goods and the Share of Manufacturing Sector Value-added in GDP, 1990–2001

|  | Ratio of services sector deflator to deflator for exports | Ratio of housing price index to deflator for exports | Share of manufacturing value added in real GDP (%) |
|---|---|---|---|
| 1990 | 0.96 | 0.87 | 24.6 |
| 1991 | 0.97 | 1.06 | 25.6 |
| 1992 | 1.02 | 1.23 | 25.1 |
| 1993 | 1.01 | 1.21 | 26.2 |
| 1994 | 0.99 | 1.24 | 26.7 |
| 1995 | 1.02 | 1.46 | 27.1 |
| 1996 | 1.05 | 1.62 | 29.1 |
| 1997 | 1.00 | 1.54 | 29.9 |
| 1998 | 0.83 | 1.12 | 27.9 |
| 1999 | 0.84 | 1.12 | 29.4 |
| 2000 | 0.84 | 1.16 | 32.3 |
| 2001 | 0.83 | 1.17 | 30.2 |

SOURCE: Bank Negara Malaysia, *Quarterly Economic Bulletin* (various issues).

On the demand side, the impetus came from economic growth in the industrial economies which raised the demand for Malaysian exports. Table 4 shows that the rising import demand in the United State and the European Union (EU) during the crucial years 1998–2000 and, in the case of Japan, 1999–2000, led to a sharp increase in Malaysian exports to these economies. These economies, together with Singapore accounted for two-thirds of the Malaysian manufactured goods exports.

Besides the adjustment in domestic relative prices, the negative output gap brought about by the contraction in economic activity eventually brought about an easing of inflationary pressure from the fourth quarter of 1998, following a four-quarterly increase in the price level that accompanied the depreciation of the exchange rate.

At the onset of the financial crisis, the Malaysian central bank sought to moderate the increase in the money market interest rate following the outflow of capital by engaging in sterilized foreign exchange market intervention. However, from the last quarter of 1997 until mid-1998, Bank Negara Malaysia reversed its policy stance and aggressively pursued a tighter monetary policy aimed not only at stabilizing the exchange rate and arresting the inflationary pressure but also to slow down domestic credit demand in order to facilitate the adjustment in the current account. Using an estimated Taylor-type interest rate reaction function, Gan and Soon (2002) have shown that the monetary policy during the first half of 1998 was much tighter than the norm for the period. In addition, Gan and Soon (2001) have shown that between July 1997 and March 1998, the economy experienced a credit crunch situation. To the extent that the high interest rate and credit retrenchment by the banking institutions affected domestic investment and consumption, the monetary and credit policies during the period contributed to the reversal of the current account. Figure 1 indicates that the real interest rate rose from 1997:4 and remained high until 1998:3. Partly reflecting the credit crunch, the growth in monetary aggregate M3 started to decelerate sharply from 1997:3.

However when the tight monetary policy failed to support the ringgit exchange rate, the Central Bank, in August 1998, reversed its policy stance and reduced the policy intervention rate three times. On 1 September 1998, the authorities announced the introduction of a system of capital controls and the fixing of the ringgit at RM3.80 to the U.S. dollar, paving the way for further easing of monetary policy.

The initial fiscal response to the currency crisis contained in the 1998 Budget (announced in October 1997) was aimed at restraining aggregate demand and reducing the current account deficit. The government had budgeted for a fiscal surplus amounting to 2.7 per cent of GNP for 1998.

**TABLE 4**
**Economic Activity and Import Growth in the United States, EU, and Japan, 1996–2001**
**(In percentage)**

| | United States | | | European Union | | | Japan | | |
|---|---|---|---|---|---|---|---|---|---|
| | Economic growth | Growth in total imports | Growth in imports from Malaysia | Economic growth | Growth in total imports | Growth in imports from Malaysia | Economic growth | Growth in total imports | Growth in imports from Malaysia |
| 1996 | 3.6 | 7.0 | 2.1 | 1.7 | 5.3 | 2.8 | 3.5 | 20.4 | 28.9 |
| 1997 | 4.4 | 9.4 | 1.1 | 2.6 | 14.0 | 18.3 | 1.8 | 7.8 | 7.6 |
| 1998 | 4.3 | 4.9 | 5.5 | 2.9 | 5.3 | 15.5 | −1.1 | −10.5 | −17.6 |
| 1999 | 4.1 | 12.4 | 12.8 | 2.8 | 9.8 | 8.8 | 0.7 | −3.8 | 9.5 |
| 2000 | 3.8 | 18.9 | 19.3 | 3.5 | 29.1 | 1.1 | 2.6 | 16.1 | 25.7 |
| 2001 | 0.2 | −6.3 | −12.6 | 1.6 | 0.3 | −10.9 | −0.3 | 3.6 | 0.0 |

SOURCE: OECD Economic Indicators; Malaysian Department of Statistics, *External Trade Statistics* (Kuala Lumpur: Department of Statistics).

The surplus was to be achieved through cutback in government current expenditure, privatization, and deferring the implementation of selective infrastructure projects. However, in March 1998, the authorities began to shift the fiscal policy stance and budgeted for a smaller surplus of only 0.5 per cent of GNP as the economy showed signs of sharper contraction than was originally projected. By July 1998, the government announced a fiscal stimulus package and projected a budgetary deficit of 3.7 per cent for 1998. The 1999 Budget, which was announced in October 1998, targetted a larger deficit of 6.1 per cent of GNP. The impact of the expansionary fiscal policy can be seen from the fact that, from 1998:2 to 2000:4, the Federal Government budget was in deficit for nine out of eleven quarters.

Hence the continued improvement in the current account surplus from the second half of 1998 was not sustained by an expenditure dampening effect of tight monetary and fiscal policies. Rather, the expansionary macroeconomic policies in combination with the expenditure-switching effect of a large real exchange rate depreciation and favourable international demand for Malaysian exports, had allowed the current account surplus to be maintained and economic activity to recover rather quickly.

## III. AN SVAR MODEL OF CURRENT ACCOUNT ADJUSTMENT

In this section, we estimate a structural VAR model to characterize the dynamics of the Malaysian current account adjustment in response to "structural" shocks to world income growth, domestic economic activity, the real exchange rate, and the real interest rate.

We assume that the structural relationship between the current account and the other macroeconomic variable can be described by the following equation

$$AY_t = C(L)Y_{t-1} + Bu_t \tag{1}$$

where $A$ is an $n \times n$ matrix of contemporaneous coefficients relating the simultaneous relationship among the $n$ variables within the same period, $Y_t$ is an $n \times 1$ vector of macroeconomic variables, $C(L)$ is a matrix polynomial in lag operator $L$ that describes the dynamic interactions between variables. $u_t$ is an $n \times 1$ vector of structural innovations with covariance matrix $\Omega$, and $B$ is a $n \times n$ matrix that describes the contemporaneous relationship among the structural shocks.

The reduced form of the model is written as:

$$Y_t = B(L)Y_{t-1} + e_t \qquad (2)$$

where $B(L) = A^{-1}C(L)$ and $e_t = A^{-1}Bu_t$ with covariance matrix $\Sigma$.

The relationship between the structural shock $u_t$ and the reduced form residual $e_t$ is therefore:

$$Ae = Bu \qquad (3)$$

Equation (3) implies the following relationship between the reduced form and the structural form covariance matrices:

$$\Sigma = A^{-1}\Omega A^{-1'} \qquad (4)$$

In order to identify the structural shocks, it is necessary to recover $u_t$ from the reduced form residuals by using (3) and (4) and imposing appropriate restrictions on matrices $A$ and $B$. The structural shocks can be identified only when the number of unknown structural parameters (in $A$ and $B$) is less than or equal to the number of estimated (known) parameters of the reduced form covariance matrix $\Sigma$.[9]

Different methodologies have been employed in the literature to identify the structural innovations. A common approach is to orthogonalize the reduced form residual $e_t$ by Cholesky decomposition, which assumes a strict recursive structure, as in Sims (1980). Bernanke (1986) and Sims (1986) have employed a generalized methodology which allows for non-recursive relationship among variables, while imposing restrictions on the contemporaneous structural parameters.

Clarida and Prendergast (1999) estimate a four-variable VAR to investigate the response of the current account to structural shocks in world income, domestic economic activity, and the real exchange rate. The authors find that a set of recursive restrictions on the contemporaneous matrix is sufficient to achieve credible identification. The impulse response analysis for three OECD economies indicates that an unexpected real appreciation creates a persistent impact on the current account, causing a deterioration in the external balance of up to two to four years.

Cushman and Zha (1997) and Kim (2001) focus on the identification of monetary policy transmission mechanism in open economies in which the exchange rate and its effects on the trade balance provide an additional channel through which monetary policy shock impacts on the economy. Eschewing the recursive ordering to structural identification, these studies make different assumptions about the kind of variables the central banks have in their information set when they set the monetary policy instruments. The main findings of these papers are that monetary policy tightening leads to a temporary real exchange rate appreciation, a transitory contraction in real income, and an initial improvement in the trade balance that is followed, subsequently, by deterioration.

Another approach, following the works of Blanchard and Quah (1989) and Clarida and Gali (1994), imposes long-run restrictions in the SVAR model in order to identify the macroeconomic shocks. Typically, the restrictions take the form that aggregate demand and nominal shocks have no long-run impact on real variables like relative output, and the nominal shocks have no long-run effects on the real exchange rate or the current account. Lee and Chinn (1998) investigate the impact of permanent productivity shock and transitory monetary shock on the dynamic adjustment of the current account and the real exchange rate. Their impulse response analysis indicates that the monetary shock simultaneously depreciates the real exchange rate and improves the current account position up to three quarters, after which the current account begins to deteriorate. Prasad and Gable (1998) estimate a three-variable SVAR to evaluate the impact of aggregate supply, demand, and nominal shocks. An expansionary nominal shock depreciates the real exchange rate, raises the domestic output moderately, and improves the trade balance for a limited duration. In a three-variable model estimated by Lane (2001), a positive monetary policy shock initially leads to deterioration in the current account, with a surplus emerging only one year after the shock.

The present SVAR model, which relies on non-recursive restrictions on contemporaneous structural parameters for identification, consists of five variables, namely the current account as percentage of GDP (CA), growth in OECD real GDP (YOECD), the ringgit real effective exchange rate (REER), domestic real income growth (Y), and the real short-term interest rate (RI). The ringgit real effective exchange rate is constructed as a geometric weighted index of ten bilateral exchange rates of the ringgit against the currencies of the ten largest trading partners of Malaysia. Each bilateral nominal exchange rate is deflated by the relative consumer price indices. The real short-term interest rate is derived as the three-month KLIBOR money market rate less the three-month consumer price inflation rate (see the Appendix).

The following restrictions are imposed on the contemporaneous structural parameters in the matrices $A$ and $B$:

$$A = \begin{bmatrix} 1 & 0 & 0 & 0 & 0 \\ 0 & 1 & 0 & 0 & 0 \\ a_{31} & a_{32} & 1 & 0 & 0 \\ a_{41} & a_{42} & a_{43} & 1 & a_{45} \\ a_{51} & a_{52} & a_{53} & a_{54} & 1 \end{bmatrix} \qquad e = \begin{bmatrix} e^{YOECD} \\ e^{Y} \\ e^{CA} \\ e^{RI} \\ e^{REER} \end{bmatrix}$$

$$B = \begin{bmatrix} 1 & 0 & 0 & 0 & 0 \\ 0 & 1 & 0 & 0 & 0 \\ 0 & 0 & 1 & 0 & 0 \\ 0 & 0 & 0 & 1 & 0 \\ 0 & 0 & 0 & 0 & 1 \end{bmatrix} \qquad u = \begin{bmatrix} u^{OECD} \\ u^{Y} \\ u^{CA} \\ u^{RI} \\ u^{REER} \end{bmatrix}$$

In specifying the contemporaneous restrictions on A, it is assumed that OECD GDP is contemporaneously exogenous to all variables in the model. In addition, it is assumed that the current account responds with a lag to shifts in the real exchange rate and the real interest rate but is influenced contemporaneously by world income and domestic activity.[10] Lastly, the restrictions on the last two rows of matrix $A$ imply that the real exchange rate and the real interest rate, being asset prices, are driven by significant development in the macroeconomic variable within the same quarter. The restrictions allow for simultaneous interaction, within the same quarter, between the real exchange rate and the real interest rate, as in the case of the popular models of the asset market approach to real exchange rate determination. The number of restrictions on the elements of the matrix $A$ has resulted in a just-identified system.[11]

We estimated the reduced form of the model using quarterly data from 1985:1 to 2000:4. Two lags of each variable are included in the estimated model.[12]

To conduct a meaningful impulse response function and variance decomposition analysis, we need to ensure that the reduced form model is stable in the sense that it does not possess unit root in the autoregressive polynomial B(L). A stable VAR would ensure that the impact of shocks on the variables is calculable and finite.

The first step in evaluating the stability of the model is to assess whether each of the variables is stationary. If the variables in the SVAR are truly non-stationary, then specifying them in level form would result in a unit root in the autoregressive polynomial. Table 5 presents the results of the unit root tests for the five variables in the model, using the augmented Dickey-Fuller and the Phillips-Perron procedures. The results indicate that the null hypothesis of unit root is rejected for both YOECD and Y, while the non-stationary hypothesis cannot be rejected for CA, REER, and RI at the 5 per cent level. However given the well-known low power of these unit root tests in a finite sample (Harris 1995), an additional test on the stability of the SVAR is required. Lutkepohl (1991) has shown that the necessary and sufficient condition for a VAR model to be stable is that all the eigenvalues of the autoregressive polynomial have modulus that is less than unity. A plot of all the inverse roots of the autoregressive polynomial shows that all of them indeed lie inside the unit circle.[13]

An additional set of diagnostic test of the residuals of the estimated model was performed. The multivariate diagnostic tests of the residuals indicate that they are normal and serially uncorrelated.[14] McCallum (1993) has argued that the estimation of a VAR model where the variable appears in level form would be appropriate if the error terms of the model are stationary and serially uncorrelated.[15]

We first examine the impulse response functions, which show the dynamic adjustment profile of the current account and other variables in response to various shocks, and later present the results of the forecast error variance decompositions.[16]

Figure 2 plots the impulse response functions of the current account to a one-standard deviation shock in world income (proxied by OECD income) growth, growth in domestic economic activity, the real exchange rate, the

**TABLE 5**
**Unit Root Tests**

| Variables | Augmented Dickey-Fuller Test | Phillips-Perron Test |
|-----------|------------------------------|----------------------|
| YOECD | −3.2651* | −4.6096* |
| Y | −3.3198* | −7.0343* |
| RI | −2.6744 | −1.9768 |
| REER | −2.6741 | −2.5057 |
| CA | −1.6978 | −1.9173 |

NOTE: * indicates rejection of null hypothesis of unit root at 5 per cent level.

## FIGURE 2
## Responses of Current Account to Shocks

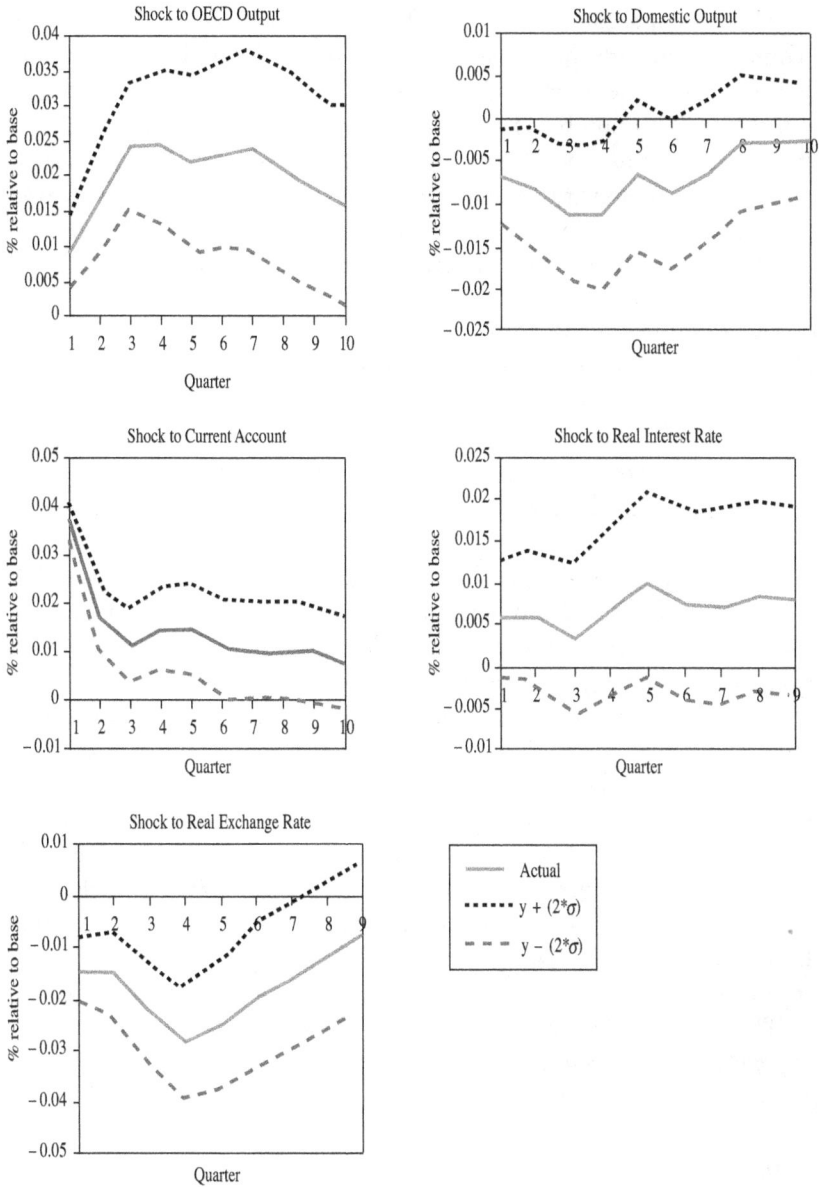

real interest rate, and its own innovation. The current account improves in response to a positive shock in the OECD income growth, with the surplus reaching its peak three quarters after the shock.

The current account deteriorates following a positive shock in domestic income growth, with the deficit growing to its maximum level four months after the shock. The observed dynamics of the current account is at variance with the consumption-based intertemporal model of current account which predicts that a transitory increase in income would lead to increase in saving as consumers attempt to smooth their consumption profile. The observed behaviour of the current account following an income shock is more in line with a current account that is largely driven by investment decision rather than saving behaviour. Therefore, to the extent that the positive income innovation represents a country-specific productivity shock, the dynamic behaviour of the current account is consistent with the intertemporal models of current account with investment behaviour (Glick and Rogoff 1995; Elliot and Fatas 1996). Such models predict that productivity shocks raise the level of domestic investment and result in current account deficit.

In response to an unexpected appreciation in the real exchange rate, the current account deteriorates for six quarters. The rapid adjustment of the current account to a real exchange rate shock confirms the absence of the J-curve effect. The speed and the duration of the current account adjustment following the exchange rate shock also demonstrate the significance of the expenditure-switching effect of exchange rate changes.[17]

A positive interest rate innovation leads to an improvement in the current account and this relationship is consistent with the basic consumption-based intertemporal model of current account. An increase in the real interest rate leads to enhancement in saving since the real interest rate represents the relative price of current goods in terms of future goods. An increase in the real interest rate implies that current goods are more expensive relative to future goods, thereby causing an intertemporal substitution in consumption. However, the large standard error bands of the impulse response function suggest that such intertemporal substitution effect is rather weak.

The dynamics of the impulse response analysis appear to be consistent with the predictions of the standard models of open economy macro-economics, and this provides comfort that we have adequately identified the structural shocks. This allows us to proceed to analyse the forecast error variance decompositions for the current account. From these decompositions, we estimate how important shocks to world income growth, domestic income growth, the real exchange rate, and the real interest rate have been in driving the movement in the current account. Such a variance decomposition exercise complements the information obtained from the descriptive analysis in Section II.

Table 6 presents the results of the variance decomposition for the current account. The shocks arising from OECD income growth explain the largest proportion of the variability of the current account, accounting for 37 per cent of the forecast error variance in the long run. The next dominant influence on the current account forecast error variance is the innovations in the real exchange rate which contribute an additional 29 per cent of the current account fluctuation. Shocks to domestic income growth and, hence, aggregate spending account for 15 per cent of the forecast error variance of movement in the current account. This finding is again consistent with investment-driven current account behaviour where income innovations can proxy for productivity shocks. In addition, where investments are partly funded by foreign capital inflows, the reversal of such funds would make domestic investment sensitive to income shocks. Real interest rate shock explains not more than 6 per cent of the current account forecast error variance. While the evidence in Section II suggests that the initial tight monetary policy pursued by the Central Bank would have significant impact on investment

**TABLE 6**
**Decomposition of Variance of Forecast Error for Current Account**

| Horizon (quarter) | Percentage variance due to | | | | |
|---|---|---|---|---|---|
| | YOECD | Y | RI | REER | CA |
| 1 | 5.7 | 3.0 | 0.0 | 0.0 | 91.3 |
| 2 | 15.7 | 4.6 | 1.4 | 8.6 | 69.7 |
| 3 | 27.6 | 16.7 | 2.0 | 12.3 | 41.4 |
| 4 | 31.2 | 17.3 | 1.6 | 19.2 | 30.7 |
| 8 | 35.5 | 19.4 | 3.2 | 30.4 | 11.5 |
| 12 | 37.9 | 14.4 | 4.7 | 28.4 | 14.6 |
| 20 | 37.3 | 14.8 | 5.5 | 29.0 | 13.4 |

NOTE: YOECD = growth in OECD real GDP; Y = growth in domestic real GDP; RI = real short-term interest rate; REER = real effective exchange rate; CA = current account in percentage of GDP.

behaviour, the small number of quarterly observations during which the tight monetary policy stance was adopted compared with the overall sample size could explain the relatively small contribution made by real interest rate shock to the forecast error variance of the current account.

Overall, the variance decomposition exercise indicates that the buoyant global economic activity, the expenditure-switching effect of the real exchange rate depreciation, and the expenditure reducing impact of the decline in the real domestic income were the key determinants in effecting the reversal in the current account from a deficit to a surplus position from 1998 onwards.

## II. SUMMARY AND CONCLUSIONS

The event-study of this paper shows that Malaysia's current account reversal started after the last quarter of 1997 and was supported initially by tight monetary and fiscal policies. The improvement in the external balance continued after September 1998 when the exchange rate was fixed and capital controls imposed. Even though such measures allowed the authorities to reflate the economy that would have impaired the current account adjustment, it did not happen. The SVAR analysis reinforced our findings that the current account adjustment was largely accomplished through the depreciation of the exchange rate, and to a lesser extent the slowdown in real income growth. The sharp depreciation of the ringgit induced the reallocation of domestic resources from the non-tradable sector to the tradable sector to take advantage of the expenditure-switching opportunities following the increase in international demand for Malaysia's exports.

It appears that Malaysia's experience with current account reversal was achieved with relatively less pain in terms of domestic contraction in output, due to the following. A low inflation environment, which limited the extent of inflationary exchange rate pass-through to domestic prices, enabled the authorities to pursue expansionary monetary and fiscal policies to limit the deflationary impact of an asset market collapse and prevented further contraction of economic activity. A low persistence in the inflationary process also enabled the nominal depreciation to be translated into a prolonged period of real depreciation and expansionary macroeconomic stance to be pursued to effect the required adjustment in the external balance with minimal loss in domestic output. Real export growth, lower investment ratio, slower economic growth, together with substantial real depreciation underpinned the substantial current account surplus.

**Appendix**

**Sources of Data**

All data on Malaysia presented in Figure 1 and used for measuring CA, Y, REER and RI in the SVAR are taken from Bank Negara Malaysia *Quarterly Economic Bulletin*. All these data are available on quarterly basis from the beginning of sample period 1985:1. The real and nominal GDP series are seasonally adjusted using the Census XII procedure. The three-month KLIBOR refers to the Kuala Lumpur inter-bank market rate.

Data on the annual current account and nominal GDP for Indonesia, Thailand and South Korea are taken from the IMF, *International Financial Statistics*. Data on U.S. and EU real GDP and imports, together with the OECD real GDP are taken from OECD Economic Indicators. The quarterly OECD real GDP adjusted using the Census XII procedure.

# Notes

1. See Eichengreen, Rose, and Wyplosz (1995) and Milesi-Ferretti and Razin (1998) for variants of the event-study methodology.
2. The criteria utilized by Milesi-Ferretti and Razin (1998) for a significant and sustained current account reversal are:
    (i)   the current account deficit exceeded 2 per cent of GDP before reversal;
    (ii)  the deficit was reduced by at least 3 per cent of GDP over a three-year period;
    (iii) the maximum deficit after the reversal was not larger than the minimum deficit in the three years before the reversal; and
    (iv)  the average deficit was reduced by one-third.
3. See Obstfeld and Rogoff (1996, Chapter 10) and Lane and Milesi-Ferretti (2000).
4. A tabulation of the pre-tax earnings of a sample of 592 companies listed on the Kuala Lumpur Stock Exchange by the end of 1997 indicated a RM15.2 billion reduction in profit arising from provisions for unhedged foreign exchange liabilities, diminution in the value of investment and bad debts. Provision for diminution in value of investments in listed shares accounted for 23 per cent of the losses. See Gan, Soon, and Soh (1999).
5. Some of the projects involved were the Bakun Hydroelectric project, KL Linear City, Cameron Highlands–Fraser Hill–Genting Highland Road, South Klang Valley Expressway, and Kuala Lumpur International Airport Dedicated Highway. Investment in office space, hotels, and shopping were scaled back as excess supply developed in the face of declining demand.
6. Between 1997:4 to 1998:4, imports of consumption goods declined by 14 per cent while imports of investment goods fell by 23 per cent.

7. Non-Malaysian owned firms accounted for 44.5 and 50 per cent of manufactured output in 1997 and 1999, respectively, and the majority are manufactures for export markets (Department of Statistics of Malaysia, *Annual Survey of Manufacturing Industries*).

8. In fact, the industrial production index for the manufacturing sector for 1999 rose to a level (167.8) that exceeded the pre-crisis level (1997: 165.6). See Bank Negara Malaysia, *Annual Report 1999*, pp. 17–18.

9. Since $\Sigma$ is a symmetric matrix, it contains $(n^2+n)/2$ known distinct moments. Matrices $A$ and $B$ each contains $n^2$ elements. Since the diagonal elements of $A$ and $B$ are all unity, the actual unknown parameters in each of the matrices is $n^2-n$. In order to identify the $2(n^2-n)$ structural parameters from $(n^2+n)/2$ independent elements of $\Sigma$, it is necessary to impose at least an additional $n(2n-1)-(n^2+n/2)=n(3n-1)/2$ restrictions on $A$ and $B$ matrices. If $B$ is assumed to be an identity matrix, as most studies do, then one is left with only $n(n-1)/2$ additional restrictions to be imposed on $A$.

10. This assumption is consistent with existing empirical evidence that the trade balance responds much more rapidly to real income changes than to real exchange movements. See Goldstein and Khan (1985) for a survey of empirical estimates.

11. The covariance matrix $\Sigma$ has 15 known moments. The number of additional restrictions required in matrices $A$ and $B$ for exact identification is 35. Since $B$ is assumed to be a diagonal matrix with 20 zero restrictions, the additional restrictions that needs to be imposed on $A$ is 15. This is satisfied by the imposition of 5 unit and 10 zero restrictions.

12. The choice of the lag length is based on minimizing the Akaike and Schwarz criteria.

13. The plot is not reproduced here but is available from the authors.

14. The multivariate Lagrange Multiplier (LM) test indicates that the null hypothesis of no serial correlation of the order 4 in the reduced form residuals cannot be rejected with $\chi^2(4) = 14.69$ and $p$-value $= 0.984$. The multivariate Jarque-Bera test indicates the null hypothesis of normality cannot be rejected with $\chi^2(4) = 96.96$ with $p$-value $= 0.707$.

15. In addition, as shown by Baxter and King (1999), first differencing the data that contain unit root, while removing the stochastic trend, tend to distort the cyclical properties of the data series.

16. SVAR was estimated using Eviews 4 (2000) software vector autoregression and error correction models programme. The identifying restrictions on the $A$ and $B$ matrices were created through the SVAR short-run pattern option. $A$ and $B$ were estimated by the maximum likelihood procedure, where the log likelihood is maximized by the Marquardt method of scoring.

17. Recent macroeconomic models with pricing-to-market behaviour predict a weak expenditure-switching effect of exchange rate changes. See Devereux and Engel (1999) and Betts and Devereux (2000).

# References

Bank Negara Malaysia. *Annual Report*. Kuala Lumpur: Bank Negara Malaysia, various issues.

————. *Quarterly Economic Bulletin*. Kuala Lumpur: Bank Negara Malaysia, various issues.

Baxter, M. and R.G. King. "Measuring Business Cycles: Approximate Band-Pass Filters for Economic Time Series". *Review of Economic and Statistics* 81 (1999): 575–93.

Bernanke, B.S. "Alternative Explanations of the Money-Income Correlation". *Carnegie-Rochester Series on Public Policy* 25 (1986): 49–99.

Betts, C. and M.B. Devereux. "Exchange Rate Dynamics in a Model of Pricing-to-Market". *Journal of International Economics* 50 (2000): 215–44.

Blanchard, O. and D. Quah. "The Dynamic Effects of Aggregate Demand and Supply Disturbances". *American Economic Review* 79 (1989): 655–73.

Clarida, R. and J. Gali. "Sources of Real Exchange Rate Fluctuations: How Important Are Nominal Shock?". *Carnegie-Rochester Conference Series on Public Policy* 44 (1994): 328–55.

Clarida, R. and J. Prendergast. "Recent G3 Current Account Imbalances: How Important Are Structural Factors". NBER Working Paper no. 6935. National Bureau of Economic Research, 1999.

Cushman, D.O. and T. Zha. "Identifying Monetary Policy in a Small Open Economy Under Flexible Exchange Rates". *Journal of Monetary Economics* 39 (1997): 433–48.

Department of Statistics. *Annual Survey of Manufacturing Industries*. Kuala Lumpur: Department of Statistics.

Devereux, M. and C. Engel. "The Optimal Choice of Exchange-Rate Regime: Price Setting Rules and Internationalized Production". NBER Working Paper no. 6992. National Bureau of Economic Research, 1999.

Eichengreen, B., A.K. Rose, and C. Wyplosz. "Exchange Market Mayhem: The Antecedents and Aftermath of Speculative Attacks". *Economic Policy* 21 (1995): 249–312.

Elliot, G. and A. Fatas. "International Business Cycles and the Dynamics of Current Account". *European Economic Review* 40 (1996): 361–87.

Freund, C.L. "Current Account Adjustment in Industrial Countries, Board of Governors of the Federal Reserve System". International Finance Discussion Paper No. 692, 2000.

Gan, W.B., L.Y. Soon, and C.C. Soh. "The Ringgit and the Malaysian Financial Crisis: An Interpretation". *Malaysian Journal of Economic Studies* 46 (1999): 45–74.

Gan, W.B. and L.Y. Soon. "Credit Crunch During a Currency Crisis: The Malaysian Experience". *ASEAN Economic Bulletin* 18 (2001): 176–92.

————. "Evaluating Monetary Policy in Malaysia: Policy Reaction Function and Transmission Mechanism". Nanyang Business School, Nanyang Technological University, 2002.

Ghosh, A.R. "International Capital Mobility Amongst the Major Industrial Countries: Too Little or Too Much?". *Economic Journal* 105 (1995): 107–28.

Glick, R. and K. Rogoff. "Global Versus Country-Specific Productivity Shocks and the Current Account". *Journal of Monetary Economics* 35 (1995): 159–92.

Goldstein, M. and M.S. Khan. "Income and Price Effects in Foreign Trade". In *Handbook of International Economics*, edited by R. W. Jones and P.B. Kenen, pp. 1041–105. Amsterdam: North - Holland, 1985.

Harris, R. *Cointegration Analysis in Economic Modelling*. London: Prentice Hall, 1995.

International Monetary Fund (IMF). *International Financial Statistics*. Washington, D.C.: IMF, various issues.

Kim, S. "International Transmission of U.S. Monetary Policy Shocks: Evidence from VAR's". *Journal of Monetary Economics* 48 (2001): 339–72.

Lane, P.R. and G.M. Milesi-Ferretti. "The Transfer Problem Revisited: Net Foreign Assets and Real Exchange Rates". CEPR Discussion Paper No. 2511, 2000.

Lane, P.R. "Money Shocks and the Current Account". In *Money, Capital Mobility and Trade*, edited by G.A. Calvo, R. Dornbusch, and M. Obstfeld, pp. 385–411. Cambridge, MA: MIT Press, 2001.

Lee, J. and M. Chinn. "The Current Account and the Real Exchange Rate". NBER Working Paper no. 6495. National Bureau of Economic Research, 1998.

Lutkepohl, H. *Introduction to Multiple Time Series*. Berlin: Springer Verlag, 1991.

McCallum, B. T. "Unit Root in Macroeconomic Time Series: Some Critical Issues". NBER Working Paper no. 4368. National Bureau of Economic Research, 1993.

Milesi-Ferretti, G.M. and A. Razin. "Current Account Reversal and Currency Crisis: Empirical Regularities". IMF Working Paper WP/98/89. International Monetary Fund, 1998.

Obstfeld, M. "International Capital Mobility in the 1990s". In *Understanding Interdependence: The Macroeconomic of the Open Economy*, edited by P.B. Kenen, pp. 201–61. Princeton, N.J.: Princeton University Press, 1994.

Obstfeld, M. and K. Rogoff. "The Intertemporal Approach to the Current Account". In *Handbook of International Economics,* edited by G. Grossman and K. Rogoff, pp. 1731–99. Amsterdam: North–Holland, 1995.

————. *Foundation of International Macroeconomics*. Cambridge, MA: MIT Press, 1996.

Organization for Economic Co-operation and Development. *OECD Economic Indicators*. Paris: OECD, <www.oecd.org>.

Prasad, E.S. and J.A. Gable. "International Evidence on the Determinants of Trade Dynamics". *IMF Staff Papers* 45 (1998): 401–39.

Sims, C.A. "Macroeconomics and Reality". *Econometrica* 48 (1980): 1–48.

————. "Are Forecasting Models Usable for Policy Analysis?". *Federal Reserve Bank of Minneapolis Quarterly Review* 10 (1986): 2–16.

# 3

# SUPPLY-SIDE CAUSES OF MACROECONOMIC FLUCTUATIONS IN A SMALL OPEN ECONOMY

## Choy Keen Meng

### I. INTRODUCTION

Empirical macroeconomic research in recent times has sought to rediscover the causes of business cycle fluctuations in the industrialized economies. Studies in this vein are provided by, *inter alia*, Shapiro and Watson (1988), Blanchard and Quah (1989), Moreno (1992), and Karras (1994). These works employed a variant of the vector autoregressive (VAR) methodology to investigate the contributions of aggregate demand and aggregate supply shocks to macroeconomic fluctuations. Typical demand shocks consist of disturbances to the goods and money markets, while supply shocks include oil price shocks, technological disturbances, and labour supply shocks. A common finding shared by the studies is that supply shocks play an important role in the business cycle fluctuations of developed countries.

Notwithstanding the renewed interest in the subject, there have been only two published studies along the above lines on business cycles in the small open economy of Singapore. The first of these, by Makrydakis (1997), recovered generic demand and supply shocks from a bivariate VAR model estimated for output and inflation. The author found that supply shocks are the dominant source of the growth cycles — fluctuations in the growth rate of economic activity — experienced by Singapore during the last two decades.

However, given the multitude of possible supply shocks and their differential impact on the economy, it is questionable whether a single aggregate supply shock recovered from the data can be meaningfully interpreted.

The second study by Choy (1999) explored the sources of macroeconomic fluctuations in Singapore through a six-variable structural VAR model, identified by Keynesian-style short-run restrictions. Of the business cycle shocks examined, three can be classified as aggregate demand disturbances and the remaining three as aggregate supply shocks. Choy (1999) showed that although demand shocks are important, supply disturbances accounted for more than half of short-run output fluctuations, thus suggesting that the latter deserve serious attention from researchers. This article, therefore, focuses on supply shocks buffeting the Singapore economy, but examines a larger number of supply-side factors which could be responsible for macroeconomic fluctuations than that considered in the earlier paper. Our emphasis on supply shocks also reflects the current popularity of the Real Business Cycle (RBC) theory.

Using VAR techniques again, our objective is to quantify the effects of supply shocks on key macroeconomic variables, in both the short and long run. The shocks we consider are oil price, foreign technology, labour supply, domestic productivity, and wage disturbances. Despite their obvious relevance to open economies, foreign productivity disturbances have not always been incorporated as a distinct class of business cycle shocks in the existing literature. This state of affairs is unsatisfactory in the specific case of the Singapore economy, with its high exposure to trade and investment flows. Hence, a notable feature of this paper is its consideration of international productivity shocks that are transmitted to domestic business cycles through technological spillovers and diffusion (for a theoretical justification, see the international RBC model of Backus, Kehoe, and Kydland 1992).

The other shocks mentioned are all potentially important for explaining fluctuations and growth in Singapore from a supply-side perspective. Following up on the significant role found for price disturbances in Choy (1999), world oil price shocks are examined directly in this study. The domestic supply shock in that paper is further decomposed into labour force increases and technological improvements, both of which have been documented by the studies cited earlier to be significant determinants of output fluctuations in the industrialized economies. In Singapore, labour supply shocks may be especially pertinent, given the economy's long-standing dependence on foreign workers as a source of labour. As in Choy (1999), we are motivated to add a wage-setting disturbance to the model, in view of the constant changes in wage policies that have characterized Singapore's economic development process. For example, wage increases were instituted by the National Wages Council (NWC) in the early 1980s to encourage higher value-added activities; conversely, reductions in wages and Central Provident Fund (CPF) contribution rates were implemented as anti-recession measures in the mid-1980s, and again during the Asian financial crisis of 1997–98.

The next section explains the empirical model and its economic rationale. This is followed by preliminary analyses of the data in Section III. Section IV presents the estimation results and the findings on the relative importance of different supply shocks for Singapore's growth cycles. These results lead to several conclusions and policy implications in Section V.

## II. EMPIRICAL MODEL

The empirical methodology used in this paper is a five-variable VAR model estimated on quarterly data over the period 1980Q1–2001Q4. Ultimately, we are interested in the following dynamic system of equations:

$$\Delta \mathbf{y}_t = \mathbf{c} + \sum_{k=0}^{\infty} \mathbf{A}_k \boldsymbol{\varepsilon}_{t-k} \tag{1}$$

where $\Delta \mathbf{y}_t$ is a vector of first-differenced macroeconomic variables, $\mathbf{c}$ is a vector of constant terms, $\boldsymbol{\varepsilon}_t$ is a vector of supply shocks and the $\mathbf{A}_k$'s are matrices of impact coefficients that measure the effects of shocks on variables at discrete time horizons. The macroeconomic variables in the system are the rate of change of the real oil price ($\Delta o$), foreign output growth ($\Delta y^f$), the change in employment ($\Delta n$), domestic output growth ($\Delta y$), and wage inflation ($\Delta w$). The uncorrelated supply innovations are interpreted accordingly as: oil price, foreign technology, labour supply, domestic productivity, and wage-setting shocks.

To recover the equations above, we first estimate the unrestricted $p$-th order VAR model:

$$\Delta \mathbf{y}_t = \mathbf{d} + \sum_{k=1}^{p} \mathbf{B}_k \Delta \mathbf{y}_{t-k} + \mathbf{u}_t \tag{2}$$

where $\mathbf{d}$ is another vector of constants, the $\mathbf{B}_k$'s are again coefficient matrices, and $\mathbf{u}_t$ is a vector of error terms. In the second step of the estimation procedure, the parameters of interest in (1) are obtained from the estimated coefficients and variances of the unrestricted model. Specifically, the relationship between the $\mathbf{A}_k$ and $\mathbf{B}_k$ matrices in Equations (1) and (2) is given by

$$\sum_{k=0}^{\infty} \mathbf{A}_k = \left( \mathbf{I} - \sum_{k=1}^{p} \mathbf{B}_k \right)^{-1} \mathbf{A}_0 \tag{3}$$

while that between the innovations is $\boldsymbol{\varepsilon}_t = \mathbf{A}_0^{-1} \mathbf{u}_t$.

In order to obtain the supply shocks, identification restrictions based on economic theory have to be imposed. Since we are investigating supply-side effects, the restrictions naturally take the form of a long-run causal ordering of the variables in the VAR model, a method employed by the seminal papers cited earlier. They are imposed recursively by constraining the infinite sums of the coefficients in the $\mathbf{A}_k$ matrices to zero. The sums, denoted as $a_{ij}$'s, summarize the cumulative long-run impact of supply shocks on macroeconomic variables, so that the restrictions effectively preclude the shocks at the bottom of the causal chain from having any permanent effects on the variables at the top. Our preferred causal ordering results in the equations below:

$$
\begin{aligned}
\Delta o &= c_1 + a_{11}\varepsilon_o \\
\Delta y^f &= c_2 + a_{21}\varepsilon_o + a_{22}\varepsilon_f \\
\Delta n &= c_3 + a_{31}\varepsilon_o + a_{32}\varepsilon_f + a_{33}\varepsilon_n \\
\Delta y &= c_4 + a_{41}\varepsilon_o + a_{42}\varepsilon_f + a_{43}\varepsilon_n + a_{44}\varepsilon_y \\
\Delta w &= c_5 + a_{51}\varepsilon_o + a_{52}\varepsilon_f + a_{53}\varepsilon_n + a_{54}\varepsilon_y + a_{55}\varepsilon_w
\end{aligned}
\tag{4}
$$

With this recursive ordering, the estimates of the $a_{ij}$'s can be calculated directly from the Choleski factor of

$$
\left(\mathbf{I} - \sum_{k=1}^{p}\mathbf{B}_k\right)^{-1}\mathbf{\Omega}\left[\left(\mathbf{I} - \sum_{k=1}^{p}\mathbf{B}_k\right)^{-1}\right]'
$$

where $\mathbf{\Omega}$ is the variance-covariance matrix of the unrestricted VAR model (see Choy 2001 for details). The $\mathbf{A}_0$ matrix is then obtained from (3).

We justify our causal ordering of variables and shocks by invoking the small open economy assumption. The assumption implies that shocks of an external origin are exogenous to Singapore, so the oil price and foreign output variables should come first in the ordering. This means that the levels of domestic employment, output, and wages, in the long run, are influenced by world energy and technology shocks, whereas the domestic shocks themselves have no lasting effects on the rest of the world. Between the two external variables, the oil price is placed before foreign real output, to allow for the possibility that oil-induced supply disturbances may have a permanent impact on global production functions.

As for the domestic variables, we assume that causation runs from employment to output to wages. While putting employment first in the ordering seems reasonable from a long-run growth accounting perspective, the direction of causality between output and nominal wages is slightly more ambiguous. Certainly, changes in wage policy can result in short-term output movements. However, the neutrality property of nominal variables would suggest that wage shocks should not affect real output in the long run. Therefore, we put the nominal wage last in the causal ordering.

## III. DATA ANALYSIS

The data employed in this study is discussed briefly below. Further details on their sources and methods of construction are found in the Appendix. To start with, the nominal oil price used is the U.S. dollar spot price of Dubai crude. This price is converted into the local currency at the prevailing exchange rate, and expressed in real terms by deflating it with Singapore's consumer price index. As no indicator of foreign output is readily available, the series is constructed as an export-weighted average of the real GDPs of Singapore's major trading partners. Domestic output is measured by Singapore's real GDP, while the employment and nominal wage time series are explained in the Appendix. In the subsequent analysis, all macroeconomic variables are expressed in logarithms; where seasonality was found to be present, the data was seasonally adjusted using the X-12 adjustment routine.

A preliminary analysis was first carried out to ascertain the unit root properties of the variables under investigation. Table 1 shows the results of the augmented Dickey-Fuller (ADF) test on the levels and first differences of the series.[1] We found unit roots to be present in the levels of every series, but not in their first differences. In other words, all variables are integrated of order one, or I(1). Hence, the growth rate specification employed in the empirical model is appropriate.

However, entering variables into the model in their first differences also entails the assumption that they are not co-integrated. To verify this, Johansen's (1988) trace and maximum Eigenvalue statistics were used to test for co-integration among the series. The outcomes of the tests reported in Table 2 do not reject the null hypothesis of no co-integration at the 5 per cent significance level.[2] Therefore, the assumption that the VAR system is driven by five independent stochastic trends, corresponding to the included supply shocks, is supported by the data. The time series plots of the relevant macroeconomic variables in Figure 1 provide visual confirmation of this result.

The last data analysis performed prior to model estimation concerns the selection of the lag length in the VAR model. Sims' (1980) modified likelihood ratio test and Akaike's information criterion (AIC) were intially used to determine the optimal number of lags to include in the model. Both

## TABLE 1
## ADF Unit Root Tests

| Variable | Levels | | Differences | |
|---|---|---|---|---|
|  | $k$ | $\tau_\tau$ | $k$ | $\tau_\mu$ |
| $o$ | 3 | −2.156 | 1 | −8.342* |
| $y^f$ | 2 | −1.674 | 4 | −3.946* |
| $n$ | 5 | −2.042 | 4 | −3.514* |
| $y$ | 4 | −1.572 | 3 | −4.434* |
| $w$ | 2 | −1.485 | 2 | −3.046** |

NOTES: $k$ is the lag length used; $\tau_\tau$ and $\tau_\mu$ are the ADF statistics with a constant and trend, and a constant only; * and ** denote significance at 1 per cent and 5 per cent levels respectively.

## TABLE 2
## Johansen Co-Integration Tests

| Null hypothesis | Trace | 95% Critical value | Max | 95% Critical value |
|---|---|---|---|---|
| $r = 0$ | 80.75 | 87.31 | 27.04 | 37.52 |
| $r \leq 1$ | 53.71 | 62.99 | 18.66 | 31.46 |
| $r \leq 2$ | 35.05 | 42.44 | 16.08 | 25.54 |
| $r \leq 3$ | 18.96 | 25.32 | 11.58 | 18.96 |
| $r \leq 4$ | 7.38 | 12.25 | 7.38 | 12.25 |

NOTES: $r$ is the number of cointegrating relationships; the model used in the tests has three lags and includes an unrestricted constant and a restricted trend; critical values are from Osterwald-Lenum (1992), Table 2*, Case 2*.

criteria picked a lag length of two, but this resulted in auto-correlated residuals in some of the VAR equations. When four lags were included in the model instead, the Lagrange Multiplier and White (1980) tests indicated that the residuals were free of serial correlation and heteroscedasticity respectively, although those in the oil, foreign output, and employment equations still failed to pass the Jarque-Bera normality test, due to the presence of isolated outliers. Consequently, a fourth order model is chosen in the next section.

## IV. ESTIMATION RESULTS

In the estimation of the VAR model, a dummy variable was added to the oil equation, to capture the sharp spike in the spot oil price during the Gulf

**FIGURE 1**
**Plot of Macroeconomic Variables**

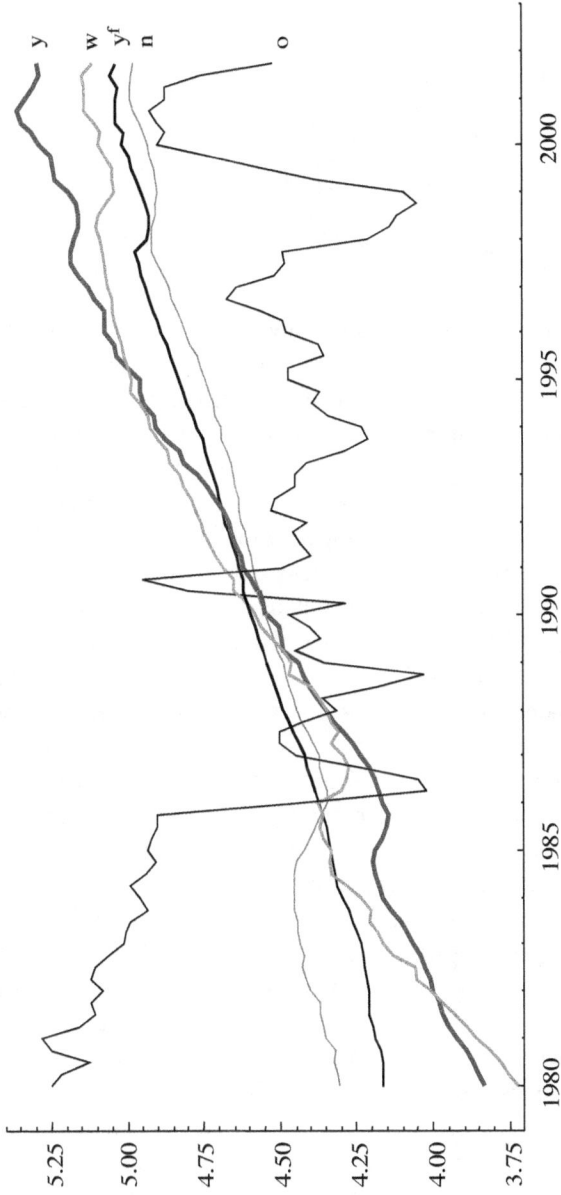

War (1990Q3). The resulting estimates of the equations in (4) are (constant terms are omitted):

$$\Delta o = 0.12\varepsilon_o$$
$$\quad\;\; (0.08)$$
$$\Delta y^f = -0.001\varepsilon_o + 0.009\varepsilon_f$$
$$\qquad\;\; (-0.01) \qquad\quad (0.98)$$
$$\Delta n = 0.007\varepsilon_o + 0.004\varepsilon_f + 0.022\varepsilon_n$$
$$\qquad (0.01) \qquad\quad (0.07) \qquad\quad (2.26)$$
$$\Delta y = -0.0003\varepsilon_o + 0.010\varepsilon_f + 0.012\varepsilon_n + 0.01\varepsilon_y$$
$$\qquad (-0.002) \qquad\;\; (0.34) \qquad\;\; (1.63) \qquad\;\; (3.82)$$
$$\Delta w = -0.013\varepsilon_o + 0.016\varepsilon_f + 0.011\varepsilon_n + 0.018\varepsilon_y + 0.018\varepsilon_w$$
$$\qquad (-0.02) \qquad\;\; (0.64) \qquad\;\; (0.73) \qquad\;\; (2.35) \qquad\;\; (5.59)$$

Figures in parentheses below the parameter estimates are $t$-statistics generated by a Monte Carlo simulation procedure, designed specifically for VAR models (Doan 1992). Unfortunately, most of the long-run $a_{ij}$ coefficients are small and statistically insignificant, even though they are estimated with the right signs. As expected, the domestic variables increase permanently after a positive foreign technology shock, and decrease after an oil price shock (the exception is the rise in employment following an oil shock). However, only the impact of domestic supply shocks is precisely estimated — in every case, they have positive effects on employment, output, and wages in the long run.

Figure 2 shows the impact of supply shocks on domestic output in the short to medium and long run. These impulse response functions trace out the dynamic effects on Singapore's GDP of a positive one-standard deviation innovation in each of the five shocks.[3] The chart shows that an adverse oil price shock causes output to decline for about three years, with the effects trending towards zero after that. On the other hand, domestic output increases significantly and permanently following a foreign technology shock, which can be interpreted in this context as a favourable global productivity shock.

In response to a labour supply disturbance, real GDP adjusts smoothly to its higher long-run level, which is reached after a mere two years. The dynamic response pattern of aggregate output to a domestic productivity innovation mimics the hump-shaped reaction to an external technology shock, with most of the shock's impact being felt within the first year. Lastly, a wage shock reduces output for only two quarters, although the estimated effects are small. Judging from Figure 2, the diverse supply shocks hitting the Singapore economy appear to be correctly identified.

Next, we turn to an examination of the relative importance of different supply shocks for Singapore's growth cycle fluctuations. In VAR analysis, forecast error variance decompositions reveal the proportions of the total

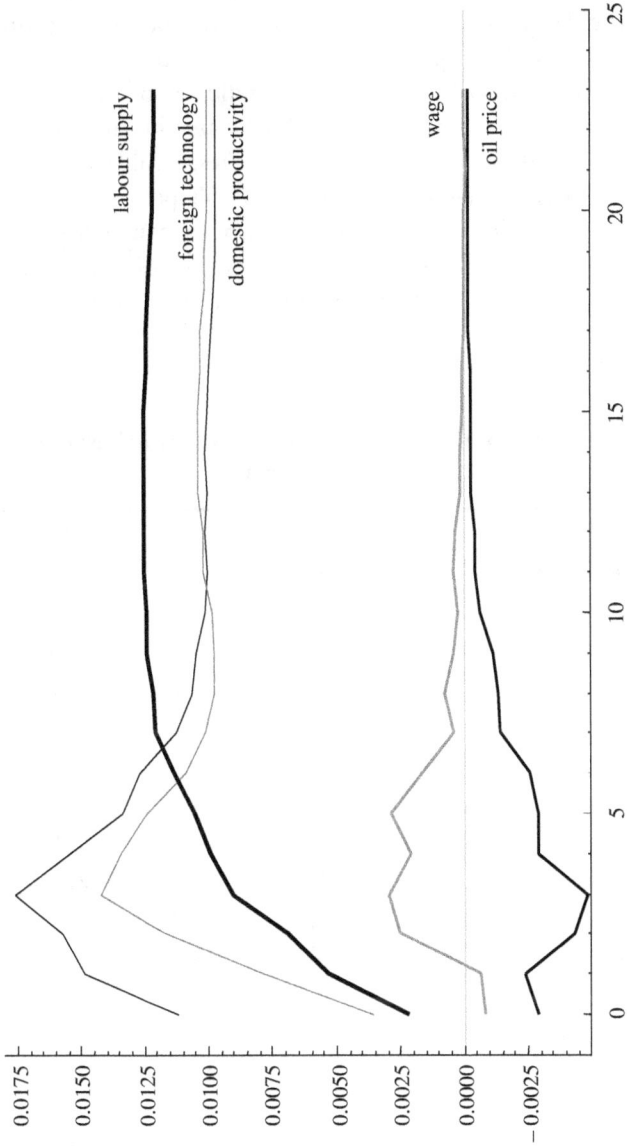

FIGURE 2
Dynamic Effects of Supply Shocks on Singapore Output

variation in macroeconomic variables that can be attributed to individual shocks. The decompositions at selected time horizons for domestic employment, output, and nominal wages are reported in Table 3. We treat the results at the 4-quarters horizon to be indicative of the short run, and those at the 24-quarters horizon to be indicative of the long run.

The variance decomposition of domestic output will be discussed first, as it is often taken to be the reference indicator of business cycles. Table 3 shows that domestic productivity shocks are the most important cause of Singapore's business cycles, as they are responsible for the lion's share of the short-term variability in output, or 58 per cent. This is followed by foreign technological disturbances, whose contribution stabilizes at roughly 30 per cent a year after the shock takes place. Labour supply shocks are much less important in the short run, with a share of about

**TABLE 3**
**Variance Decompositions for Domestic Variables**
**(Per cent)**

| Shock | $\varepsilon_o$ | $\varepsilon_f$ | $\varepsilon_n$ | $\varepsilon_y$ | $\varepsilon_w$ |
|---|---|---|---|---|---|
| *Domestic Output* | | | | | |
| 1 quarter | 5.8 | 8.4 | 3.2 | 82.2 | 0.4 |
| 4 quarters | 3.7 | 26.7 | 10.5 | 58.0 | 1.0 |
| 12 quarters | 1.8 | 28.6 | 26.3 | 42.6 | 0.7 |
| 24 quarters | 1.0 | 29.0 | 34.1 | 35.5 | 0.4 |
| | | | | | |
| *Employment* | | | | | |
| 1 quarter | 2.6 | 9.3 | 73.3 | 5.9 | 8.8 |
| 4 quarters | 0.4 | 2.7 | 72.1 | 21.4 | 3.5 |
| 12 quarters | 2.9 | 3.9 | 85.7 | 6.1 | 1.4 |
| 24 quarters | 5.9 | 3.1 | 88.1 | 2.3 | 0.5 |
| | | | | | |
| *Nominal Wage* | | | | | |
| 1 quarter | 32.2 | 1.5 | 13.0 | 1.5 | 51.8 |
| 4 quarters | 24.1 | 4.3 | 10.2 | 17.4 | 44.0 |
| 12 quarters | 19.5 | 15.6 | 3.1 | 33.6 | 28.2 |
| 24 quarters | 16.7 | 18.5 | 6.4 | 31.3 | 27.0 |

NOTE: Numbers may not add up to 100 per cent at each horizon, due to rounding errors.

11 per cent in economic fluctuations, but their role increases in the medium term. In the long run, local productivity shocks account for just over one-third of output growth. This is matched by the contributions of foreign productivity and labour supply shocks, at 34 per cent and 29 per cent respectively.

Interestingly, world oil price shocks play a very small part in output fluctuations at all time horizons. Indeed, such disturbances explain at most 4 per cent of real GDP gyrations in the short run. This finding is consistent with the empirical evidence presented in Abeysinghe (2001*b*) and Ito and Tay (1994), demonstrating that oil price shocks have a relatively small impact on Singapore's economic growth — an intuitively plausible result in the light of Singapore's status as a net exporter of refined oil products. Less expected is the negligible role of wage shocks in output fluctuations, which is at odds with the conventional view that cost-cutting measures are an efficacious instrument of macroeconomic demand management in Singapore.

Fluctuations in employment are mainly explained by labour supply shocks. In the short run, domestic productivity disturbances are another determinant of employment changes. Again, wage-setting shocks do not seem to matter much for employment; this is true not just in the long run, where they have no bite by assumption, but also in the short run. Although not conclusive, this result suggests that reductions in labour costs have not had much success in minimizing job retrenchments in economic downturns, such as during the Asian financial crisis.

Wage shocks are nevertheless the predominant sources of cyclical movements in the wage rate itself. Nominal wages are also depressed by oil price and labour supply shocks in the short run, albeit for different reasons: a fall in output in the first case, and an expansion of the labour force in the second (see the impulse responses of nominal wages in Figure 3). In contrast, productivity gains arising from external and domestic technology shocks contribute to a higher nominal wage mainly in the long run.

## V. CONCLUSION

This study has provided empirical evidence on the supply-side causes of business cycle fluctuations in the small open economy of Singapore. The analysis is carried out by estimating a VAR model that includes externally induced oil and technology shocks on the one hand, and domestic labour supply, productivity, and wage shocks on the other. Despite the diversity of the shocks considered, their dynamic effects on domestic macroeconomic variables have been identified, by imposing economic restrictions on the empirical model.

**FIGURE 3**
**Dynamic Effects of Supply Shocks on Singapore Wage**

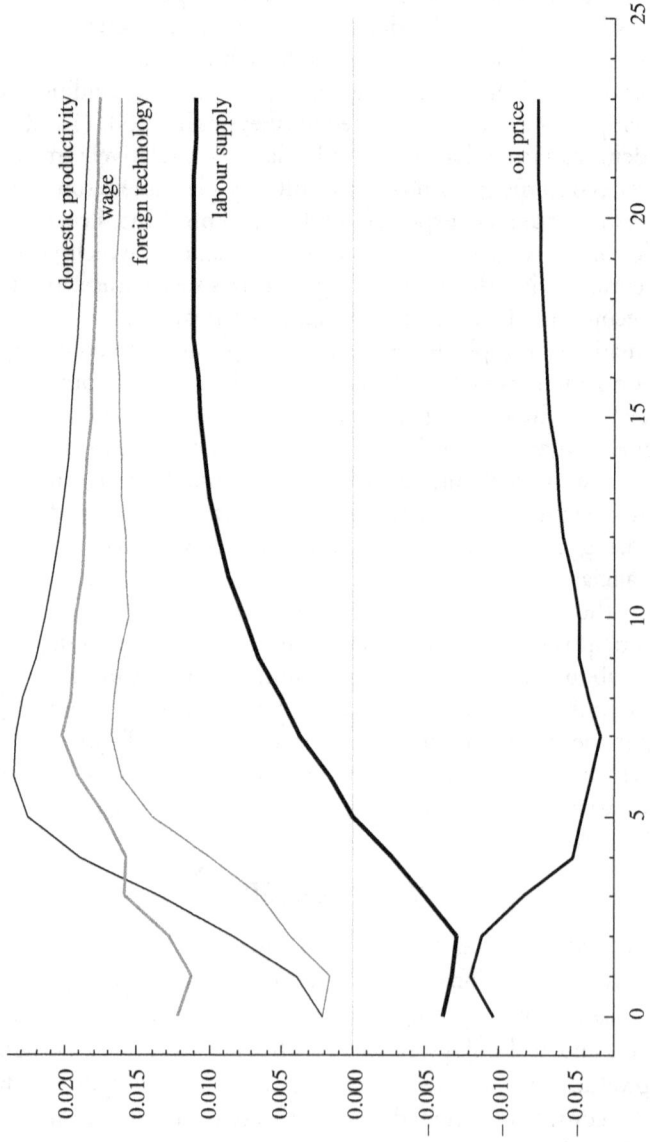

A major conclusion of the paper is that domestic productivity shocks are the principal driving force behind Singapore's macroeconomic fluctuations, as far as supply-side shocks are concerned. Not surprisingly, however, foreign technological disturbances are also important in explaining Singapore's short-run fluctuations as well as long-term growth. These findings compare well with the results reported for the Organization for Economic Co-operation and Development (OECD) economies by Ahmed and Park (1994). Our conclusions are generally supportive of the view that Singapore business cycles are caused by both domestic and international factors. With regard to foreign shocks, we also found that world oil price increases have only a small negative impact on output fluctuations.

Labour supply shocks originating in Singapore play a more important role in long-run output growth than in short-run cycles; this is in contrast to Shapiro and Watson's (1988) finding that these shocks strongly influenced American business cycles. The result suggests that the government's foreign worker policy has aided the secular expansion of the Singapore economy over the past twenty years, by allowing for a steady augmentation of the domestic labour force. More unexpectedly, wage-setting shocks seem to have small effects on both output and employment. Thus, another policy implication could be that wage policy is not as potent an instrument of macroeconomic management as commonly envisaged by policy-makers and economists alike, though a definitive conclusion can only be reached through further research — for example, by estimating the aggregate demand for labour in Singapore.[4] It is instructive to note that a recent report by the Economic Review Committee calls for avoiding the use of changes in CPF contribution rates as a counter-cyclical tool, save as a last resort in exceptional economic circumstances (Economic Review Committee 2002).

In conclusion, one caveat of the study must be pointed out. This is the recognition that aggregate demand shocks are also important for understanding Singapore's growth cycles. Such disturbances have not been included in the VAR model because the focus of the paper is on supply shocks, and in any event, demand shocks were examined by Choy (1999). However, the exclusion of these disturbances from the empirical model calls for caution in interpreting the results of this article.

**Appendix**

The data sources and methods of construction of the macroeconomic variables used in the paper are detailed below.

*o*: The nominal oil price is the U.S. dollar Dubai Fateh spot price from the *International Financial Statistics* CD-ROM. To convert the price into real domestic currency terms, it is multiplied by the Singapore dollar/U.S. dollar exchange rate and divided by the Singapore consumer price index. These two series are extracted from the Singapore Department of Statistics' (DOS) TREND database.

$y^f$: The foreign output series is obtained from Tilak Abeysinghe of the Department of Economics, National University of Singapore. It is constructed as a geometrically-weighted average of real GDP in a group of ten countries and one region which constitute Singapore's main export destinations, viz., Malaysia, Indonesia, Thailand, the Philippines, South Korea, Taiwan, Hong Kong, China, Japan, the United States, and the OECD group (excluding the United States and Japan). The weights used are the respective export shares of the countries/region in Singapore's total nominal exports. To capture changing trends in market shares over time, a 12-quarter moving average is used to compute the weights. The data sources drawn upon are given in Abeysinghe (2001*a*).

*n*: Total employment is calculated from data on changes in employment published on a quarterly basis by DOS and extending back to 1979. The starting value for the series is obtained by adding the change in employment in 1979Q1 to the level of total employment at the end of 1978, which is published as an annual statistic. All data are sourced from TREND.

*y*: Domestic output is Singapore's real GDP at 1990 market prices from the TREND database.

*w*: A nominal wage time series is not available for Singapore from the official sources. The series used is derived from unit labour costs data in TREND and a productivity series obtained by dividing real GDP by employment.

## Notes

The author is grateful to Tilak Abeysinghe for providing data and helpful suggestions. The comments of two anonymous referees on an earlier draft of this paper are also much appreciated.
1. Both constant and trend terms were included in the level regressions. For the first differences regressions, only a constant was used. Lag lengths were chosen by a sequential testing procedure.
2. The test statistics are based on three lags, an unrestricted constant, and a restricted trend.
3. The impulse responses are the impact coefficients in the $\mathbf{A}_k$ matrices of

Equation (1), while the variance decompositions are functions of the same coefficients.
4. The author is indebted to a referee for this suggestion.

## References

Abeysinghe, T. "Thai Meltdown and Transmission of Recession within ASEAN4 and NIE4". In *International Financial Contagion*, edited by S. Claessens and K. Forbes, pp. 225–40. Boston, MA: Kluwer Academic Publishers, 2001*a*.

———. "Estimation of Direct and Indirect Impact of Oil Price on Growth". *Economics Letters* 73 (2001*b*): 147–53.

Ahmed, S. and J.H. Park. "Sources of Macroeconomic Fluctuations in Small Open Economies". *Journal of Macroeconomics* 16 (1994): 1–36.

Backus, D.K., P.J. Kehoe, and F.E. Kydland. "International Real Business Cycles". *Journal of Political Economy* 100 (1992): 745–75.

Blanchard, O.J. and D. Quah. "The Dynamic Effects of Aggregate Demand and Supply Disturbances". *American Economic Review* 79 (1989): 655–73.

Choy, K.M. "Sources of Macroeconomic Fluctuations in Singapore: Evidence from a Structural VAR Model". *Singapore Economic Review* 44 (1999): 74–98.

———. *Macroeconomic Fluctuations in Singapore: An Empirical Study*. Ph.D. dissertation, National University of Singapore, 2001.

Doan, T.A. *RATS User's Manual Version 4*. Evanston, Illinois: Estima, 1995.

Economic Review Committee, Sub-Committee on Policies Related to Taxation, the CPF System, Wages and Land. "Refocusing the CPF System for Enhanced Security in Retirement and Economic Flexibility". Singapore, 2002. Available at <http://www.mti.gov.sg>.

Ito, S. and B.N. Tay. "The Impacts of the Oil Shock on the Singaporean Economy: Simulation Results of a CGE Model". *Asian Economic Journal* 8 (1994): 59–84.

Johansen, S. "Statistical Analysis of Cointegrating Vectors". *Journal of Economic Dynamics and Control* 12 (1988): 231–54.

Karras, G. "Sources of Business Cycles in Europe 1960–1988: Evidence from France, Germany, and the United Kingdom". *European Economic Review* 38 (1994): 1763–78.

Makrydakis, S. "Sources of Macroeconomic Fluctuations in the Newly Industrialized Economies: A Common Trends Approach". *Asian Economic Journal* 11 (1997): 361–83.

Moreno, R. "Macroeconomic Shocks and Business Cycles in Australia". Federal Reserve Bank of San Francisco, *Economic Review*, No. 3 (1992): 34–52.

Osterwald-Lenum, M. "A Note on Quantiles of the Asymptotic Distribution of the Maximum Likelihood Cointegration Rank Test Statistic". *Oxford Bulletin of Economics and Statistics* 54 (1992): 461–72.

Shapiro, M.D. and M. Watson. "Sources of Business Cycle Fluctuations". *NBER Macroeconomics Annual* (1988): 111–56.

Sims, C.A. "Macroeconomics and Reality". *Econometrica* 48 (1980): 1–49.

White, H. "A Heteroskedastic-Consistent Covariance Matrix Estimator and a Direct Test for Heteroskedasticity". *Econometrica* 48 (1980): 817–38.

# 4

# EFFECTIVENESS OF FISCAL STIMULI

## Tsangyao Chang, Wen Rong Liu, and Henry Thompson

The Asian financial crisis of 1997 led to output declines in South Korea, Taiwan, and Thailand. In response, the three countries have turned to fiscal policy to stimulate output. This study investigates the empirical evidence on the viabiltiy of fiscal policy for these three Asian countries using data starting in the 1950s. While fiscal expansion can raise output under certain theoretical conditions, deficit spending implies higher taxes that could eliminate even transitory effects. This article explores these issues, and examines the empirical relationships between government spending, taxes, and output in these three Asian "tigers".

The literature includes varying views on the links between fiscal policy, government spending, and output. The tax-and-spend hypothesis of Buchanan and Wagner (1978) and Friedman (1978) is that taxes lead to government spending. On the other hand, according to the spend-and-tax hypothesis of Peacock and Wiseman (1979), temporary increases in government spending lead to permanent tax increases. Meltzer and Richard (1981), describe fiscal synchronization and state that spending and taxes would adjust as the public chooses an optimal package of taxes and government spending. The related literature using Granger (1988) causality includes von Furstenberg, Green, and Jeong (1986), Owoye (1995), Hasan and Lincoln (1997), and Darrat (1998). In addition, Koren and Stiassny (1998) consider whether taxes and spending are cointegrated.

The dynamic responses of taxes, spending, and income are examined in this article using vector autoregression (VAR) analysis. Impulse response and variance decomposition are also included as in Baffes and Shah (1994) and Koren and Stiassny (1998), because coefficients of a VAR are difficult to gauge. Impulse responses trace the reaction of an endogenous variable to an innovation, capturing dynamic interactions and adjustment speeds. Variance decomposition measures the share of forecast error variance due to a shock to the system and own innovations would explain the forecast error variance of exogenous variables.

This article focuses on real government spending, taxes, and gross domestic product. Fiscal policy could affect interest rates, and in turn investment spending. Interest rates could be included in the study, but it is not clear which rate to use and expected inflation clouds the issue. The empirical links between the fiscal variables and output may provide some indication of the viability of a more active fiscal policy stance in these Asian economies.

The article is organized as follows. The next section briefly describes the recent history of fiscal policy in South Korea, Taiwan, and Thailand. Section II presents empirical tests of fiscal policy and output, while Section III concludes.

## I. THE RECENT HISTORY OF FISCAL POLICY IN SOUTH KOREA, TAIWAN, AND THAILAND

South Korea, Taiwan, and Thailand have achieved relatively high growth since the 1960s and in all three countries, macroeconomic policies have focused on export-led growth. Thailand's growth, in particular, was very high during the 1990s. Among the three countries, South Korea and Taiwan share many similar features in terms of economic growth, size, population, and dependency on energy imports. With regard to their characteristics, public spending patterns are also similar in these three countries. Mundle (1999) points out that public spending has been under 30 per cent of gross domestic product (GDP) in Taiwan, 25 per cent in South Korea, and 20 per cent in Thailand, relative to an average of about 50 per cent for the Organization for Economic Co-operation and Development (OECD) countries. The relatively low spending levels in these three countries has been combined with government surpluses or low deficits. Episodes of inflation have generally been followed by fiscal restraint, at least up to the financial crisis of 1997. Since the crisis, along with structural reforms, South Korea and Thailand have been pursuing expansionary fiscal policy to revive economic growth.

In Taiwan, the "Forecasters of Aggregate Supply and Demand" of the central government have been responsible for providing a basis for government budgeting since 1968. Taiwan had a balanced government budget from 1955 to 1988, but has since experienced a deficit. As a consequence, recent budget deficits in Taiwan have sparked debate over fiscal policy, as discussed by Rao (1998). The government has sold public properties, issued debts, and borrowed from private banks. A six-year macroeconomic stability plan adopted in 1990, but abandoned in 1993, produced large budget deficits financed by bonds (Wu 1998).

The year 2000 introduced a new political era for Taiwan with a change in political parties after the fifty-year reign of the Kuomintang (KMT), and the political situation has become unusually unstable. Related to this, stock markets were quite volatile during 2000. Labour costs have caused some enterprises to leave for China and the overall economic situation has worsened. As a consequence, the new administration has decided to increase government spending to stimulate aggregate demand.

The debate between supporters of market versus government-led development in Korea and Taiwan is discussed by Hattori and Sato (1997). They conclude that growth in South Korea has been mostly government-led, while growth in Taiwan has been led by trade and productivity. Budget deficits had not been an issue for South Korea until 1997. Furthermore, after a lull, South Korea has regained its momentum, and output grew over 10 per cent in 1999.

Similarly, Thailand's output grew about 8 per cent annually during the 1990s until the crisis in 1997 that started with the collapse of the Thai baht. The Thai Government has since pursued structural reform of the financial system and expansionary fiscal policy to revive growth. For all three countries, it might be worthwhile to look at the history of the viability of fiscal policy to forecast its potential for success.

## II. EMPIRICAL TESTS OF FISCAL POLICY AND OUTPUT

Annual data include gross domestic product Y, government spending G, and tax revenue T for South Korea (1954–96), Taiwan (1951–96), and Thailand (1951–95), all in real terms. Data are from AREMOS of the Taiwan Ministry of Education and are transformed to logarithms to achieve stationarity in variance.

Macroeconomic time series generally contain unit roots and are dominated by stochastic trends, as developed by Nelson and Plosser (1982). Unit root tests detect nonstationarity that would invalidate standard empirical results. The present study uses augmented Dickey-Fuller (1991, ADF) and Kwiatowski-Phillips-Schmidt-Shin (1992, KPSS) tests to detect unit roots. The Akaike (1974) information criterion (AIC) determines the optimal specification.

Table 1 reports the results of ADF tests with a constant but no time trend. Nonstationarity cannot be rejected for levels according to the test statistics of MacKinnon (1991), but nonstationarity can be rejected with differenced data. Every series is integrated of order one. Table 2 reports KPSS results confirming the ADF results.

Given the presence of unit roots, the question becomes whether there is some long-run equilibrium cointegrating relationship between variables. A variable $x_t$ is cointegrated of order $(d, b)$ if it is integrated of order $d$ and there is a vector $b$ such that $bx_t$ is integrated of order $(d - b)$. Cointegration tests are conducted with the Johansen and Juselius (1990) method. A VAR model is fitted to the data to find the appropriate lag structure. The Schwartz criterion and the likelihood ratio test suggest two lags, and a Ljung-Box Q test on residuals indicates no residual autocorrelation. The Lagrange multiplier test indicates no ARCH effects in systems.

**TABLE 1**
**ADF Unit Root Tests**

|  | Level | AIC(n) | First-difference | AIC(n) |
|---|---|---|---|---|
| **South Korea** (1954–96) |  |  |  |  |
| Y | 1.07 | −6.70(1) | −3.98* | −6.82(1) |
| G | −0.61 | −3.67(1) | −7.16* | −3.90(1) |
| T | −1.01 | −3.70(1) | −4.70* | −3.70(1) |
| **Taiwan** (1951–96) |  |  |  |  |
| Y | −0.81 | −7.26(1) | −4.21* | −7.24(1) |
| G | −1.10 | −4.55(1) | −5.19* | −4.51(1) |
| T | −1.63 | −4.70(1) | −5.19* | −4.68(1) |
| **Thailand** (1951–95) |  |  |  |  |
| Y | 1.47 | −7.07(1) | −3.46* | −7.05(1) |
| G | 0.02 | −4.73(1) | −5.59* | −4.90(1) |
| T | 1.25 | −5.58(1) | −4.57* | −5.53(1) |

NOTE: * indicates 5 per cent level of significance.
SOURCE: Author's estimations.

## TABLE 2
## KPSS Unit Root Tests

| | | Level (l = 3) | | 1st-difference (l = 3) | |
|---|---|---|---|---|---|
| | | $h_u$ | $h_l$ | $h_u$ | $h_l$ |
| **South Korea** | | | | | |
| | Y | 1.17* | 0.14** | 0.31 | 0.11 |
| | G | 1.17* | 0.04 | 0.05 | 0.05 |
| | T | 1.16* | 0.10 | 0.04 | 0.04 |
| **Taiwan** | | | | | |
| | Y | 1.25* | 0.18* | 0.21 | 0.17 |
| | G | 1.25* | 0.04 | 0.08 | 0.05 |
| | T | 1.25* | 0.10 | 0.20 | 0.05 |
| **Thailand** | | | | | |
| | Y | 1.22* | 0.12** | 0.33 | 0.07 |
| | G | 1.22* | 0.08 | 0.05 | 0.05 |
| | T | 1.22* | 0.20* | 0.27 | 0.05 |

NOTE: * and ** indicate 5 and 10 per cent levels of significance respectively.
SOURCE: Author's estimations.

Table 3 presents the results from the Johansen cointegration tests. Trace and L-max statistics suggest two cointegrating vectors for South Korea and one for Taiwan. For Thailand, the null hypothesis of no cointegration is not rejected at the 5 per cent level. There are long-run relationships between fiscal variables and output in South Korea and Taiwan, but there is none in Thailand. This long-run independence of the variables in Thailand suggests immediately that fiscal policy will be ineffective. Thailand's economy is based more on natural resources and that may account for the lack of a long-run relationship between fiscal policy and output.

If nonstationary variables are cointegrated, vector autoregression (VAR) in first differences would be misspecified. Since cointegration relationships are found for South Korea and Taiwan, an error correction model (ECM) is used to test for statistical causality. Granger (1988) points out that cointegration would imply statistical causality in at least one direction. The error correction model (ECM) of Engle and Granger (1987) takes into account information

## TABLE 3
## Cointegration Tests

**South Korea**    Y, T, G (VAR lag = 2)

|                | Tr    | L-max | Tr (5%) | L-max (5%) |
|----------------|-------|-------|---------|------------|
| $H_0$: r = 0   | 48.0* | 27.2* | 30.0    | 21.0       |
| $H_0$: r =1    | 21.0  | 20.6* | 15.4    | 14.1       |
| $H_0$: r = 2   | 20.3  | 0.27  | 3.76    | 3.76       |

Estimates of cointegrating relation (asymptotic standard errors)
lrgdp – 1.833 lrge + 0.742 lrgr ~ I(0)
(0.23)        (0.19)

**Taiwan**        Y, T, G (VAR lag = 2)

|                | Tr    | L-max | Tr (5%) | L-max (5%) |
|----------------|-------|-------|---------|------------|
| $H_0$: r = 0   | 35.4* | 21.4* | 30.0    | 21.0       |
| $H_0$: r =1    | 15.2  | 13.5  | 15.4*   | 14.1       |
| $H_0$: r = 2   | 0.59  | 0.59  | 3.76    | 3.76       |

Estimates of cointegrating relation (asymptotic standard errors)
lrgdp – 4.074 lrge + 3.143 lrgr ~ I(0)
(2.11)        (1.20)

**Thailand**      Y, T, G (VAR lag = 2)

|                | Tr    | L-max | Tr (5%) | L-max (5%) |
|----------------|-------|-------|---------|------------|
| $H_0$: r = 0   | 16.7  | 11.3  | 30.0    | 21.0       |
| $H_0$: r =1    | 5.38  | 3.93  | 15.4    | 14.1       |
| $H_0$: r = 2   | 1.46  | 1.46  | 3.76    | 3.76       |

NOTES: Given the restricted test results, the trend is not incorporated for Thailand.
* indicates 5 per cent level of significance.
SOURCE: Author's estimations.

provided by cointegrated properties. Lag lengths are determined with Hsiao's (1979) sequential procedure based on the Granger definition of causality and Akaike's (1974) minimum final prediction error (FPE). For Thailand, the variables are not cointegrated and causality is analysed without an error correction term.

Table 4 summarizes the ECM results. Numbers in brackets indicate minimum FPE lag length. For South Korea, unidirectional causality from G to T supports the spend-and-tax hypothesis. Income has led to government spending, not vice versa, while there is feedback between income and taxes. This evidence suggests expansionary fiscal policy has no history of success in South Korea.

**TABLE 4**
**Granger Causality Tests:**
**Multivariate ECMs for South Korea and Taiwan,**
**VAR in differences for Thailand**

| South Korea | Taiwan | Thailand |
|---|---|---|
| G [1] ⇒ T [1] | T [3] ⇒ G [1] | Y [1] ⇒ T [2] |
| Y [1] ⇒ G [1] | Y [1] ⇔ G [1] | Y [1] ⇒ G [2] |
| Y [1] ⇔ T [1] | Y [1] ⇒ T [3] | |

NOTE: Details about the estimates of ECM and VAR in difference are available upon request.
SOURCE: Author's estimation.

For Taiwan, there is unidirectional causality from T to G, supporting the tax-and-spend hypothesis. There is feedback between Y and G, suggesting that expansionary fiscal policy may have some impact on Y. Also, higher income causes increased taxes.

For Thailand, the first differenced VAR model suggests no causality between government spending and taxes, while higher income causes both increased government spending and higher taxes. There is no evidence of a viable fiscal policy in Thailand, a link between either G or T and Y.

Table 5 reports cumulative impulse responses after ten years indicating the direction of the impact of an innovation. The effects gradually build up over ten years. Focusing on the established causality, in South Korea the impact of G on T has an elasticity of 0.25, a moderate spend-and-tax. The causal impact of Y on G is close to zero. The feedback between Y and T is dominated by the effect of T on Y.

For Taiwan, the elasticity of T on G is only 0.07, indicating a very weak tax-and-spend property. The elasticity of G on Y is 0.26, and the reverse of this feedback mechanism reveals a much weaker elasticity of 0.07. A 10 per cent increase in government spending in Taiwan would lead to a 2.6 per cent increase in income after ten years. Such a small impact suggests fiscal policy would not be recommended. Higher income leads to slightly lower taxes in Taiwan.

For Thailand, all cumulative responses are negligible and the two causal impacts are close to zero.

Table 6 presents variance decompositions after ten years. Forecast error variance is decomposed into the proportion attributed to each random shock. For South Korea, the forecast error variance of T, attributed to G is only 7 per cent. The variance of G attributed to Y is 57 per cent, and for T, the

### TABLE 5
### Cumulative Impulse Responses after Ten Years

|  | *Response to Y* | | | *Response to G* | | | *Response to T* | | |
|---|---|---|---|---|---|---|---|---|---|
|  | Y | G | T | Y | G | T | Y | G | T |
| **South Korea** | 0.41 | −0.04 | 0.09 | 0.47 | −0.01 | 0.25 | 0.75 | 0.48 | −0.18 |
| **Taiwan** | 0.25 | 0.07 | −0.04 | 0.26 | 0.09 | 0.08 | 0.24 | 0.07 | 0.03 |
| **Thailand** | 0.04 | −0.00 | 0.01 | 0.04 | 0.00 | 0.02 | 0.04 | 0.04 | −0.01 |

SOURCE: Author's estimation.

### TABLE 6
### Variance Decompositions after Ten Years

|  | *Variance decomposition of Y* | | | *Variance decomposition of G* | | | *Variance decomposition of T* | | |
|---|---|---|---|---|---|---|---|---|---|
|  | Y | G | T | Y | G | T | Y | G | T |
| **South Korea** | 0.92 | 0.02 | 0.06 | 0.57 | 0.25 | 0.18 | 0.58 | 0.07 | 0.35 |
| **Taiwan** | 0.89 | 0.08 | 0.03 | 0.42 | 0.13 | 0.45 | 0.50 | 0.05 | 0.45 |
| **Thailand** | 0.92 | 0.04 | 0.04 | 0.08 | 0.88 | 0.05 | 0.30 | 0.05 | 0.65 |

SOURCE: Author's estimation.

variance attributed to Y is 58 per cent. The feedback from T to Y is much weaker, only 6 per cent.

In Taiwan, the forecast error variance of G attributed to T is relatively large, 45 per cent. The variance of G attributed to Y is 42 per cent but the "fiscal policy" forecast error variance from Y to G is only 8 per cent. While increased G causes an increase in Y in Taiwan, the effect is very small. The variance of T attributed to Y is 50 per cent.

For Thailand, variables are accounted for mostly by their own innovations, confirming the lack of causal links. The variance of T attributed to Y is relatively high, at 65 per cent. Output in all three countries is predominantly exogenous as indicated by the high own variance decomposition terms.

### III. CONCLUSION

Output growth has not depended on any particular approach to fiscal policy in these three quickly growing Asian economies, and there is little evidence to support a belief that expansionary fiscal policy will be effective in the future. More active fiscal policy would seem likely to have different effects on the three economies. In South Korea, there would be moderate output effects that would gradually build up, and higher taxes can be expected according to its spend-and-tax character. In Taiwan, only very weak output responses can be anticipated in response to government spending. Taiwan has a cautious approach to fiscal policy, establishing a tax base before spending. In Thailand, taxes and spending have been independent and fiscal policy has had no output effects.

In summary, more active efforts at fiscal policy stimulation are not recommended for these three Asian economies. The three have relatively small public sectors and no history of successful fiscal policy. The 1997 crisis was financial and it would be wise to concentrate on correcting the underlying inefficiencies in the financial systems.

## References

Akaike, H. "A New Look at the Statistical Model Identification". *IEEE Transaction on Automatic Control* AC-19 (1974): 716–23.

Baffes, John and Anwar Shah. "Causality and Comovement between Taxes and Expenditures: Historical Evidence from Argentina, Brazil, and Mexico". *Journal of Development Economics* (1994): 311–31.

Buchanan, James and Richard Wagner. "Dialogues Concerning Fiscal Religion". *Journal of Monetary Economics* 4 (1978): 627–36.

Darrat, Ali. "Tax and Spend, or Spend and Tax? An Inquiry into the Turkish Budgetary Process". *Southern Economic Journal* (1998): 940–56.

Dickey, David. A. and W.A. Fuller. "Likelihood Ratio Statistics for Autoregressive Time Series with A Unit Root". *Econometrica* (1991): 1057–72.

Engle, R.F. and C.W.J. Granger. "Co-integration and Error-Correction: Representation, Estimation and Testing". *Econometrica* (1987): 251–76.

Friedman, Milton. "The Limitations of Tax Limitation". *Policy Review* (1978): 7–14.

Granger, C.W.J. "Some Recent Developments in a Concept of Causality". *Journal of Econometrics* (1988): 199–211.

Granger, C.W.J. and P. Newbold. "Spurious Regressions in Econometrics". *Journal of Econometrics* (1974): 111–20.

Hasan, Mohammad and Ian Lincoln. "Tax then Spend or Spend then Tax? Experience in the UK, 1961–93". *Applied Economics Letters* (1997): 237–39.

Hattori, Tamio and Yukihito Sato. "A Comparative Study of Development Mechanisms in Korea and Taiwan: Introductory Analysis". *Developing Economies* 35 (1997): 341–57.

Hsiao, Cheng. "Causality Tests in Econometrics". *Journal of Economic Dynamics and Control* 4 (1979): 321–46.

Johansen, S. and K. Juselius. "Maximum Likelihood Estimation and Inference on Cointegration: With Applications to the Demand for Money". *Oxford Bulletin of Economics and Statistics* (1990): 169–210.

Koren, Stephan and Alfred Stiassny. "Tax and Spend, or Spend and Tax? An International Study". *Journal of Policy Modeling* (1998): 163–91.

Kwiatkowski, D., P.C. Phillips, P. Schmidt and Y. Shin. "Testing the Null Hypothesis of Stationarity against the Alternative of a Unit Root". *Journal of Econometrics* (1992): 159–78.

MacKinnon, James. "Critical Values for Cointegration Tests in Long-Run Economic Relationships". In *Readings in Cointegration*, edited by Engle and Granger. Oxford: Oxford University Press, 1991.

Meltzer, Allan and Scott Richard. "A Rational Theory of the Size of Government". *Journal of Political Economy* 89 (1981): 914–27.

Mundle, S. "Symposium: Fiscal Policy and Growth — Some Asian Lessons for Asia". *Journal of Asian Economics* 10 (1999): 15–36.

Nelson, C.R. and C.I. Plosser. "Trends and Random Walks in Macroeconomic Time Series: Some Evidence and Implications". *Journal of Monetary Economics* (1982): 139–62.

Owoye, Oluwole. "The Causal Relationship between Taxes and Expenditures in The G-7 Countries: Cointegration and Error-Correction Models". *Applied Economics Letters* (1995): 19–22.

Peacock, Alan and Jack Wiseman. "Approaches to the Analysis of Government Expenditure Growth". *Public Finance Quarterly* 7 (1979): 3–23.

Rao, M.G. "Accommodating Public Expenditure Policies: the Case of Fast Growing Asian Economies". *World Development* 26, no. 4 (1998): 673–94.

von Furstenberg, George M., R. Jeffery Green, and Jin-Ho Jeong. "Tax and Spend, or Spend and Tax?". *Review of Economics and Statistics* (1986): 179–88.

Wu, J.L. "Are Budget Deficits 'Too Large'? The Evidence from Taiwan". *Journal of Asian Economics* 9 (1998): 519–28.

# 5

# PUBLIC DEBT SUSTAINABILITY AND ITS MACROECONOMIC IMPACTS

## Anthony J. Makin

### I. INTRODUCTION

Capital flight from the emerging economies of East Asia in 1997–98 precipitated the most notable geo-financial crisis of the second half of the twentieth century with lasting international economic and political effects. Thailand, Malaysia, the Philippines, and Indonesia (the ASEAN-4) in particular were severely distressed by near simultaneous exchange rate and asset price collapses that devastated banking and financial sectors, slashed real investment and induced recessions (see, for instance, Chang and Velasco 1999, Eichengreen 2002, Furman and Stiglitz 1998, Glick, Moreno and Spiegel 2001, Goldstein 1998, Makin 1999 and Radelet and Sachs 1998). South Korea, an advanced economy, also suffered directly although quickly recovered, while Hong Kong, Taiwan, and Singapore were punished indirectly through associated trade shocks that dampened or negated previously strong growth rates.

Numerous factors triggered the international capital flow reversals that caused financial crisis in the ASEAN-4. These included poor corporate governance, overvalued exchange rates and excessive foreign borrowing by domestic banks for unproductive projects. However, fiscal balances had generally been sound and inflation rates moderate. In contrast, overall budget balances measured as a proportion of GDP have deteriorated markedly in the ASEAN-4 economies since the crisis, turning pre-crisis fiscal surpluses to deficits that remain high by the standards of developed economies (Makin 2005). Most notably, Malaysia and the Philippines have posted persistent deficits between 4 to 6 per cent of GDP since 2000 (see Figure 1).

The consolidated public debt (inclusive of the debt of all tiers of government and non-financial public enterprises) to income ratios of the ASEAN-4 economies have accordingly risen well above pre-crisis levels (see Figure 2) to historically high levels across the region. They are generally well in excess of the average public debt to income ratio of advanced economies of around 25 per cent (IMF 2003).

Public debt grew strongly because the ASEAN-4 governments actively deployed fiscal policy as a post-crisis counter-cyclical measure to boost domestic demand in the context of a global economic slowdown. Accelerated domestic financial liberalization also facilitated issuance of public debt instruments in home markets over this time.

In addition, the ASEAN-4 financial sectors experienced balance sheet distress after the currencies collapsed. Due to implicit guarantees to protect depositors and other creditors, as well as taking on the foreign exchange debt of certain corporations, the public sectors of these economies subsumed significant commercial bank liabilities. The recapitalization of failed banks in particular was either recorded explicitly in the budget accounts or recorded off-budget through the quasi-fiscal activities of central banks (see Brixi and Schick 2002). Of course, to the extent that nationalized banks remained commercial, governments also acquired bank assets.

High public debt levels raise numerous macroeconomic risks for emerging economies. For instance, excess public sector demand for domestic funds raises domestic interest rates that crowd out private investment and limit economic growth. Moreover, an escalating stock of public debt increases the probability of default, raising the interest risk premium charged by creditors. This further enlarges public debt interest obligations, accelerating budget outlays. Governments facing uncontrollable interest servicing costs are tempted to default or monetize public debt.

Outright debt default then makes further government borrowing on reasonable terms very difficult, whereas monetization subsequently generates higher inflation. Should default or monetization occur, either course of action is likely to precipitate capital flight, sparking further financial crisis. Indeed, capital flight can occur before the domestic authorities actually default or monetize if investors suddenly judge such events inevitable, or when they realize crowding out is crippling economic growth.

FIGURE 1
ASEAN-4: Central Government Budget Balances

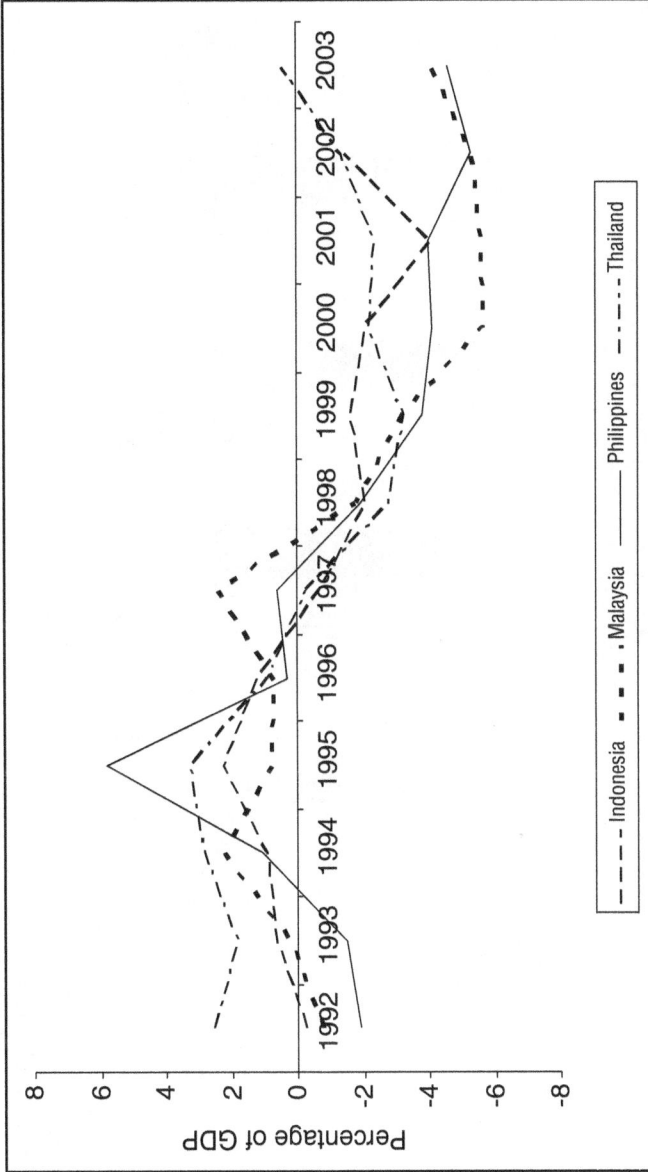

SOURCES: Based on data from International Monetary Fund, *International Financial Statistics* and IMF-Singapore Training Institute.

FIGURE 2
ASEAN-4: Consolidated Public Debt to GDP

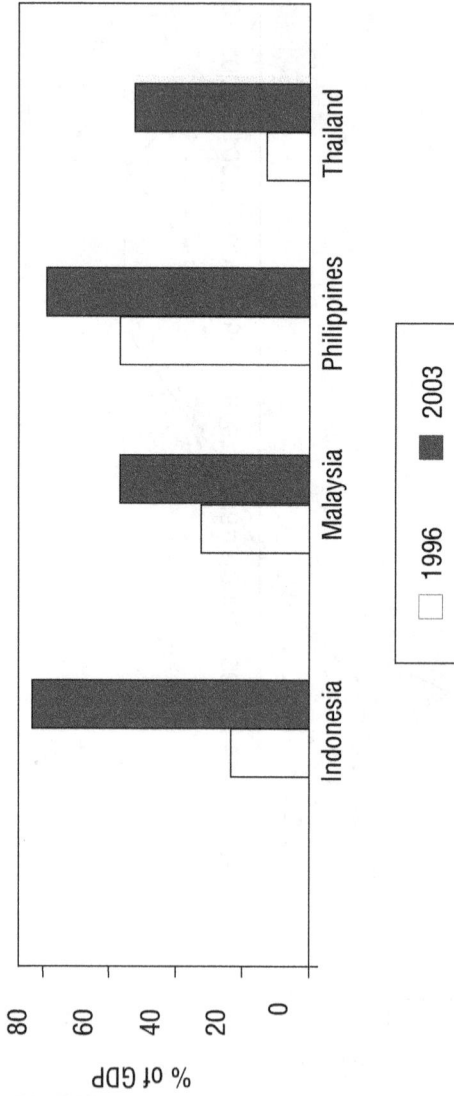

SOURCE: IMF-Singapore Training Institute.

## II. PUBLIC DEBT SUSTAINABILITY

Using a range of mathematical methods, numerous authors have examined the dynamic macroeconomic interrelationship between budget balances and public debt (see, for instance, Blanchard 1990, Bohn 1998, Buiter 1985, Fischer and Easterly 1990, Frederiksen 2001). In what follows, we focus strictly on the sustainability dimension. This is first outlined algebraically, then interpreted using new graphical techniques.

A fiscal stance is ultimately not sustainable if it leads to an ever-increasing ratio of debt to income. To assess fiscal sustainability, it is necessary to estimate whether this ratio will rise, fall, or remain stable in the immediate period ahead. Since the primary budget balance (the conventional fiscal balance less interest payments) determines the rate at which new debt accumulates or old debt can be retired, it plays the central role in assessing fiscal sustainability. Fiscal authorities directly control the primary fiscal balance through discretionary fiscal measures affecting public expenditure and revenue.

A given fiscal stance becomes untenable if public debt to income exceeds a level financial markets will tolerate. Precisely what this level is in percentage terms is a matter for judgement, however, and may vary from country to country, given levels of economic development and the underlying strength of financial systems (see Aiyagari and McGrattan 1998). Faced with rapidly rising public debt, fiscal authorities need to decide whether merely stabilizing debt to national income is sufficient. If not, then the primary balance to national income ratio that would ensure a lower targeted debt to GDP ratio has to be estimated.

A straightforward method for assessing the fiscal effort required to stabilize or lower this ratio is founded on the government intertemporal budget constraint whereby the stock of public debt in the current period equals pre-existing debt minus the primary budget surplus (or plus the primary budget deficit) plus accrued public debt interest. Budget deficits are not money-financed by the central bank. In other words, there is no seigniorage, since money-financing can be highly inflationary.

The budget accounting relation can be expressed algebraically in discrete time as

$$D_t = D_{t-1} + iD_{t-1} - PB_t \tag{1}$$

where $D$ is public debt, $i$ is interest rate, and $PB$ is primary balance.

Dividing equation (1) by nominal *GDP* (or *Y*)

$$\frac{D_t}{Y_t} = (1+i)\frac{D_{t-1}}{Y_t} - \frac{PB_t}{Y_t} \tag{2}$$

$$\frac{D_t}{Y_t} = \frac{(1+i)}{(1+g)}\frac{D_{t-1}}{Y_{t-1}} - \frac{PB_t}{Y_t} \tag{3}$$

where *g* is rate of GDP growth.

Taking the change in the public debt to national income ratio

$$\frac{D_t}{Y_t} - \frac{D_{t-1}}{Y_{t-1}} = \frac{(1+i)}{(1+g)}\frac{D_{t-1}}{Y_{t-1}} - \frac{D_{t-1}}{Y_{t-1}} - \frac{PB_t}{Y_t} \tag{4}$$

Setting

$$\Delta(\frac{D}{Y}) = \frac{D_t}{Y_t} - \frac{D_{t-1}}{Y_{t-1}} \tag{5}$$

and simplifying

$$\Delta(\frac{D}{Y}) = \left[\frac{i-g}{1+g}\right]\frac{D_{t-1}}{Y_{t-1}} - \frac{PB_t}{Y_t} \tag{6}$$

Equation (6) shows that public debt to GDP rises, the higher the primary deficit, the higher the interest rate (*i*) and the lower the rate of growth (*g*), whereas the public debt to income ratio falls, the lower the interest rate, the higher the rate of growth and the higher the primary surplus. If GDP growth is relatively small, the (1+*g*) term may be omitted to simplify the expression.

To stabilize public debt to national income,

$$\frac{PB_t}{Y_t} = \left[\frac{i-g}{1+g}\right]\frac{D_{t-1}}{Y_{t-1}} \tag{7}$$

or simply

$$pb = \alpha\left[\frac{i-g}{1+g}\right] \tag{8}$$

where *pb* is the primary balance to income ratio and $\alpha$ is the previous period debt to income ratio.

The relationship between nominal and real interest rates is

$$i = (1+r^*)(1+\pi) - 1 \tag{9}$$

where $r^*$ is the real interest rate and $\pi$ is the inflation rate, and the relationship between nominal and real growth is

$$g = (1+g^*)(1+\pi) - 1 \tag{10}$$

Hence, through substitution, and assuming small product terms are negligible, equation (8) can also be written as

$$pb = \alpha \left[ \frac{r^* - g^*}{1 + g^* + \pi} \right] \tag{11}$$

If the interest rate exceeds the growth rate, a primary surplus is required for debt stabilization, whereas if the growth rate exceeds the interest rate, a primary deficit is possible. If a primary surplus is necessary for debt stabilization, its size rises directly with the magnitude of the initial debt to income ratio. Hence, the higher the initial debt stock is, the more difficult it is to stabilize the debt to income ratio and the higher this ratio, the greater is the fiscal effort required.

The relationship between primary balances, interest rates, growth and debt stabilization can usefully be illustrated with reference to Figure 3. In the figure, the horizontal axis shows possible primary budget balances ranging from deficit to surplus that the fiscal authorities can choose for time $t$.

The vertical axis shows public debt to GDP values over the same period, with debt levels rising above the horizontal axis and falling below it. At the origin, the primary budget balance is zero and the debt ratio is $\frac{D_{t-1}}{Y_{t-1}}$.

The $BB$ schedule passing through the intersection point $a \frac{(i-g)}{(1+g)}$ on the vertical axis and through the point $pb$ on the horizontal axis relates discretionary primary balances for period $t$ to corresponding changes in the debt ratio, for given interest and economic growth rates. Since the value of the debt to GDP ratio at the point of intersection of both axes is the pre-existing debt to income ratio, $\frac{D_{t-1}}{Y_{t-1}}$, the vertical distance to any point on the vertical axis from the intersection is also the value of $\Delta(\frac{D}{Y})$.

## FIGURE 3
## The Primary Budget Balance and Debt to Income Ratio

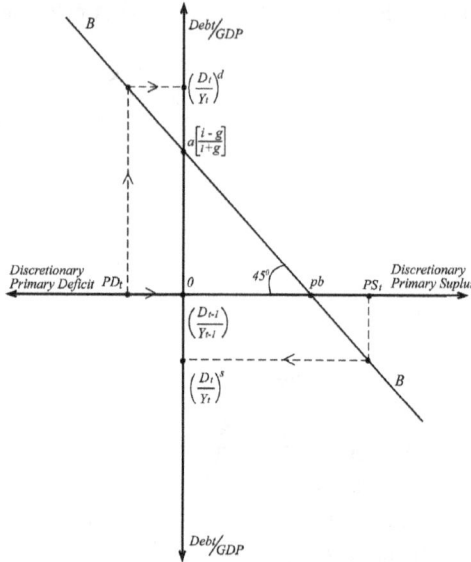

The negative slope of the $BB$ schedule, derived by differentiating equation (4), has a value of minus one and intercepts the vertical axis above intersection point $\dfrac{D_{t-1}}{Y_{t-1}}$ if $i > g$, and would intercept below this point if $i < g$.

Taking the case where $i > g$, the figure shows that a primary deficit of say $PD_t$ in excess of the stabilizing primary balance $pb$ implies a rising debt ratio of $(\dfrac{D_t}{Y_t})^d$ whereas a primary surplus of $PS_t$ in excess of $pb$ reduces the debt ratio to $(\dfrac{D_t}{Y_t})^s$.

In the opposite case where $i < g$, the $BB$ schedule would intersect below the horizontal axis as $a\dfrac{(i-g)}{(1+g)}$ would be negative. Although not drawn in the figure, a lower $BB$ schedule reflecting a lower interest rate and/or higher growth rate could show that it is possible to run primary deficits without raising the debt ratio, up to the point where the *BB* line intersects the deficit section of the primary balance line.

This analysis can also be used to highlight the vicious cycle effects of higher deficits and debt as shown in Figure 4. For instance, a primary deficit in period $t$ of $pb_t$ raises the debt ratio to $\dfrac{D_t}{Y_t}$. As creditors become more concerned about public sector solvency and the probability of default, a higher risk premium for holding the larger debt stock in period $t + 1$ raises the interest rate for that period. Other things equal, a higher interest rate and increased uncertainty would reduce private investment and hence $g$ for $t + 1$.

The $B_{t+1}B_{t+1}$ schedule of Figure 4 has a larger intercept value than the $B_tB_t$ schedule, implying an even larger primary surplus of $pb_{t+1}$ is necessary to stabilize higher public debt level at end $t + 1$. The debt trajectory is, therefore, unstable and primary fiscal deficits of $PD_{t, t+1}$ (or larger) repeated in $t + 2$, $t + 3 \ldots t + n$ make a fiscal and financial crisis inevitable. On the contrary, a virtuous cycle can arise if a sufficiently large primary surplus in $t$ reduces the debt ratio. In this case, it may be surmised that lower debt

## FIGURE 4
## Persistent Primary Deficits and Debt Instability

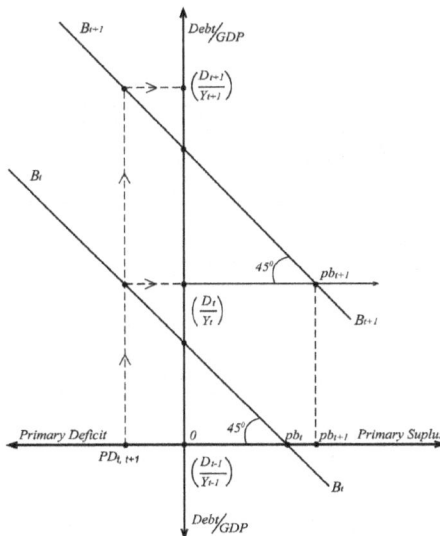

implies a lower interest rate, reduced uncertainty, higher investment, higher economic growth and a shrinking debt to income ratio.

## III. HOW SUSTAINABLE IS PUBLIC DEBT IN ASEAN-4 ECONOMIES?

With these foundations, it is possible to assess the sustainability of the fiscal positions of the ASEAN-4 economies using recent data on budget imbalances, public debt levels, GDP, and relevant interest rates. To assess the fiscal effort required to stabilize debt levels in accordance with the foregoing theory, it is first necessary to combine recent data on the debt to income ratio with the effective interest rate on public debt and the economic growth rate.

Public debt, budget deficit, and interest data for the central government sectors of the ASEAN-4 economies is available from IMF publications *Government Finance Statistics* and *International Financial Statistics* and central banks. As prescribed by equation (8), this data yields values for central government primary balances as a proportion of GDP that stabilize debt levels. These values can then be compared to actual primary balances. If the actual values exceed the stabilizing values, public debt ratios are falling whereas if actual values are less than stabilizing values, public debt ratios are rising.

Table 1, based on official data compiled from various sources, compares computed primary (non-interest) budget balances that satisfy the stability condition with actual primary budget balances. Estimates of the nominal

### TABLE 1
### Debt Stabilization and Primary Budget Balances, 2003–04

| | Public Debt/ GDP | Nominal Effective Interest Rate | Nominal Growth Rate | Stabilizing Primary Balance | Estimated Primary Balance |
|---|---|---|---|---|---|
| Indonesia | 80.5 | 9.5 | 13.6 | −2.9 | 3.8 |
| Malaysia | 51.9 | 4.8 | 10.5 | −2.7 | −1.8 |
| Philippines | 71.7 | 7.0 | 10.2 | −2.1 | 0.9 |
| Thailand | 28.8 | 4.7 | 6.5 | −0.5 | 5.4 |

SOURCES: Based on data sourced from IMF, *International Financial Statistics, Government Finance Statistics (various), Bank Negara Malaysia* and IMF-Singapore Regional Training Institute staff estimates.

effective interest rate, the ratio of public debt interest paid to the relevant stock measure of public debt, are based on the average of estimates for the most recent three years. Nominal economic growth estimates are also based on the most recent three years data.

This data illustrate whether public debt positions are stable or unstable. It shows that public debt levels for the ASEAN-4 economies are not automatically increasing, but decreasing. Indeed, debt to GDP ratios should continue to fall under the assumed macroeconomic conditions characterized by nominal growth rates greater than effective interest rates and actual primary balances exceeding the critical values necessary for stabilization. Nonetheless, conventional budget deficits inclusive of public debt interest remain significant, except for Thailand, because public debt interest payments still represent a major expenditure item on the outlays side of the public accounts.

Interestingly, the effective interest rate data shown in the table also reflect interest risk premia in the ASEAN-4 economies which, as mentioned earlier, act to crowd out real domestic private investment. A measure of the size of any country's interest risk premium is the difference between interest rates prevailing in that country and comparable international interest rates.

In all the ASEAN-4 economies, effective interest rates paid on public debt were at least 2 per cent higher than those payable on long-term bonds in Europe, Japan, and the United States. Indonesia and the Philippines, clearly the ASEAN-4 economies with the highest public debt levels, not surprisingly have the highest effective interest rates and hence risk premia. By implication, these sizeable interest risk premia could reduce domestic capital accumulation, resulting in an economic growth rate that is below potential.

The foregoing analysis has estimated the primary balances necessary to stabilize debt ratios at existing levels. However, if too high, public debt that has been stabilized may not necessarily be sustainable into the future. Since financial markets in emerging economies are more volatile, institutions weaker and credit histories poorer, default risk is higher in emerging economies than in advanced economies.

For instance, the public debt ratio limit of 60 per cent set for European Union (EU) members is too high for emerging economies. This is because over half of recent debt defaults of emerging economies have occurred at public debt levels below the EU limit (IMF 2003). Based on previous fiscal crises in other emerging economies, a much lower debt to income limit for ASEAN economies of less than half the EU limit may therefore be appropriate. Except for Thailand, the ASEAN-4 economies are presently well above this limit.

Indeed, to minimize crisis risk the International Monetary Fund has proposed a debt to income ceiling of 25 per cent (IMF 2003, Chapter 3).

This proposed limit is informed by analysis of financial crises experienced over the past decade by transition economies in Europe (Bulgaria, the Czech Republic, Russia, and Ukraine) and by emerging economies in Latin America (Argentina, Brazil, Ecuador, and Mexico). In all of these countries, fiscal problems that manifested in high public debt levels were the root causes of financial instability (see Hemming, Kell and Schimmelfennig 2003).

With reference to Figure 3, if the current level of debt was at $(\frac{D_t}{Y_t})^d$ and a desired level of 25 per cent corresponded to $(\frac{D_t}{Y_t})^s$, the fiscal turnaround to achieve the lower ratio in one year would require a turnaround from deficit $PD_t$ to surplus $PS_t$. The large fiscal reversals necessary to reduce debt to this particular target level may not, however, be feasible in the short term if debt levels significantly exceed the target level.

To estimate fiscal effort required to achieve the IMF's proposed 25 per cent ratio within a given number of years, it is possible to apply the following general formula.

$$pb = \beta \frac{(1+i)^n - (1+g)^n \rho}{\sum_{j=1}^n (1+i)^{n-j}}$$

$$(12)$$

where $\beta$ is the current debt to income ratio, $\rho$ is the targeted debt to GDP ratio and $n$ is the number of years allowed to achieve the target ratio. A full derivation of equation (12) is contained in Appendix 1.

Using spreadsheet analysis founded on relation (12), it is possible to estimate the constant primary balances required each year to achieve the 25 per cent limit in ASEAN-4 economies over particular time frames. For each of the ASEAN-4 economies, the tables in Appendix 2 show the central government primary surpluses as a proportion of GDP necessary to meet the target 25 per cent debt level. In general of course, the more time fiscal authorities have to achieve this target, the smaller their annual primary surpluses need be.

For comparative purposes, Figure 5 illustrates the values of annual primary surpluses that the central governments of ASEAN-4 economies need to run to reduce central government debt to 25 per cent of GDP within three, five, and ten year horizons, based on recent macroeconomic performance. Of the ASEAN-4, the central governments of Indonesia and the Philippines clearly have to exert the most fiscal effort to attain a target ratio of 25 per cent, given the size of their debt.

FIGURE 5

ASEAN-4: Primary Balances Required to Stabilize Debt at 25 per cent of GDP

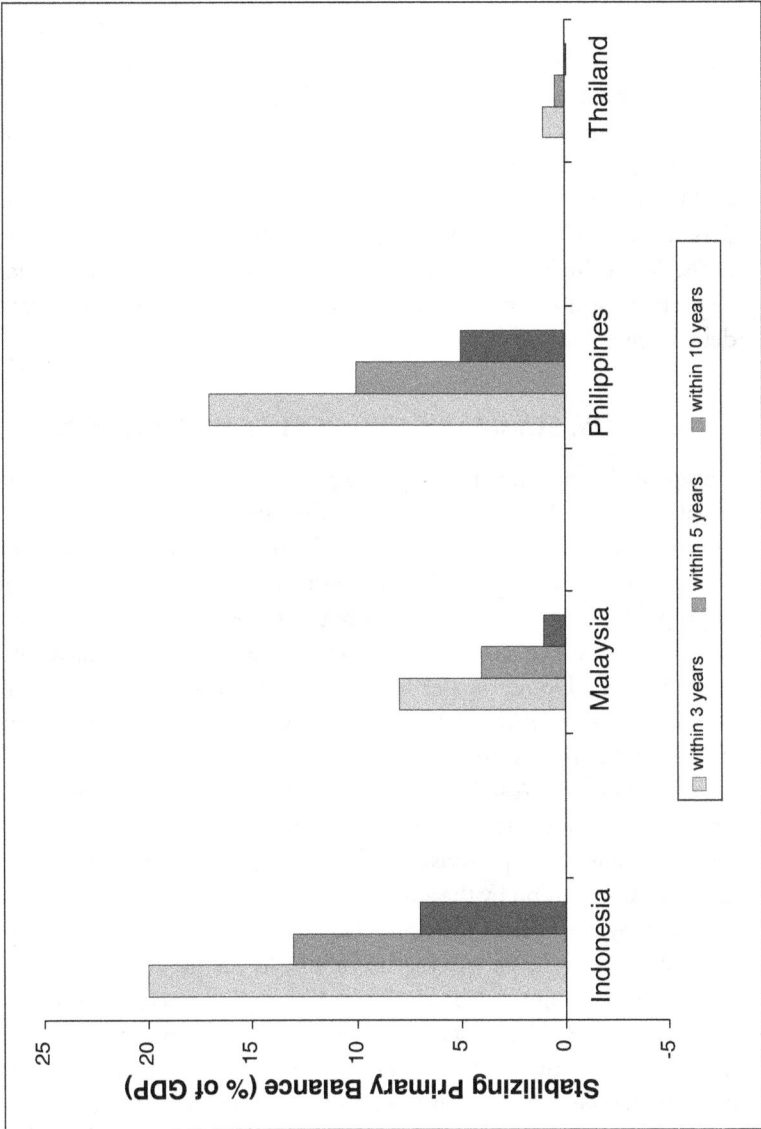

The very large primary surpluses of between 15 and 20 per cent of GDP required to drastically lower public debt would obviously be infeasible within a five-year time-frame. Yet, under recent economic conditions, if the central governments of Indonesia and Thailand ran primary surpluses averaging around 5 per cent of GDP, the 25 per cent target could be reached within a decade. Malaysia could quite easily achieve this limit within five years and Thailand even sooner with minimal effort.

It should be noted that the above estimates are based on recent central government debt data which does not include debt of relevant provincial and local governments, all public enterprises, or the outstanding off-budget debt of central banks for recapitalizing financial institutions post-Asian crisis. Accordingly, the above debt scenarios may significantly understate the respective fiscal efforts required to stabilize and reduce consolidated public debt levels.

## IV. SUMMARY AND POLICY IMPLICATIONS

This paper has outlined fundamental principles for analysing the sustainability of public debt in emerging economies. Examining public debt ratios is important because high levels increase the risk of financial crisis either through outright default or capital flight in response to a rising probability of default. High public debt levels also crowd out domestic spending as the interest risk premium rises and create monetization pressures which have inflationary consequences. Domestic and foreign investors need only rightly or wrongly anticipate future debt monetization or default for immediate capital flight to spark a financial crisis.

The emerging ASEAN-4 economies were at the centre of the East Asian financial crisis of the late 1990s. In the wake of the crisis, however, public debt has risen well above pre-crisis levels due to persistently large budget deficits and the capitalization by the authorities of financial institutions (mainly banks) damaged by the crisis. Questions therefore arise as to whether the post-crisis fiscal stance raises new macroeconomic risks for the region.

ASEAN-4 public debt levels are high by advanced economy standards and unexpected rises in world interest rates or sharp currency depreciations in the region would severely test public debt sustainability. Under recent current macroeconomic conditions and fiscal settings, the public debt levels are being stabilized in the region. However, to lower public debt levels to more prudent levels, the Philippines and Indonesia, in particular, require larger primary budget surpluses.

In principle, these larger primary budget surpluses could be achieved either through expenditure restraint or higher revenue-raising. Given the deadweight losses associated with raising tax, improving the effectiveness of public expenditure and its allocation between consumption and investment activities should be a priority. Accordingly, there is scope to further involve the private sector in the provision of infrastructure and related public services to alleviate budgetary pressures on the spending side. Strengthening private–public partnership could entail better assignment of property rights, further privatization of public assets, which of course also temporarily boosts revenue, and the use of market mechanisms, such as contracting out and more widespread application of the "user pays" principle.

Many issues arise when contemplating fiscal consolidation. For instance, what is the risk that large public expenditure cuts may restrict aggregate demand and growth, especially if vital capital, rather than more politically difficult current expenditures are cut? Meanwhile, what scope exists for widening revenue bases and improving tax administration, given that revenue shares as a proportion of GDP are much lower in ASEAN economies than in advanced economies?

Each ASEAN economy considered in this article has, of course, its own unique fiscal characteristics and institutions, so answers to these questions and recommendations about specific policy measures require further research. However, as politics and fiscal policy are inseparable, political factors will also evidently play an important role in determining the precise nature and speed of fiscal adjustment in the region.

## Appendix 1
## Derivation of the Debt Reduction Relationship

Solvency requires that present debt, $D_t$, can eventually be repaid at some time in the future, $t+n$, such that $D_{t+n}=0$. This means that the present value of budget surpluses over the period must equal the debt stock at $t$. Hence,

$$D_t = \frac{PB_{t+1}}{(1+i)} + \frac{PB_{t+2}}{(1+i)^2} + \frac{PB_{t+3}}{(1+i)^3} + \dots + \frac{PB_{t+n}}{(1+i)^n}$$

(1a)

or

$$D_t = \frac{\sum_{j=1}^{n} (1+i)^{n-j} PB_{t+j}}{(1+i)^n}$$

(2a)

Solving for the constant primary balance $\overline{PB}$ to achieve solvency,

$$\overline{PB} = \frac{D_t (1+i)^n}{\sum_{j=1}^{n} (1+i)^{n-j}}$$

(3a)

Since $D_{t+n} = D_t(1+i)^n$, it follows from equation (2a) that the solvency condition is

$$D_{t+n} = D_t (1+i)^n - \sum_{j=1}^{n} (1+i)^{n-j} PB_{t+j} = 0$$

(4a)

Dividing equation (4a) by $Y_{t+n}$ and noting that

$$(1+g)^n Y_t = Y_{t+n}$$

(5a)

yields

$$\frac{D_{t+n}}{Y_{t+n}} = \frac{D_t (1+i)^n - \sum_{j=1}^{n} (1+i)^{n-j} PB_{t+j}}{(1+g)^n Y}$$

(6a)

If the debt to income ratio is reduced to a proportion $\rho$ of the existing ratio between $t$ and $t+n$

$$\frac{D_{t+n}}{Y_{t+n}} = \rho(\frac{D_t}{Y_t}) \quad \text{where } 0 \le \rho \le 1$$

(7a)

Hence, substituting in equation (6a)

$$\rho\left(\frac{D_t}{Y_t}\right) = \frac{D_t\,(1+i)^n - \sum_{j=1}^{n}(1+i)^{n-j}\,PB_{t+j}}{(1+g)^n\,Y_t}$$

(8a)

Solving for $D_t$ and redividing by $Y_t$, it follows that

$$\frac{D_t}{Y_t} = \frac{-\sum_{j=1}^{n}(1+i)^{n-j}\,PB_{t+j}}{[\rho(1+g)^n - (1+i)^n]Y_t}$$

(9a)

Solving equation (9a) for the constant primary balance $(\overline{PB})$ as a proportion of national income that would satisfy condition (7a)

$$\frac{\overline{PB}}{Y_t} = \frac{D_t}{Y_t} \cdot \frac{(1+i)^n - (1+g)^n \cdot \rho}{\sum_{j=1}^{n}(1+i)^{n-j}}$$

(10a)

## APPENDIX 2
### ASEAN-4: Primary Balances Required to Achieve
### a 25 Per Cent Debt Ratio

|  | Indonesia | Malaysia | Philippines | Thailand |
|---|---|---|---|---|
| General Government Debt to GDP (%)[a] | 80.5 | 51.9 | 71.7 | 28.8 |
| Nominal Effective Interest Rate (%)[b] | 9.5 | 4.8 | 7.0 | 4.7 |
| Nominal Growth Rate (%)[b] | 13.6 | 10.5 | 10.2 | 6.5 |
| Primary Balance to GDP (%) required to reach 25% debt to GDP target by end of: |  |  |  |  |
| Year 2 | 30.4 | 12.9 | 25.0 | 1.6 |
| Year 3 | 20.1 | 8.2 | 16.9 | 0.9 |
| Year 4 | 15.9 | 5.9 | 12.9 | 0.6 |
| Year 5 | 13.0 | 4.4 | 10.4 | 0.4 |
| Year 6 | 11.1 | 3.4 | 8.8 | 0.2 |
| Year 7 | 9.6 | 2.7 | 7.6 | 0.1 |
| Year 8 | 8.6 | 2.1 | 6.7 | 0.0 |
| Year 9 | 7.7 | 1.6 | 6.0 | −0.1 |
| Year 10 | 7.0 | 1.2 | 5.4 | −0.1 |
| Year 11 | 6.4 | 0.9 | 5.0 | −0.2 |
| Year 12 | 5.9 | 0.5 | 4.5 | −0.2 |
| Year 13 | 5.4 | 0.2 | 4.2 | −0.3 |
| Year 14 | 5.0 | −0.1 | 3.9 | −0.3 |
| Year 15 | 4.7 | −0.3 | 3.6 | −0.4 |

NOTES:

a. Data sources as for Table 1.

b. Effective interest rate is derived by dividing public debt interest payments by the stock of public debt. Effective interest rates and growth rates are in nominal terms and represent averages of the most recent three years.

c. Estimates of the constant primary balances required to achieve the 25 per cent ratio within the specified years are based on a spreadsheet formulation of equation (12).

## Note

This article is based on research undertaken while the author was at the IMF Singapore Training Institute in 2003–04. The author gratefully acknowledges the extensive constructive comments provided by two anonymous reviewers.

## References

Aiyagari, R. and E. McGrattan. "The Optimum Quantity of Debt". *Journal of Monetary Economics* 42, no. 4 (1998): 447–69.

Asian Development Bank. *Asian Development Bank Outlook*. Manila: ADB, 2003.

Blanchard, O. "Suggestions for a New Set of Fiscal Indicators". OECD Working Paper No. 79. Paris: Organization for Economic Cooperation and Development, 1990.

Bohn, H. "The Behavior of U.S. Public Debt and Deficits". *Quarterly Journal of Economics* 113, no. 3 (1998): 949–63.

Brixi, P. and A. Schick. *Government at Risk: Contingent Liabilities and Fiscal Risk*. Washington, D.C.: World Bank, 2002.

Buiter, W. "Guide to Public Sector Debt and Deficits". *Economic Policy: A European Forum* 1 (November 1985): 13–79.

Chang, R. and A. Velasco. "Liquidity Crises in Emerging Markets: Theory and Policy". In *NBER Macroeconomics Manual*, edited by B. Bernanke and J. Rotemberg. Cambridge, Masachusetts: MIT Press, 1999.

Eichengreen, B. *Financial Crises and What to Do About Them*. Oxford: Oxford University Press, 2002.

Fischer, S. and W. Easterly. "The Economics of the Government Budget Constraint". *World Bank Research Observer* 5, no. 3 (1990): 127–42.

Frederiksen, N. "Fiscal Sustainability in the OECD: A Simple Method and Some Preliminary Results". OECD Working Paper No. 3/2001. Copenhagen: Finansministeriet, 2001.

Furman, J. and J. Stiglitz. "Economic Crises: Evidence and Insights from East Asia". *Brookings Papers on Economic Activity* 2 (1998): 11–35.

Glick, R., R. Moreno, and M. Spiegel. *Financial Crises in Emerging Markets*. Cambridge: Cambridge University Press, 2001.

Goldstein, M. *The Asian Crisis: Causes, Cures and Systemic Implications*. Washington, D.C.: Institute for International Economics, 1998.

Hemming, R., M. Kell, and A. Schimmelfennig. *Fiscal Vulnerability and Financial Crisis in Emerging Market Economics*. IMF Occasional Paper 218. Washington, D.C.: IMF, 2003.

International Monetary Fund. "Public Debt in Emerging Markets: Is It Too High?". *World Economic Outlook*, chapter 3. Washington, D.C.: IMF, September 2003.

―――. *Government Finance Statistics*. Washington, D.C.: IMF, 2005a.

―――. *International Financial Statistics*. Washington, D.C.: IMF, 2005*b*.

Makin, T. "Preventing Financial Crises in East Asia". *Asian Survey* 39, no. 4 (1999): 668–78.

―――. "Fiscal Risk in ASEAN". *Agenda* 12, no. 3 (2005): 235–46.

Radelet, S. and J. Sachs. "The East Asian Financial Crisis: Diagnosis, Remedies, Prospects". *Brookings Papers on Economic Activity* 1 (1998): 1–90.

# PART II

# ECONOMIC CO-OPERATION IN SOUTHEAST ASIA

# 6

# GAINS FROM INTRA- AND INTER-REGIONAL TRADE AND ECONOMIC CO-OPERATION

## Sasatra Sudsawasd and Prasopchoke Mongsawad

### I. INTRODUCTION

Despite the progress in tariff reductions initiated by the World Trade Organization (WTO) over the past twenty years, there still exist a number of trade barriers and other problems needed to be addressed. Besides, there are conflicts among WTO country members in several issues. All these delay the trade liberalization process, which will take a long time for trade to be fully liberalized. As a result, several countries have moved ahead of the WTO by initiating regional and/or bilateral free trade agreements (FTAs).

By end May 2004, more than 200 agreements have been enforced; 80 per cent of these numbers are bilateral agreements. Recently, ASEAN members have been very active in forming bilateral FTAs with non-ASEAN members. For example, Singapore enacted the Japan-Singapore FTA in 2002 and the U.S.-Singapore FTA in 2003; and Singapore has been negotiating with several countries such as Canada, Mexico, and South Korea.[1] Thailand also signed the free trade agreements with Australia and New Zealand in 2004 and 2005, respectively; and it has been initiating FTAs with several countries.

Many concerns have been raised whether it is the most beneficial to each ASEAN member to sign the agreements separately, rather than collectively. Even though a bilateral agreement may broaden market access, reduce trade barriers, increase investment opportunity and strengthen other cooperation between the two countries, it appears that a small country often loses bargaining power over a big country in arranging the agreement. ASEAN, as a group, would have more bargaining powers in negotiating with big FTA partners such as the United States, China, and Japan. Moreover, bilateral FTAs that ASEAN members have engaged in may lead to welfare losses while trade liberalization among ASEAN has yet fully be honoured. These losses are partly caused by in-efficient resource utilization and possible negative terms-of-trade effects, arising from the FTAs.

Another concern of the bilateral agreements that ASEAN members are engaging in, as Sally and Sen (2005) point out, is that these agreements might hinder rather than encourage the ASEAN economic integration due to the diversity of the agreements. To promote and expedite the ASEAN integration, those bilateral agreements need to have some consistency and complement the liberalization within ASEAN.

The objective of this paper is to show the potential gains from stronger economic cooperation, such as comprehensive trade liberalization, within ASEAN. Such liberalization would yield ASEAN greater benefits from the FTAs that already concluded and currently under negotiation, which are ASEAN-China FTA, ASEAN-South Korea FTA, ASEAN-India FTA, ASEAN-Australia and New Zealand FTA, ASEAN-Japan CEP, and ASEAN-U.S. TIFA.[2] In addition, since ASEAN plus 3 FTA (China, Japan, and South Korea) has been the main interest in recent years, this study therefore incorporates ASEAN plus 3 FTA into the investigation.

The above objective can be achieved by, first, using the gravity model of bilateral trade to show evidences that the formation of ASEAN results in more trade among ASEAN members. Second, the study estimates the trade potentials between ASEAN-5 members[3] and seven FTA partners. Then, a Computable General Equilibrium (CGE) model is employed to evaluate and compare the impacts of bilateral FTAs on ASEAN-5 members between the case where each ASEAN-5 country signed FTAs separately and the case where ASEAN-5, with free trade among themselves, as a group signed FTAs. Finally, this paper suggests some trade policy recommendations for ASEAN-5.

The structure of this paper is as follows. The literature reviews are in Section II. Section III presents the gravity model results. Section IV shows the results from the CGE model. Finally, the concluding remarks are presented in Section V.

## II. LITERATURE REVIEWS

The Association of Southeast Asian Nations (ASEAN) founded in 1967 currently has ten country members.[4] Not only the political security rationale, but the economic cooperation among members is also the main objective. The ASEAN Free Trade Area (AFTA) was initiated in 1992 to enhance economic cooperation and eliminate trade barriers. Regarding the tariff reduction schedule, some ASEAN members have yet to comply with it (Derosa 2004).

To point out the benefit of FTAs, there are many empirical studies on the issue using both eco-nometric models (such as a gravity model) and CGE models (such as the Global Trade Analysis Project, or GTAP model.) Some studies have focused on the free trade agreements (FTAs) between ASEAN and several trading partners to the extent where there is fully trade liberalization among ASEAN members. Ballard and Cheong (1997) suggest that FTAs initiated in the Pacific Rim (Australia-New Zealand, ASEAN-4, China, Canada, Mexico, NIEs, and the United States) do promise economic welfare gains. Both perfectly-competitive and imperfectly-competitive GTAP models have been used and both confirm the finding. Moreover, the result indicates that the larger the FTA becomes the more welfare the country gains. For ASEAN-4 (Malaysia, Indonesia, Philippines and Thailand), they would gain the most from the trade liberalization in APEC and the least from the East-Asia FTA in the case of the perfectly-competitive model. In the case of imperfectly-competitive model, the result is fairly similar with higher values of welfare gains.

Many studies suggested that ASEAN would benefit more from the FTAs if they engaged in trade liberalization among themselves. Kawasaki (2003) employs the GTAP model to show the impacts of free trade in Asia, concerning mainly on the prospective Japan's FTAs. The results indicate that ASEAN members would significantly gain more from the bilateral FTAs if there is trade liberalization among the members. Besides, most ASEAN members would gain more from the Japan-China-ASEAN FTA than the Japan-ASEAN and China-ASEAN FTAs.

Derosa (2004) investigates the economic impacts of U.S.-ASEAN FTA using the gravity model and the GTAP model. The results from the gravity model show that U.S.-ASEAN FTA would increase ASEAN's total exports, led by the expansion of Philippines, Malaysia, and Thailand, while the import would rise from the import expansion of Philippines, Malaysia, and Singapore. However, if ASEAN members have free trade among themselves, the U.S.-ASEAN FTA would benefit much more to ASEAN members. There would be around 70 per cent jump in both ASEAN exports and imports, led by the expansions of the same countries. The economic impact of U.S.-ASEAN FTA from the GTAP model shows much smaller magnitudes than those from the gravity model. For the ASEAN-5, both import and export increases are in the range of 0.5 to 6 per cent. The nominal GDPs grow by about 0.5 to 3 per cent. Philippines would benefit the most while Singapore would gain the least, as tariff barriers are already trivial.

To extend those previous studies, this paper will employ the gravity model and the GTAP model to investigate the potential gains of ASEAN from FTAs in both cases where there is free trade among ASEAN and where there is not. The gravity model will show the trade potential compared with those of ASEAN exporting competitors. The GTAP result will clarify the GDP and welfare gains from the FTAs. In addition, the impacts on the sectoral production will be examined.

## III. GRAVITY MODEL

### III.1 Methodology and Estimation

The gravity model of international trade is well known as an empirical framework to analyse the patterns of bilateral trade flows between countries. It offers a systematic mechanism for measuring what normal bilateral trade should be. The basic idea of the gravity model is that bilateral trade flows are basically determined by potential demand of importing country, potential supply of exporting country, and transportation costs between importing and exporting countries.

The gravity model is widely used to estimate the effects of various variations in the international trade. To estimate the effects of joining the same regional FTAs on bilateral trade flows, the dummy variables account for belonging in the same preferential trade agreements are added to the standard gravity model (Rose 2005; Greenaway and Milner 2002). The specification of the gravity model is as follows:

$$
\begin{aligned}
\ln(T_{ijt}) = {} & \beta_0 + \beta_1 \ln(RGDP_{it}) + \beta_2 \ln(RGDP_{jt}) + \beta_3 \ln(RGDPPC_{it}) \\
& + \beta_4 \ln(RGDPPC_{jt}) + \beta_5 \ln(DIST_{ij}) + \beta_6 LANG_{ijt} + \beta_7 GSP_{ijt} \\
& + \beta_8 FTA_{ijt} + \mathring{a}_{ijt},
\end{aligned}
$$

where $i$ and $j$ denote trading partners, and $t$ denotes time.

$T$         = bilateral trade between countries $i$ and $j$,
$RGDP$    = real GDP,
$RGDPPC$ = real GDP per capita,
$DIST$     = distance between $i$ and $j$,

*LANG*    = dummy variable equals to one when two countries $i$ and $j$ have a common language,

*GSP*    = dummy variable equals to one if country $i$ extends GSP concession to country $j$,

*FTA*    = dummy variable equals to one if both $i$ and $j$ belong to the same free trade agreement.

The dependent variable is total bilateral trade, the sum of exports and imports between countries $i$ and $j$. As described, in the gravity model, bilateral trade is basically determined by potential demand of the importing country, potential supply of the exporting country, transportation cost, and transaction cost. The variable incomes $RGDP_i$ and $RGDP_j$ capture the potential demand of the importing country $i$ and the potential supply of the exporting country $j$, respectively. These two variables are expected to be positive. As Frankel, Stein, and Wei (1995) points out, for a given size of overall income, a country with higher income per capita tends to be more specialized in production and trade. Thus, the variable income per capita $RGDPPC$ is expected to have a positive impact on trade. The variables $DIST$ and $LANG$ capture transportation cost and transaction cost, respectively.[5] One can see that the variable $DIST$ should have a negative effect on trade; whereas $LANG$ is expected to have a positive value. Similarly, the variable $GSP$ is expected to influence trade flows positively. Finally, by using Rose (2005) data set, the $FTA$ dummy variable can be classified into eleven major trade agreements to capture the effect of each trade agreement. These trade agreements are ASEAN, EU, NAFTA, U.S.-Israel FTA, CARICOM, PATCRA, ANZCERTA, CACM, Mercosur, and SPARTECA.

The difference between the predicted and the observed bilateral trade flows is interpreted as the remaining trade potential. This study defines the bilateral trade potential as the ratio of the remaining trade potential to the observed trade flows. The low ratio value indicates the high level of existing bilateral trade flows. On the other hand, the high ratio value may reflect high trade barriers. The high ratio value suggests large potential gains from the FTA, especially if the FTA has yet existed. Therefore, it would be strategically wise to initiate an FTA with countries of the high ratios.

## III.2 Data and Empirical Issues

The panel data used in this study cover 12,150 bilateral merchandise trading partners from 1948 to 1999. The data are mainly from the World Bank's

*World Development Indicators*, the IMF's *International Financial Statistics* and *Direction of Trade Statistics*, and Rose (2005) data set. The data set is an unbalanced panel, since the data for each trading country are perhaps not available for all time periods. Thus, the unbalance panel regressions are estimated in this study.

To estimate the model, this study runs the standard OLS regression. However, due to the nature of the panel data, there might be country specific effects and/or time specific effects. Therefore, the fixed effect and the random effect estimators are estimated by using both one-way and two-way effects. The results from the F-test indicate that the fixed effects model outperform the standard OLS model. The Hausman (1978) test is performed to test whether the fixed or random effect model is more appropriate. The results suggest that the fixed effect model is more appropriate for this data set. Therefore, the results from the one-way fixed effect model are analysed and discussed in the next section, as the benchmark. Table 1 reports estimated results from all five models.

## III.3 Gravity Model Results

In general, the estimated results are consistent with the results from others (Rose 2005; Derosa 2004). The signs of the coefficients are as expected and most of them are significant. The potential demand and the potential supply expand trade flows. A country with higher income per capita tends to trade more. The distance between trading countries significantly reduces trade, while the effects of a common language and the GSP on trade flows are positive.

The results confirm that the formation of FTAs significantly creates trade. Trade flows among countries within the group are estimated to expand between 129 per cent and 600 per cent.[6] In case of ASEAN, the effects of free trades within ASEAN members significantly boost intra-trade to be approximately 182 per cent.[7]

Next, the potential trades between ASEAN-5 and each of the seven FTA partners are estimated as illustrated in Figures 1 to 7. In order to analyse trade potential, the study considers and compares the trade performances of ASEAN-5 with China and India, the two major ASEAN trade competitors. The major finding is that there are large trade potentials between ASEAN-5 and the four major trading partners (China, Japan, India, and the United States), in which the reasons can be explained as in Table 1.

In the U.S. market, China has already been over-traded. The trade flow between China and the United States in 1999 is above their trade potential by more than 1,100 per cent; whereas, ASEAN-5 trade potential, on average,

**TABLE 1**
**Gravity Model Regression Results: Dep. Var. ln($T$)**

| Variable | OLS | | One-Way Fixed | | One-Way Random | | Two-Way Fixed | | Two-Way Random | |
|---|---|---|---|---|---|---|---|---|---|---|
| Constant | −26.270 | *** | −8.265 | *** | −6.512 | *** | −14.620 | *** | −18.852 | *** |
| | (0.10) | | (0.23) | | (0.27) | | (0.62) | | (0.34) | |
| ln$RGDP$ | 0.830 | *** | 0.269 | *** | 0.510 | *** | 0.447 | *** | 0.816 | *** |
| | (0.00) | | (0.01) | | (0.01) | | (0.02) | | (0.01) | |
| ln$RGDPPC$ | 0.384 | *** | 0.336 | *** | 0.102 | *** | 0.236 | *** | 0.080 | *** |
| | (0.00) | | (0.01) | | (0.01) | | (0.02) | | (0.01) | |
| ln$DIST$ | −1.198 | *** | | | −1.285 | *** | | | −1.323 | *** |
| | (0.01) | | | | (0.03) | | | | (0.02) | |
| LANG | 0.611 | *** | | | 0.261 | *** | | | 0.566 | *** |
| | (0.01) | | | | (0.05) | | | | (0.05) | |
| GSP | 0.341 | *** | 0.108 | *** | 0.013 | | 0.173 | *** | 0.298 | *** |
| | (0.01) | | (0.01) | | (0.01) | | (0.01) | | (0.01) | |
| EU | −0.020 | | 0.829 | *** | 0.801 | *** | 0.882 | *** | 1.017 | *** |
| | (0.06) | | (0.05) | | (0.05) | | (0.05) | | (0.05) | |
| U.S.-Israel FTA | 1.000 | * | 0.556 | | 0.461 | | 0.575 | | 0.488 | |
| | (0.56) | | (0.41) | | (0.42) | | (0.41) | | (0.41) | |
| NAFTA | 0.451 | | 0.927 | *** | 0.801 | *** | 0.832 | *** | 0.860 | *** |
| | (0.45) | | (0.30) | | (0.31) | | (0.30) | | (0.30) | |
| CARICOM | 1.638 | *** | −0.112 | | −0.184 | ** | −0.063 | | 0.365 | *** |
| | (0.06) | | (0.10) | | (0.09) | | (0.09) | | (0.09) | |
| PATCRA | 3.062 | *** | −0.091 | | 0.047 | | −0.282 | | −0.162 | |
| | (1.08) | | (0.70) | | (0.71) | | (0.70) | | (0.70) | |
| ANZCERTA | 2.060 | *** | 0.521 | | 0.400 | | 0.695 | * | 0.875 | ** |
| | (0.53) | | (0.39) | | (0.40) | | (0.39) | | (0.39) | |
| CACM | 1.362 | *** | 1.946 | *** | 1.584 | *** | 1.975 | *** | 1.934 | *** |
| | (0.11) | | (0.15) | | (0.15) | | (0.15) | | (0.15) | |
| Mercosur | 0.783 | *** | 1.100 | *** | 0.898 | *** | 0.969 | *** | 1.026 | *** |
| | (0.24) | | (0.16) | | (0.16) | | (0.15) | | (0.16) | |
| ASEAN | 1.372 | *** | 1.037 | *** | 0.939 | *** | 0.766 | *** | 0.665 | *** |
| | (0.20) | | (0.16) | | (0.15) | | (0.15) | | (0.15) | |
| SPARTECA | 2.472 | *** | −0.035 | | 0.039 | | 0.084 | | 0.268 | * |
| | (0.13) | | (0.15) | | (0.15) | | (0.14) | | (0.14) | |
| $R^2$ | 0.577 | | 0.4578 | | 0.5137 | | 0.5132 | | 0.5957 | |
| No. of Obs. | 234,597 | | 234,597 | | 234,597 | | 234,597 | | 234,597 | |
| Hausman test | | | Fixed Effects | | | | Fixed Effects | | | |

NOTE: ***, **, * denote 1 per cent, 5 per cent, 10 per cent significant levels respectively.

exceeds the predictions by 85 per cent. Hence, compared to China, ASEAN-5 countries still have much more trade potential with the United States. In case of China market, ASEAN-5 members have more trade potentials compared with India, whose trade with China has already exceeded the potential by more than 2,000 per cent. For the same argument, ASEAN-5 can expand trade

FIGURE 1
Potential Trade between Australia and the Candidate Countries (Percents)

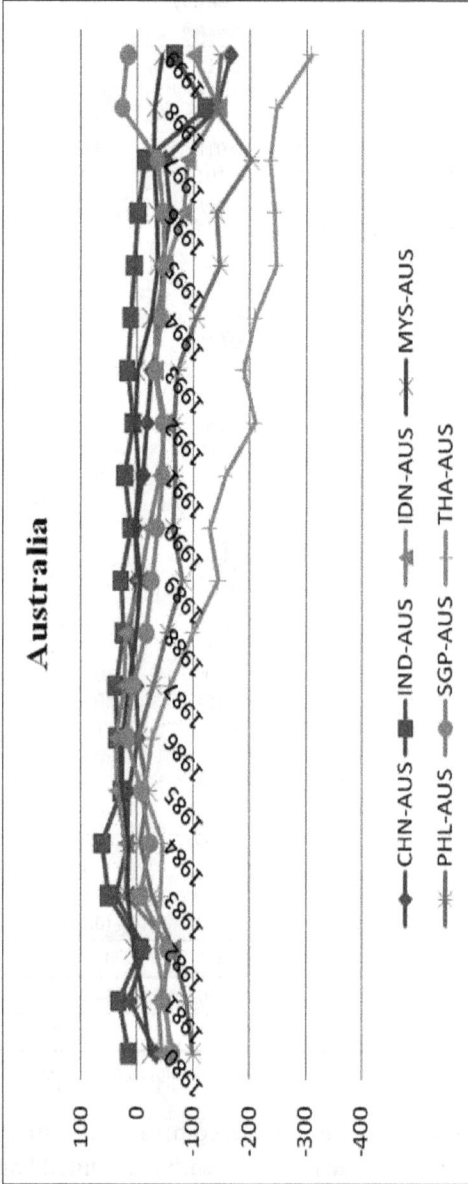

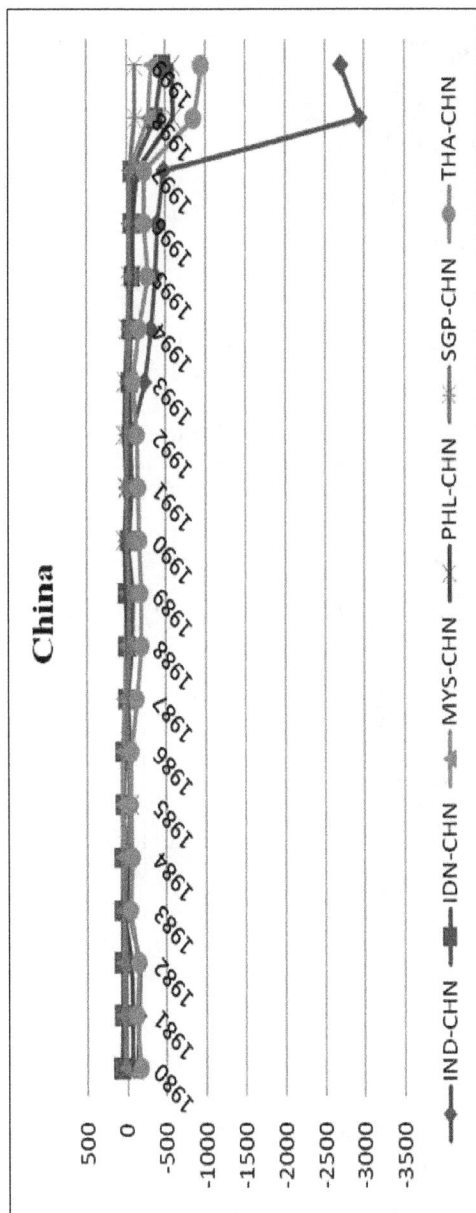

FIGURE 2
Potential Trade between China and the Candidate Countries (Percents)

FIGURE 3
Potential Trade between India and the Candidate Countries (Percents)

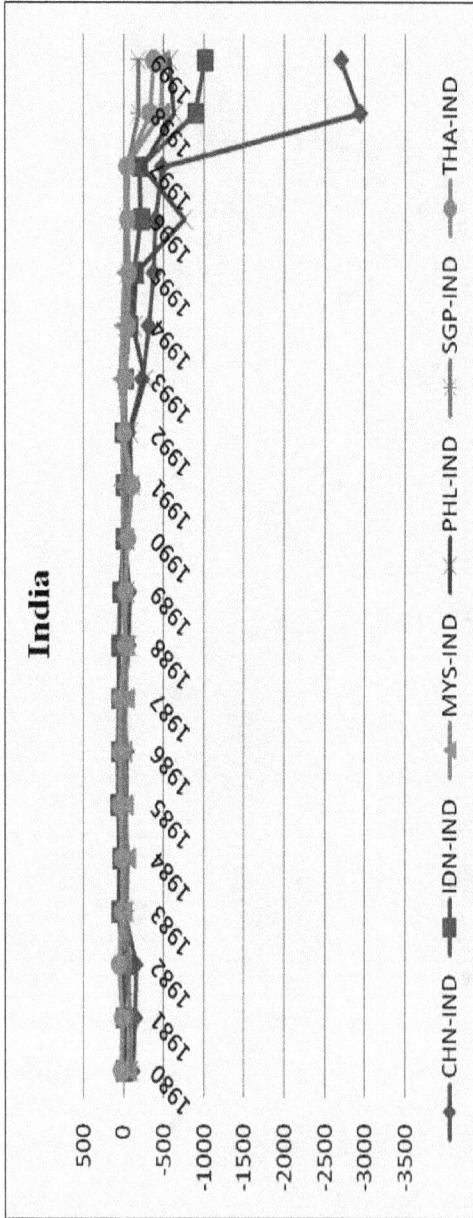

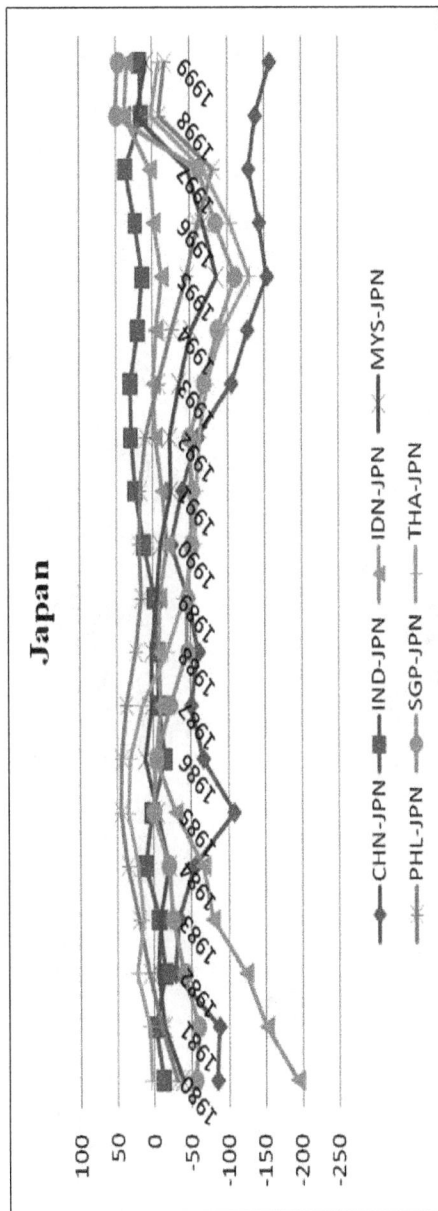

FIGURE 4
Potential Trade between Japan and the Candidate Countries (Percents)

FIGURE 5
Potential Trade between New Zealand and the Candidate Countries (Percents)

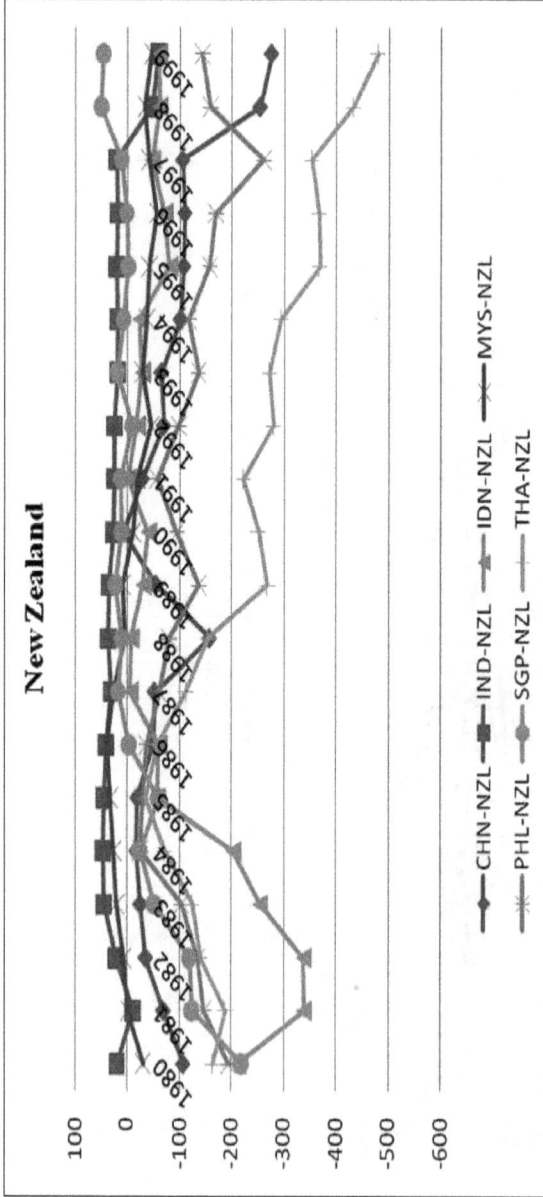

New Zealand

**FIGURE 6**
**Potential Trade between South Korea and the Candidate Countries (Percents)**

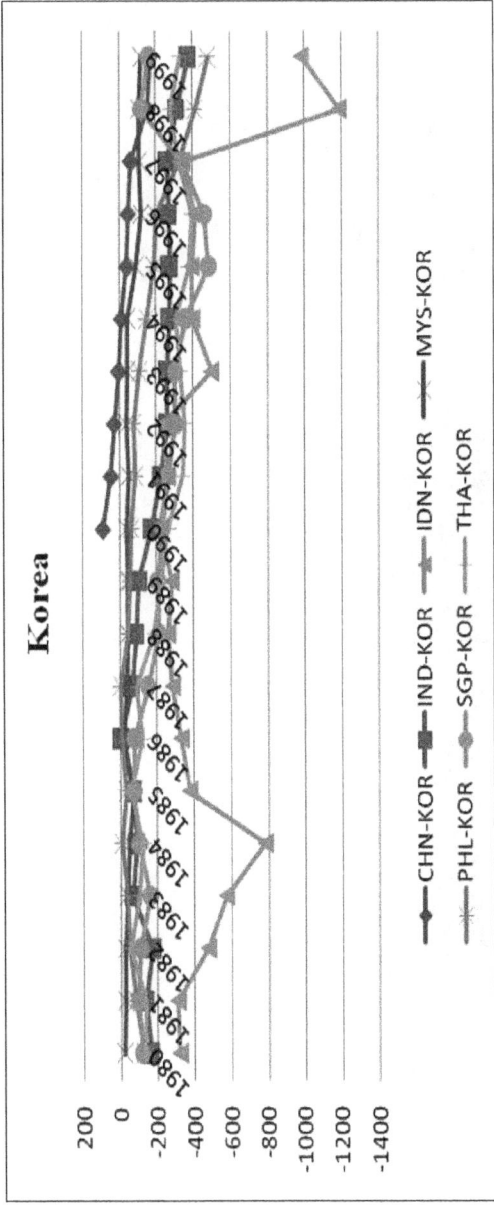

**FIGURE 7**
**Potential Trade between the US and the Candidate Countries (Percents)**

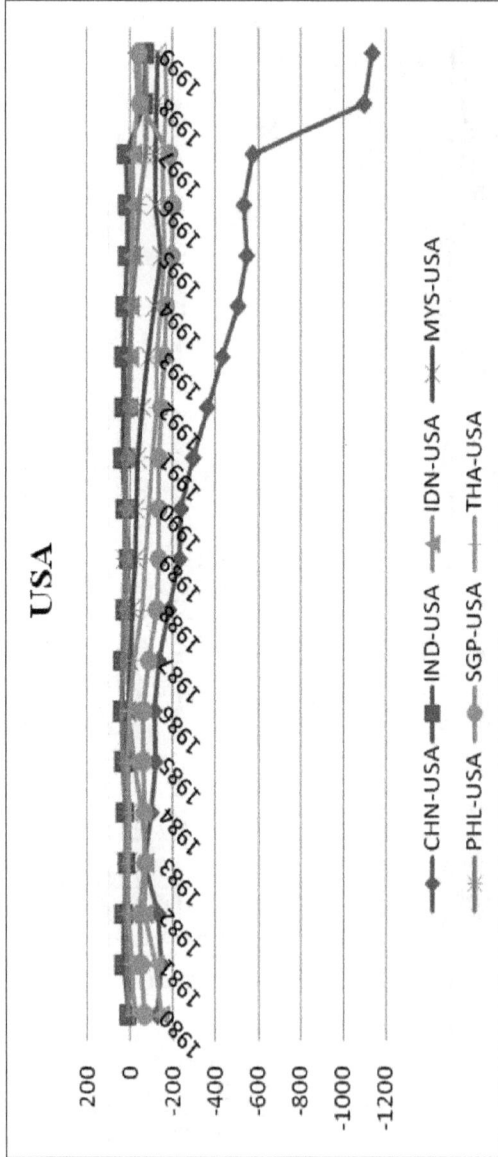

dramatically in India market. Finally, trades between ASEAN-5 members and Japan are still under their trade potentials as indicated by the model.

It is worth noting that ASEAN-5 countries have been losing market shares in these four major trading markets to their competitors, especially to China. This can be seen from the widening gaps between trade potentials of ASEAN-5 countries and those of their competitors in recent years. This emphasizes the necessity and the benefit of the FTAs.

## IV. COMPUTABLE GENERAL EQUILIBRIUM (CGE) MODEL

### IV.1 Framework of Model Simulations

A computable general equilibrium (CGE) model has been widely used for evaluating the effects of policy changes. Basically, a CGE model is based on a general equilibrium theory with a system of simultaneous equations. One of the benefits of the CGE model is that it can calculate the magnitudes of the effects from policy changes.

To measure the effects of changes in trade policy, this study uses the GTAP model, which is one of the most widely used global trade CGE models. The GTAP model is a comparative static model with optimizing behaviour of all economic agents. Based on the recent updated GTAP database version 6 employed in this analysis, the GTAP model is a multi-regional and multi-sectoral CGE model comprising 87 regions and 57 sectors.

In this study, a static GTAP model is used. The static model assumes a perfect competition in each market, a constant return to scale, a full employment, a fixed amount of capital, and the Armington assumption.[8] The representative household demands are assumed to be non-homothetic preference. In addition, in 2005, the Multi-Fibre Agreement (MFA), a system of bilateral import quotas on textile, leather, and wearing apparels from low-cost exporting countries, was eliminated. The MFA import quotas are converted to export tax equivalents in the GTAP data set.[9] Therefore, taking this into account, export taxes on textiles and apparel products are removed in each model simulation.

For FTA model simulations, this study considers mainly on the impacts of the seven FTA candidates that are either already concluded or currently under negotiation with ASEAN. Those seven FTA candidates are Australia-New Zealand FTA, China FTA, India FTA, Japan FTA, South Korea FTA, U.S. FTA, and China-India-Japan (plus 3) FTA. In all FTA model simulations, they are simulated and compared between the following two scenarios.

In Scenario 1, each of ASEAN-5 members initiates the bilateral FTAs independently. Thus, the simulation results reflect an isolated impact of the

FTAs on each ASEAN-5 member. Scenario 2 is the case where ASEAN-5 members implement FTAs simultaneously. In addition, all import tariffs among ASEAN-5 are eliminated.

All the GTAP model simulation results are reported in Tables 2 to 4. Note that, each FTA scenario is restricted to only the removal of all import tariffs on goods, trade in services and other kinds of barriers are left unchanged.

## IV.2 Simulation Results

The effects of trade liberalization among ASEAN-5 and the FTA candidate partners, in Scenario 2, on ASEAN-5 economies in terms of total production growth and welfare gains (equivalent variation) are better than those in Scenario 1. The welfare effects in the GTAP model are decomposed into several components. Reported here are the two major components: allocative efficiency and terms-of-trade effects. The allocative efficiency measures the change in national welfare attributable to efficiency changes from resource utilization across economic activities. The higher value of allocative efficiency implies the larger trade creation after trade liberalization, whereas the lower value may reflect the higher trade diversion. A country with high market distortion would be expected to have large positive gains in this component. The terms-of-trade effect component measures the change in national welfare attributable to the price increase resulting from tariff eliminations.

The simulation results from Scenario 2 suggest that regional free trade in ASEAN-5 has improved terms-of-trade effect and allocative efficiency, reducing the problem of trade diversion beyond those of the bilateral FTAs in Scenario 1. It is not surprising that the trade balances of ASEAN-5 countries worsen under Scenario 2 as the weighted average tariffs within ASEAN-5, approximately 3 per cent, has been removed.[10] Therefore, the worsening trade balance is partly caused by an increase in imports among ASEAN-5, reflecting more efficient resource utilization. This is confirmed by the higher value of welfare in Scenario 2.

In prioritizing FTA partners, this study determines the sum of total ASEAN-5 country welfare gains in Scenario 2. The results suggest the ranking orders as follows: (1) Plus 3 FTA ($5,262 million), (2) China FTA ($4,710 million), (3) U.S. FTA ($3,906 million), (4) Japan FTA ($3,174 million), (5) India FTA ($2,992 million), (6) Korea ($2,578 million), and (7) Australia-New Zealand FTA ($2,233 million). One of the reasons behind a significant increase in welfare of ASEAN-5 from free trade with China is that China is a large trading partner that has moderately high weighted average tariff rate of 12.6 per cent. For the United States, even if the weighted average tariff rate is relatively low at 2.67 per cent, it is ranked third since it is the largest

## TABLE 2
## The Macroeconomic Impacts of Bilateral FTAs on ASEAN-5
## (Scenario 1)

| Country | Indonesia | Malaysia | Philippines | Singapore | Thailand |
|---|---|---|---|---|---|
| Australia-New Zealand FTA | | | | | |
| Nominal GDP (%) | 0.43 | 0.16 | 0 | −0.07 | 0.45 |
| Trade Balance (US$ million) | −41.78 | 22.02 | −9.66 | −4.95 | −181.21 |
| Equivalent Variation (US$ million) | 103.38 | 108.68 | 18.92 | −51.35 | 105.75 |
| – Allocative Efficiency (US$ million) | 340.78 | 109.83 | 117.8 | −6.55 | 193.43 |
| – Term of Trade (US$ million) | −135.72 | 77.87 | −107.03 | −65.71 | −20.69 |
| China FTA | | | | | |
| Nominal GDP (%) | 1.24 | 1.24 | 1.06 | 1.8 | 1.84 |
| Trade Balance (US$ million) | −27.34 | 254.43 | −209.84 | −370.37 | −413.01 |
| Equivalent Variation (US$ million) | 432.83 | 933.18 | 217 | 774.58 | 832.89 |
| – Allocative Efficiency (US$ million) | 423.96 | 233.88 | 167.52 | 26.75 | 394.13 |
| – Term of Trade (US$ million) | 200.27 | 841.68 | 25.38 | 677.63 | 580.48 |
| India FTA | | | | | |
| Nominal GDP (%) | 1.04 | 0.78 | 0.16 | 0.74 | 0.55 |
| Trade Balance (US$ million) | 42.5 | 142.19 | −31.94 | −152.28 | −152.35 |
| Equivalent Variation (US$ million) | 266.95 | 505.73 | 38.36 | 310.07 | 167.21 |
| – Allocative Efficiency (US$ million) | 304.82 | 104.5 | 110.64 | 11.87 | 219.2 |
| – Term of Trade (US$ million) | 157.39 | 543.55 | −82.89 | 256.07 | 22.62 |
| Japan FTA | | | | | |
| Nominal GDP (%) | 0.5 | 0.1 | 0.55 | 0.03 | 1.03 |
| Trade Balance (US$ million) | −214.32 | −456.51 | −212.57 | −24.7 | −1,234.66 |
| Equivalent Variation (US$ million) | 221.37 | 510.73 | 52.68 | −10.83 | 794.26 |
| – Allocative Efficiency (US$ million) | 362.37 | 288.92 | 125.38 | −7.05 | 495.11 |
| – Term of Trade (US$ million) | −114.38 | −4.01 | −71.11 | −27.18 | 174.4 |
| South Korea FTA | | | | | |
| Nominal GDP (%) | 0.56 | 0.27 | 0.37 | 0.06 | 0.58 |
| Trade Balance (US$ million) | −57.68 | 19.01 | −81.04 | −29.15 | −255.93 |
| Equivalent Variation (US$ million) | 197.32 | 246.88 | 52.49 | 5.8 | 201.99 |
| – Allocative Efficiency (US$ million) | 394.05 | 168.06 | 116.44 | −3.77 | 249.25 |
| – Term of Trade (US$ million) | −91.6 | 121.53 | −76.91 | −14.7 | 5.68 |
| U.S. FTA | | | | | |
| Nominal GDP (%) | 1.54 | 0.58 | 2.73 | 0.26 | 1.6 |
| Trade Balance (US$ million) | 68.98 | 90.46 | −563.83 | −57.71 | −537.63 |
| Equivalent Variation (US$ million) | 426.19 | 556.8 | 520.36 | 92.17 | 665.85 |
| – Allocative Efficiency (US$ million) | 370.65 | 381.88 | 163.27 | 2.17 | 274.52 |
| – Term of Trade (US$ million) | 346.08 | 229.96 | 297.52 | 60.47 | 518.6 |
| China, Japan, and South Korea (Plus 3)  FTA | | | | | |
| Nominal GDP (%) | 1.08 | 1.03 | 0.86 | 1.76 | 2.38 |
| Trade Balance (US$ million) | −265.67 | −307.34 | −310.51 | −327.47 | −1,542.04 |
| Equivalent Variation (US$ million) | 575.97 | 1,322.89 | 114.81 | 790.24 | 1,531.02 |
| – Allocative Efficiency (US$ million) | 467.68 | 441.33 | 173.48 | 21.55 | 729.95 |
| – Term of Trade (US$ million) | 200.63 | 730.87 | −70.65 | 680.85 | 752.56 |

Source: Authors' simulation.

## TABLE 3
### The Macroeconomic Impacts of Trade Liberalization among ASEAN-5 plus FTA partner
### (Scenario 2)

| Country | Indonesia | Malaysia | Philippines | Singapore | Thailand |
|---|---|---|---|---|---|
| Australia-New Zealand FTA | | | | | |
| Nominal GDP (%) | 0.78 | 0.57 | 0.66 | 1.53 | 1.01 |
| Trade Balance (US$ million) | −78.39 | −120.20 | −213.33 | −291.59 | −751.21 |
| Equivalent Variation (US$ million) | 263.68 | 657.09 | 158.92 | 645.95 | 507.69 |
| – Allocative Efficiency (US$ million) | 392.71 | 406.73 | 177.46 | 26.14 | 464.78 |
| – Term of Trade (US$ million) | 26.98 | 221.04 | −34.62 | 556.64 | 85.68 |
| China FTA | | | | | |
| Nominal GDP (%) | 1.55 | 1.55 | 1.62 | 3.04 | 2.33 |
| Trade Balance (US$ million) | −55.54 | 102.72 | −392 | −586.09 | −963.03 |
| Equivalent Variation (US$ million) | 563.92 | 1,368.93 | 326.55 | 1,277.45 | 1,173.31 |
| – Allocative Efficiency (US$ million) | 475.75 | 523.3 | 223.78 | 44.13 | 653.83 |
| – Term of Trade (US$ million) | 328.59 | 887.1 | 72.55 | 1,125.78 | 630.98 |
| India FTA | | | | | |
| Nominal GDP (%) | 1.25 | 1.08 | 0.83 | 2.22 | 1.1 |
| Trade Balance (US$ million) | 5.73 | 6 | −235.52 | −414.02 | −707.92 |
| Equivalent Variation (US$ million) | 387.11 | 958.71 | 177.95 | 930.13 | 538.28 |
| – Allocative Efficiency (US$ million) | 369.12 | 402.43 | 171.35 | 36.85 | 485.4 |
| – Term of Trade (US$ million) | 247.76 | 592.01 | −12.82 | 809.23 | 102.87 |
| Japan FTA | | | | | |
| Nominal GDP (%) | 0.76 | 0.44 | 0.94 | 1.24 | 1.48 |
| Trade Balance (US$ million) | −256.24 | −615.88 | −364.13 | −245.74 | −1,789.17 |
| Equivalent Variation (US$ million) | 344.07 | 1,012.58 | 143.13 | 529.62 | 1,144.06 |
| – Allocative Efficiency (US$ million) | 404.15 | 573.27 | 178.42 | 16.33 | 754 |
| – Term of Trade (US$ million) | 12.2 | 109.25 | −37.77 | 459.3 | 236.53 |
| South Korea FTA | | | | | |
| Nominal GDP (%) | 0.90 | 0.67 | 0.98 | 1.58 | 1.12 |
| Trade Balance (US$ million) | −91.31 | −124.68 | −275.88 | −300.72 | −822.18 |
| Equivalent Variation (US$ million) | 353.44 | 783.87 | 182.1 | 665.73 | 592.39 |
| – Allocative Efficiency (US$ million) | 443.92 | 461.84 | 173.85 | 27.45 | 518.17 |
| – Term of Trade (US$ million) | 66.99 | 255.26 | −11.71 | 573.76 | 100.67 |
| U.S. FTA | | | | | |
| Nominal GDP (%) | 1.79 | 0.97 | 3.13 | 1.62 | 2.07 |
| Trade Balance (US$ million) | 7.81 | −46.35 | −724.89 | −297.59 | −1,099.03 |
| Equivalent Variation (US$ million) | 554.2 | 1,065.1 | 614.26 | 667.36 | 1,004.83 |
| – Allocative Efficiency (US$ million) | 421.48 | 672.83 | 222.54 | 26.24 | 538.64 |
| – Term of Trade (US$ million) | 469.4 | 350.98 | 329.07 | 572 | 563.63 |
| China, Japan, and South Korea (Plus 3) FTA | | | | | |
| Nominal GDP (%) | 1.28 | 1.23 | 1.02 | 2.47 | 2.67 |
| Trade Balance (US$ million) | −294.68 | −485.39 | −410.24 | −443.79 | −2,061.99 |
| Equivalent Variation (US$ million) | 635.88 | 1,663.13 | 140.44 | 1,048.32 | 1,774.03 |
| – Allocative Efficiency (US$ million) | 502.61 | 709.85 | 217.48 | 23.42 | 968.73 |
| – Term of Trade (US$ million) | 258.11 | 705.86 | −87.73 | 914.89 | 714.8 |

Source: Authors' simulation.

## TABLE 4
### The Impacts of Trade Liberalization among ASEAN-5 plus FTA partner on ASEAN-5 Sectoral Productions (percentage changes)
### (Scenario 2)

| Sector | AUS&NZL | CHN | IND | JPN | USA | KOR | Plus3* |
|---|---|---|---|---|---|---|---|
| Paddy rice | −0.28 | −0.13 | 0.12 | −2.04 | −0.16 | −1.72 | −4.33 |
| Wheat | −1.45 | −0.27 | 0.41 | 0.04 | 0.96 | 0.55 | −0.04 |
| Cereal grains NEC | −0.29 | −0.32 | 0.22 | −0.6 | −0.01 | 0.5 | −0.02 |
| Vegetables, Fruits and Nuts | −0.18 | −0.16 | −0.41 | −0.16 | −0.01 | 0.21 | 0.27 |
| Oil seeds | −1.11 | −1.32 | −3.9 | 0.09 | 0.33 | 1.2 | 2.42 |
| Sugar cane and Sugar beet | −0.14 | −0.13 | 0.28 | −4.49 | −0.08 | 0.38 | −2.02 |
| Plant-based fibres | 3.34 | 11.8 | 4 | 0.18 | −0.2 | 1.6 | 10.3 |
| Crops NEC | 0.62 | −3.87 | −0.58 | −0.07 | 0.61 | 0.42 | −0.72 |
| Cattle, Sheep, Goats and Horses | −0.78 | −0.71 | −0.51 | −0.19 | −0.03 | −0.04 | 0.04 |
| Animal products NEC | −0.39 | −0.5 | 0.38 | −0.11 | −0.03 | −0.05 | 0.36 |
| Raw milk | −0.63 | −0.6 | 0.49 | −0.15 | 0 | 0.25 | 0.26 |
| Wool and Silk-worm cocoons | 0.51 | 7.08 | 0.8 | 0.16 | −0.52 | 1.87 | 6.29 |
| Forestry | −1.83 | −1.85 | −0.63 | −0.25 | 0.04 | −0.3 | −1.11 |
| Fishing | −0.08 | −0.3 | 0.33 | −0.02 | 0.04 | −0.07 | 0.11 |
| Coal | −0.43 | −0.65 | −1.25 | −0.04 | 0.03 | −0.16 | −0.61 |
| Oil | −0.31 | −0.89 | −1.48 | −0.12 | 0.05 | −0.15 | −0.87 |
| Gas | −0.55 | −0.48 | −0.41 | −0.06 | 0.12 | −0.2 | −0.62 |
| Minerals NEC | −0.42 | −1.76 | −0.5 | 0.14 | 0.14 | 0.05 | −0.6 |
| Meat: Cattle, Sheep, Goats and Horses | −0.9 | −2.52 | 4.4 | −0.18 | 0 | 0.6 | −1.06 |
| Meat products NEC | −0.87 | −3.24 | 55.7 | −0.85 | 0.1 | −0.68 | −0.45 |
| Vegetable oil and Fat | −2.35 | −4.28 | −34.6 | 0.06 | 0.16 | −0.44 | −0.99 |
| Dairy Products | −0.44 | −4.67 | 0.48 | −0.23 | 0.03 | 0.12 | −0.42 |
| Processed rice | −0.22 | −0.12 | 0.18 | −2.35 | 2.61 | 0.13 | −3.07 |
| Sugar | −0.11 | −3.39 | 0.45 | −4.51 | −0.08 | 0.19 | −3.78 |
| Food products NEC | −0.13 | −0.63 | 1.78 | 0 | 0.08 | −0.11 | 0.61 |
| Beverages and Tobacco products | 0.45 | −0.14 | 0.07 | 0.06 | 0.06 | 0.12 | 0.31 |
| Textiles | 11.5 | 12.3 | 5.51 | −2.3 | −4.53 | 4.12 | 12 |
| Wearing apparel | 2 | 26.3 | 13.9 | −0.88 | −5.76 | −1.29 | 17.3 |
| Leather products | −2.72 | −4.62 | −1.49 | −1.11 | −1.62 | 0.28 | −1.27 |
| Wood products | −2.42 | −3.98 | −0.72 | −0.52 | 0.15 | −1.3 | −2.69 |
| Paper products and Publishing | −0.18 | −1.96 | −1.28 | 0.01 | 0.09 | −0.27 | −0.51 |
| Petroleum and Coal products | 0.16 | −1.75 | 0.87 | −0.01 | 0.01 | 0.37 | −0.22 |
| Chemical, Rubber and Plastic products | 1.41 | −2.78 | −0.63 | 0.26 | 0.05 | 0.57 | −0.73 |
| Mineral products NEC | 0.82 | −0.51 | 0.45 | 0.22 | 0.25 | 0.01 | 0.01 |
| Ferrous metals | 1.79 | −2.21 | −0.64 | 1.05 | 0.23 | 0.57 | −1.01 |
| Metals NEC | −1.31 | −3.82 | −2.47 | 0.6 | 0.39 | 1.42 | −1.96 |
| Metal products | 1.61 | −2.05 | 0.02 | 0.42 | 0.17 | 0.04 | −0.75 |
| Motor vehicles and Parts | 1.85 | −1.48 | −0.11 | 0.61 | 0.17 | 0.6 | −1.48 |
| Transport equipment NEC | 0.2 | −1.4 | 0.2 | 0.23 | 0.24 | −2.34 | −4.03 |
| Electronic equipment | −0.98 | −1.89 | −5.23 | −0.63 | 0.45 | −0.64 | −2.33 |
| Machinery and Equipment NEC | 3.04 | −2.88 | −0.57 | −0.11 | 0.25 | −0.71 | −1.97 |
| Manufactures NEC | −0.94 | −3.88 | −1.15 | 0.02 | 0.4 | 0.51 | −1.89 |

NOTE: * Plus 3 is China, Japan, and South Korea FTA.
SOURCE: Authors' simulation.

trading partner with ASEAN-5. Japan stands on the fourth place as its tariff rates are already at the very low level with the exception of tariff rates on agricultural products. Thus, welfare gains from free trade with Japan mainly come from the elimination of the trade protections on agricultural sector. India is ranked fifth mainly due to a very high weighted average tariff rate of 40.46 per cent and the lower trade flows with ASEAN-5 compared with those trade flows between ASEAN-5 and Japan.

For the impacts on ASEAN-5 sectoral productions, the results from both scenarios show that the textile and wearing apparel sectors would benefit significantly from eliminating import tariffs. Some sectors (such as meat products, plant-based fibres, wool and silk-worm cocoons, etc.) would gain much more benefits if ASEAN-5 were to trade freely among them. This implies the better resource allocation and less trade diversion among ASEAN-5.

## IV.3 Limitations

It is important to emphasize that the static GTAP model simulated in this paper confronts several limitation. One of the most common criticisms on the static model is that it is bias in certain underlying assumptions and ignores the dynamic effects, such as capital accumulation, increase return to scale, and imperfect competition. However, as found in previous studies (Francois 1998; Ballard and Cheong 1997), the simulation results from both static and dynamic models indicate the same direction of economic impacts. There is a relatively small difference in the magnitude of the impacts such that the simulation effects on the welfare are larger under the dynamic models. Thus, the simulation results from the static model should be used as lower bounds.

Another limitation is that the scope of most ASEAN FTAs is not only limited to just about liberalizing merchandise trade or just about removing import tariff barriers, as they are simulated in this study. In reality, most ASEAN FTAs move forward to the comprehensive economic partnership agreements that involve more liberalizing services and investment, as well as lowering non-tariff barriers. Hence, it should be noted that, since at present the GTAP database does not incorporate this information, the simulation results should be analysed to only the extent of tariff liberalization of trade in merchandise goods.

However, the evidence of the benefits resulting from merchandise trade liberalization showed here should encourage and speed up service trade and investment liberalizations. Both service trade and investment liberalizations enable countries to enjoy more benefits of globalization and more economic efficiency improvement as well as term of trade improvements, similar to those gains from merchandise trade liberalization.

## V. CONCLUDING REMARKS

The results from the gravity model confirm that the formation of FTAs, in general, increases trade flows significantly. The effect of ASEAN economic cooperation is estimated to increase trade flows by 182 per cent among ASEAN members. Note that this number could be remarkably higher if there is less trade restriction, tariff and non-tariff barriers.

There are two major findings from the GTAP model. First, ASEAN-5 members would benefit from the FTAs. One such benefit is higher GDP growth for ASEAN-5 members. However, there could be some welfare losses from the FTAs, since FTAs may increase trade diversion and cause negative terms-of-trade effects such as those in Australia-Zealand FTA, China FTA, and Korea FTA. Second, as suggested by the GTAP model, the first five FTA candidates, ranked according to the ASEAN-5 welfare gains, are ASEAN plus 3 FTA, ASEAN-China FTA, ASEAN-U.S. FTA, ASEAN-Japan FTA, and ASEAN-India FTA. This finding is consistent with that of the unexplored trade potentials from the gravity model. Thus, this second major finding could be one of the vital criteria in choosing strategic FTA partners for ASEAN trade policies.

The FTA partners that ASEAN has been involved are mainly industrialized countries and/or large trading country partners. This follows the traditional north-south pattern of trade. Most of the trade agreements are focused on inter-regional trade, while intra-regional trade, which has yet to be fully explored as indicated by some remaining trade barriers is given less priority. This study emphasizes the significant role of intra-regional trade, specifically that within ASEAN. The results clearly indicate the considerable economic potential gains from the intra-regional free trade in ASEAN. If ASEAN countries fully liberalized trade among themselves, they would achieve greater benefits from the FTAs. This study also shows the higher welfare gains for ASEAN from a regional tariff removal. These gains arise from better resource allocation, less trade diversion, and terms-of-trade effect improvement among ASEAN members. Indeed, another important policy implication drawn from this study is the importance of policies inducing more intra-regional trade, which leads to more south-south pattern of trade. Moreover, if regional trade liberalization is extended to other countries outside the region, the benefits to ASEAN may be significantly higher.

## TABLE 5
## Tariffs Structure: FTA Partner Import Tariffs on ASEAN-5 Exports (%)

| Sector | Australia | New Zealand | China | India | Japan | South Korea | USA |
|---|---|---|---|---|---|---|---|
| Paddy rice | 0 | 0 | 0.4 | 0 | 965.3 | 960.9 | 8 |
| Wheat | 0 | 0 | 1 | 0 | 0 | 2.2 | 2 |
| Cereal grains NEC | 0 | 0 | 1 | 34.2 | 40.4 | 434.3 | 0.3 |
| Vegetables, Fruits and Nuts | 0.4 | 0 | 22.3 | 51.3 | 12.3 | 34 | 1.8 |
| Oil seeds | 1.4 | 0 | 19.8 | 44.2 | 0 | 17.1 | 11.1 |
| Sugar cane and Sugar beet | 0 | 0 | 1.2 | 0 | 0 | 0 | 0 |
| Plant-based fibres | 0 | 0 | 5.9 | 6.7 | 0 | 1.4 | 0 |
| Crops NEC | 0 | 0.6 | 12.9 | 34.8 | 0.7 | 7.1 | 3.1 |
| Cattle, Sheep, Goats and Horses | 0 | 0 | 0 | 22.6 | 37.7 | 0 | 0 |
| Animal products NEC | 0 | 0 | 9 | 18 | 0.4 | 6.5 | 0.5 |
| Raw milk | 0 | 0 | 0 | 0 | 0 | 0 | 0 |
| Wool and Silk-worm cocoons | 1.7 | 0 | 2.6 | 24.4 | 1 | 1.4 | 0 |
| Forestry | 0.4 | 0 | 0.8 | 8.2 | 0 | 1.7 | 0.1 |
| Fishing | 0.1 | 0.1 | 19.2 | 13.6 | 3 | 18.7 | 0.2 |
| Coal | 0 | 0 | 4.4 | 49.8 | 0 | 1 | 0 |
| Oil | 5.6 | 0 | 0 | 15 | 0 | 5 | 0 |
| Gas | 0 | 0 | 6 | 0 | 0 | 1 | 0 |
| Minerals NEC | 0.1 | 0 | 0.9 | 6.7 | 0 | 1.1 | 0 |
| Meat: Cattle, Sheep, Goats, Horses | 0 | 0 | 12.3 | 33.4 | 12.5 | 10.9 | 1 |
| Meat products NEC | 0 | 2.1 | 17 | 64.3 | 9.3 | 23.4 | 2.8 |
| Vegetable oil and Fat | 1 | 0.8 | 12.2 | 99 | 0.9 | 5 | 0.9 |
| Dairy Products | 1.1 | 3.3 | 30.8 | 38.1 | 161.9 | 54.2 | 16.3 |
| Processed rice | 0 | 0 | 1 | 56.1 | 904.9 | 439.7 | 3.7 |
| Sugar | 0.3 | 0 | 18.7 | 56.2 | 300.4 | 3.8 | 40.1 |
| Food products NEC | 1.6 | 1.7 | 20.8 | 44 | 7.8 | 25.1 | 2 |
| Beverages and Tobacco products | 17.2 | 4.8 | 47.6 | 75.9 | 10.5 | 37.6 | 3.8 |
| Textiles | 8.6 | 1.8 | 18.3 | 22.8 | 4.6 | 8.2 | 11.3 |
| Wearing apparel | 22.3 | 11 | 24.3 | 34.9 | 8.7 | 12.6 | 13.3 |
| Leather products | 11.4 | 8.8 | 8.3 | 29 | 13.4 | 10.3 | 13.4 |
| Wood products | 4.8 | 3.5 | 9.8 | 29.9 | 2.5 | 6.2 | 0.8 |
| Paper products and Publishing | 3.4 | 0.7 | 7.5 | 21 | 0.2 | 2.7 | 0 |
| Petroleum and Coal products | 0 | 1 | 8.5 | 23.2 | 2.9 | 5.9 | 1.9 |
| Chemical, Rubber & Plastic products | 4.4 | 1.8 | 23.8 | 28 | 0.3 | 5.2 | 2.2 |
| Mineral products NEC | 4.1 | 1.8 | 15 | 34.9 | 0 | 8 | 2.4 |
| Ferrous metals | 5 | 2.2 | 8.3 | 35 | 0 | 2.3 | 1.2 |
| Metals NEC | 0.3 | 2.4 | 4.7 | 30.8 | 0.1 | 3.7 | 0.6 |
| Metal products | 5.2 | 3.4 | 13.3 | 34 | 0 | 7.4 | 0.8 |
| Motor vehicles and Parts | 10.3 | 6.1 | 33.5 | 36 | 0 | 7.2 | 0.7 |
| Transport equipment NEC | 1.5 | 0.8 | 9.1 | 18.7 | 0 | 1.2 | 0.3 |
| Electronic equipment | 0.8 | 0.8 | 9.1 | 13.3 | 0 | 0.8 | 0.2 |
| Machinery and Equipment NEC | 4.6 | 2.2 | 14.6 | 25.4 | 0 | 6.2 | 0.9 |
| Manufactures NEC | 3.3 | 2.5 | 21.7 | 34.1 | 0.8 | 8.2 | 0.5 |
| Weighted Average Tariffs | 3.56 | 1.62 | 12.60 | 40.46 | 11.79 | 7.17 | 2.69 |

SOURCE: Authors' calculation from GTAP data set version 6.

## TABLE 6
## Tariffs Structure: ASEAN-5 Import Tariffs on FTA Partner's Exports (%)

| Sector | Within ASEAN | Australia | New Zealand | China | India | Japan | South Korea | USA |
|---|---|---|---|---|---|---|---|---|
| Paddy rice | 14 | 5.1 | 0 | 2.5 | 5.5 | 14.2 | 25.5 | 1.9 |
| Wheat | 2.2 | 2.9 | 5 | 5 | 3.7 | 1.6 | 5 | 5.9 |
| Cereal grains NEC | 0.6 | 9.7 | 0 | 0.8 | 1.4 | 1.7 | 0.3 | 6.8 |
| Vegetables, Fruits and Nuts | 3.6 | 4.1 | 5.6 | 4.8 | 0.9 | 12.8 | 10.6 | 4.7 |
| Oil seeds | 1.3 | 8.1 | 7.5 | 7.5 | 4.9 | 11.8 | 0.7 | 5.4 |
| Sugar cane and Sugar beet | 0 | 0 | 0 | 1.1 | 0 | 0 | 0 | 0 |
| Plant-based fibres | 0.8 | 1.7 | 0 | 1 | 0.3 | 1.7 | 0.8 | 1.6 |
| Crops NEC | 40.6 | 38 | 17.5 | 12.8 | 13.2 | 14.6 | 9.8 | 84.3 |
| Cattle, Sheep, Goats, Horses | 0.4 | 1.7 | 0 | 6.5 | 0 | 0.2 | 3.2 | 3.4 |
| Animal products NEC | 0.9 | 1.6 | 0.9 | 9.2 | 5.2 | 1 | 4.5 | 2.4 |
| Raw milk | 0 | 0 | 0 | 0 | 0 | 0 | 0 | 0 |
| Wool and Silk-worm cocoons | 1.4 | 0.8 | 1.4 | 21.2 | 1.5 | 17.2 | 0.7 | 3.5 |
| Forestry | 0.4 | 0.2 | 0.3 | 3.7 | 6 | 2.5 | 2.1 | 0.2 |
| Fishing | 2 | 3.7 | 2.3 | 3.3 | 10.7 | 3.4 | 0.5 | 30.8 |
| Coal | 2.2 | 3.1 | 0 | 4.6 | 4.3 | 2.1 | 4.7 | 1.6 |
| Oil | 0.2 | 0.2 | 0 | 0.1 | 0 | 0.2 | 0 | 0.1 |
| Gas | 0 | 0 | 0 | 0 | 0 | 1 | 0 | 0 |
| Minerals NEC | 1.4 | 1.4 | 1.7 | 1.9 | 3 | 2.3 | 0.9 | 1.9 |
| Meat: Cattle, Sheep, Goats, Horses | 4.3 | 4.8 | 3.4 | 2 | 4.3 | 5.4 | 15.7 | 6.2 |
| Meat products NEC | 9.2 | 1.5 | 4.8 | 6.3 | 2 | 11.5 | 26.9 | 13.5 |
| Vegetable oil and Fat | 1.3 | 1.6 | 1.1 | 2 | 5 | 1.8 | 2.7 | 0.9 |
| Dairy Products | 4.3 | 3.9 | 3.8 | 1.3 | 4.1 | 1.3 | 2.8 | 4 |
| Processed rice | 14.4 | 0.4 | 0 | 9.7 | 10.7 | 6 | 3 | 43 |
| Sugar | 13 | 2 | 22 | 28.2 | 9.7 | 9.1 | 16.2 | 15.8 |
| Food products NEC | 10.6 | 9.8 | 11.7 | 10.9 | 22 | 21.7 | 23.1 | 8.7 |
| Beverages & Tobacco products | 15.5 | 17 | 13.7 | 136.4 | 67.2 | 5.9 | 46 | 73.5 |
| Textiles | 5.6 | 4.2 | 5.5 | 9.7 | 7.6 | 8.6 | 9.7 | 7.5 |
| Wearing apparel | 3.8 | 8.5 | 8.6 | 7.6 | 9.4 | 13.2 | 12.9 | 12.2 |
| Leather products | 4 | 4.4 | 2.3 | 8.5 | 3.3 | 7 | 2.7 | 4.7 |
| Wood products | 3.4 | 8.5 | 5 | 4.8 | 8.6 | 11.6 | 9.1 | 4.8 |
| Paper products and Publishing | 4.3 | 4.5 | 2.9 | 6.4 | 4.3 | 6.6 | 4.8 | 4.3 |
| Petroleum and Coal products | 1.2 | 0.1 | 0.5 | 0.2 | 1.7 | 0.9 | 3 | 0.1 |
| Chemical, Rubber and Plastic products | 4.7 | 4 | 4 | 5.6 | 4.1 | 6.8 | 6.1 | 4 |
| Mineral products NEC | 5.6 | 6.7 | 10 | 8.8 | 11.3 | 6.3 | 9.2 | 10.4 |
| Ferrous metals | 5.1 | 5.2 | 2.3 | 5.6 | 6.5 | 9.8 | 7.4 | 3.4 |
| Metals NEC | 2.5 | 1.8 | 1.9 | 1.5 | 1.5 | 5.1 | 6.2 | 5.4 |
| Metal products | 5.5 | 6.9 | 3.5 | 8.3 | 8.8 | 10.5 | 7.9 | 6 |
| Motor vehicles and Parts | 18.3 | 29.8 | 4.9 | 11 | 19.7 | 24.3 | 32.4 | 18.7 |
| Transport equipment NEC | 2.5 | 2 | 0.6 | 11.4 | 9 | 7.8 | 0.9 | 0.4 |
| Electronic equipment | 0.8 | 1.6 | 1 | 1.9 | 0.1 | 0.5 | 1.1 | 0.2 |
| Machinery & Equipment NEC | 2.8 | 2.8 | 2.9 | 4.5 | 2.6 | 3.4 | 4.4 | 1.9 |
| Manufactures NEC | 2.9 | 5.3 | 4.2 | 6.7 | 0.6 | 7.7 | 6.3 | 5.1 |
| Weighted Average Tariffs | 3.05 | 3.79 | 4.65 | 5.53 | 5.99 | 5.77 | 4.98 | 3.12 |

SOURCE: Authors' calculation from GTAP data set version 6.

Whether ASEAN chooses to cooperate more within the region or moves forward to bilateral FTAs, this may be a good time for ASEAN to look at its stand on trade policy. The results from this study indicate that ASEAN could gain great benefits from regional cooperation such as ASEAN Free Trade Area (AFTA) as it could promote faster growth and enhance welfare gains from those bilateral FTAs. However, presently AFTA has yet to be fully honoured and sufficiently utilized by the members. Efforts on encouraging the uses of AFTA by ASEAN countries would, therefore, be considered as one of the important trade policies. This recommendation may not be different from those of others; nonetheless, it is one of the policy recommendations that should not be ignored.

## Notes

The authors would like to thank the anonymous referees for their valuable comments, Kanassanant Lertlalitkul and Varachat Numchaisri for their helpful research assistance, and Dr Wisuwat Plodpradista for his encouragement.

1. For more information, see http://www.fta.gov.sg.
2. The current status of the ASEAN FTA is from the U.S.-ASEAN Business Council, ASEAN FTA Matrix, available from www.us-asean.org dated 1 June 2007.
3. ASEAN-5 members are Indonesia, Malaysia, Philippines, Singapore, and Thailand.
4. Today ten ASEAN member countries are Brunei, Cambodia, Indonesia, Laos, Malaysia, Myanmar, the Philippines, Singapore, Thailand, and Vietnam.
5. Note that if data is available, the freight rate can be used as a proxy of the transportation cost.
6. The values 129 per cent and 600 per cent are calculated from is $\exp(0.829)-1$ and $\exp(1.946)-1$, respectively.
7. The value 182 per cent is calculated from $\exp(1.037)-1$.
8. Armington (1969) suggests that products are differentiated by locations of production to capture imperfect substitutions in products across countries.
9. See Hertel (1997), pp. 94–95.
10. For tariff structures, see Tables 5 and 6.

## References

Armington, P. "A Theory of Demand for Products distinguished by the Place of Production". *IMF Staff Papers* 16 (1969): 159–78.
Ballard, C.L. and I. Cheong. "The Effects of Economic Integration in the Pacific Rim: A Computational General Equilibrium Analysis". *Journal of Asian Economics* 8 (1997): 505–24.

Derosa, D. "U.S. Free Trade Agreement with ASEAN". In *Free Trade Agreements US Strategies and Priorities*, edited by Jeffery S. Washington, D.C.: Institute for International Economics, 2004.

Francois, J.F. "Scale Economics and Imperfect Competition in the GTAP Model". *GTAP Technical Paper* 14 (1998).

Frankel, J., E. Stein, and S. Wei. "Trading Blocs and the Americas: The Natural, the Unnatural, and the Super-Natural". *Journal of Development Economics* 47 (1995): 61–95.

Greenaway, D. and C. Milner. "Regionalism and Gravity". *Scottish Journal of Political Economy* 49 (2002): 574–85.

Hausman, J.A. "Specification Tests in Econometrics". *Econometrica* 46 (1978): 1251–71.

Hertel, T.W. *Global Trade Analysis: Modeling and Applications*. Cambridge: Cambridge University Press, 1997.

Kawasaki, K. "The Impact of Free Trade Agreement in Asia". *Research Institute of Economy, Trade and Industry Discussion Paper Series#* 03-E-018, 2003.

Rose, A. "Which International Institutions Promote International Trade?". *Review of International Economics* 13 (2005): 682–98.

Sally, R. and R. Sen. "Whither Trade Policies in Southeast Asia? The Wider Asian and Global Context". *ASEAN Economic Bulletin* 22 (2005): 92–115.

# 7

# FROM ECONOMIC REFORM TO CLOSER ECONOMIC TIES
## Regional- and National-Level Issues

Jenny D. Balboa, Erlinda M. Medalla, and Josef T. Yap

## I. INTRODUCTION

Over the past decade, efforts at promoting closer regionalism in East Asia have been stepped up for various reasons, including: (i) a response to the experience and lessons of the 1997 financial crisis; (ii) the gridlock in the Doha round, success of North American Free Trade Agreement (NAFTA), and expansion of the EU; (iii) the mitigation of political factors that prevented closer co-operation in the past, for example, competition between China and Japan; and (iv) the perception that ASEAN economic integration will not progress far unless other East Asian economies are involved.

One major constraint to this process is the large disparity in economic development in East Asia. Table 1 depicts the situation for fourteen countries of East Asia and the ASEAN member countries including Timor Leste. In terms of per capita income in PPP$, East Asia has the largest disparity when compared to other regional groupings: Latin America, Europe, South Asia, and North Africa. Studies have shown (for example, Venables 2003) that a large disparity in economic development will hinder efforts towards greater economic integration.

This paper examines various policies at the regional and national level that can help narrow the development gap and at the same time increase the chances for effective and meaningful economic integration. At the national

## TABLE 1
## Summary Measures for Europe 34, East Asia 14, SEA 11
## and Other Regions, 2003

|  | Mean | CV |
|---|---|---|
| Per Capita GDP (PPP$) SEA 11 | 6,937 | 113.1 |
| Per Capita GDP (PPP$) East Asia 14 | 9,090 | 101.9 |
| Per Capita GDP (PPP$) Europe 34 | 18,286 | 71.3 |
| Per Capita GDP (PPP$) Accession-12 | 13,491 | 29.7 |
| Per Capita GDP (PPP$) South Asia | 2,321 | 37.3 |
| Per Capita GDP (PPP$) North Africa | 5,306 | 30.0 |
| Per Capita GDP (PPP$) Latin America | 8,223 | 32.0 |

NOTES:
1. CV is the coefficient of variation. The higher is the measure, the higher the disparity.
2. SEA 11 are the ASEAN member countries plus Timor Leste. The East Asia 14 are the SEA 11 plus Japan, Korea and China. 2002 value was used for Myanmar.
3. Europe 34 is composed of the 15 EU member countries, the 12 Accession countries (including Bulgaria and Romania which will follow in 2007) and the so-called CIS-7 (Armenia, Azerbaijan, Georgia, Kyrgystan, Moldova, Tajikistan, and Uzbekistan).
4. South Asia covers India, Pakistan, Nepal, Bangladesh, Sri Lanka, Bhutan, and Maldives.
5. The North African countries are Algeria, Egypt, Morocco, and Tunisia.
6. The Latin American countries included are Argentina, Brazil, Chile, Mexico, Paraguay, Peru and Uruguay.
SOURCE: Basic Data from 2005 UNDP Human Development Report (implying that the data are for 2003).

level, these policies can be considered as *necessary conditions* for successful trade liberalization and financial co-operation. Free flow of goods and services is a minimum requirement for ASEAN to function as a single market. On the other hand financial co-operation and integration of financial markets provides a valuable window of opportunity to foment macroeconomic stability and reduce vulnerabilities.

In this context, the following questions will be considered: What are the structural constraints to growth in the Philippines? What institutional and economic reforms, thus far, have been implemented? What factors prompted these reforms? What institutional and economic reforms are needed or lacking?

## II. THE ECONOMIC DISPARITY IN ASEAN

The ten ASEAN member countries significantly vary in several social and economic indicators (Tables 2 and 3). In general, they can be classified into four clusters based on Human Development Index (HDI) rankings and

## TABLE 2
## Poverty and Income Inequality

| | National Poverty Line | | | | International Poverty Line | | | | | |
| | Survey year | Population below the poverty line (%) | | | Survey year | Population below $1 a day (%) | Poverty gap at $1 a day (%) | Population below $2 a day (%) | Poverty gap at $2 a day (%) | Gini coefficient |
| --- | --- | --- | --- | --- | --- | --- | --- | --- | --- | --- |
| | | Rural | Urban | National | | | | | | |
| Cambodia | 1999 | 40.1 | 13.9 | 35.9 | 1997[a] | 34.1 | 9.7 | 77.7 | 34.5 | 0.450 |
| China | 1998 | 3.1 (2003) | <2 | 4.6 | 2001[a] | 16.6 | 3.9 | 46.7 | 18.4 | 0.447 |
| Indonesia | 2002 | 21.1 | 14.5 | 18.2 | 2002[a] | 7.5 | 0.9 | 52.4 | 15.7 | 0.343 |
| Lao PDR | 1997–98 | 41.0 | 26.9 | 38.6 | 2002[a] | 27 | 6.1 | 74.1 | 30.2 | 0.370 |
| Malaysia | 1999 | 12.4 | 3.4 | 7.5 | 1997[b] | <2 | <0.5 | 9.3 | 2 | 0.440 |
| Myanmar | 1997 | 22.4 | 23.9 | 22.9 | — | — | — | — | — | — |
| Philippines | 2000 | 47.4 | 20.4 | 34.0 | 2000[a] | 15.5 | 3 | 47.5 | 17.8 | 0.461 |
| Singapore | — | — | — | — | — | — | — | — | — | 0.425 |
| Thailand | 2002 | 12.6 | 4 | 9.8 | 2002[a] | <2 | <0.5 | 25.2 | 6.2 | 0.432 |
| Vietnam | 2002 | 35.6 | 6.6 | 28.9 | 2002 | 13.1 | — | — | — | 0.376 |

NOTES: a. Expenditure base.
       b. Income base.
SOURCE: World Development Indicators, 2006; ADB Key Indicators, 2004.

socio-economic indicators. Singapore and Brunei belong to the upper cluster, being in the "high human development" category along with Japan, Republic of Korea, and the United States.

The second cluster is categorized as upper "medium development countries" and includes Malaysia, Thailand, and the Philippines. Vietnam and Indonesia belong to the medium "medium human development" countries, while Cambodia, Myanmar, and Lao PDR belong to the fourth group of countries referred to as lower "medium human development" countries.

The Philippines actually straddles the second and third groups since many of its socio-economic indicators are closer to Indonesia and Vietnam rather than Thailand and Malaysia. Among the ASEAN-6, the Philippines has the highest incidence of poverty — even higher than Vietnam — as measured by the proportion of population living below $1 per day, and the highest income inequality (Table 3). Its only distinct advantage is in the education index, reflecting its tradition of having a highly qualified workforce that is proficient in the English language.

The Philippines is an enigma in this context. It has not lived up to its enormous potential, which is reflected not only in its level of education but also in the vast natural resources of the country. Despite the economic reforms that have been implemented, issues of poor governance and a weak state have hampered economic progress (Fabella 1999; Llanto and Gonzalez 2006). This issue will be further explained later.

An existing large disparity in the level of development will likely lead to divergence or greater disparity in development when an FTA among the member countries is formed. Systematic analyses of the comparative advantage of customs union members[1] show that countries with an "extreme" comparative advantage do worse than those with comparative advantage intermediate between partner and the rest of the world (Venables 2003). The analysis shows the possible drawbacks of "South-South" integration schemes, showing how they may draw manufacturing production into richer countries at the expense of poorer members of the region. It also suggests that low-income countries are better served by integration with high-income countries.

This analysis can be dovetailed with evidence that countries that trade intensively tend to exhibit a relatively high incidence of income convergence. The initial large disparity may likely indicate that some countries are not in a position to absorb the new technology that goes with greater trade and investment and hence these countries may not be able to take advantage of the opportunities provided by a more liberalized trade regime. Another way of viewing it is that the less developed countries should attain a minimum

## TABLE 3
## Development Gap Indicators

| Development Gap Indicators[a] | ASEAN-6 | | | | | | CLMV Region | | | | China |
|---|---|---|---|---|---|---|---|---|---|---|---|
| | Brunei | Indonesia | Malaysia | Philippines | Singapore | Thailand | Cambodia | Lao PDR | Myanmar | Vietnam | China |
| **Economic Performance** | | | | | | | | | | | |
| GDP (US $ billion) | 5.5 | 257.6 | 118.3 | 84.6 | 106.8 | 161.7 | 4.9 | 2.5 | 10.1 | 45.2 | 1,931.7 |
| PPP (US$ billion) | — | 785.2 | 255.8 | 376.6 | 119.1 | 515.3 | 33.4 | 11.3 | — | 225.5 | 7,642.3 |
| Per Capita GDP (US$) | 15,122.3 | 1,184.0 | 4,753.0 | 1,036.0 | 25,191.0 | 2,539.0 | 354.0 | 423.0 | 201.2 | 550.0 | 1,490.0 |
| Per Capita PPP GDP (US$) | 19,210.0 | 3,609.0 | 10,276.0 | 4,614.0 | 28,077.0 | 8,090.0 | 2,423.0 | 1,954.0 | 1,027.0 | 2,745.0 | 5,896.0 |
| Population (million), 2005 | 0.4 | 222.8 | 26.0 | 83.1 | 4.2 | 64.2 | 14.1 | 5.9 | 54.0 | 84.2 | 1,315.8 |
| **Structure of Economy, 2005 (At Current Prices)** | | | | | | | | | | | |
| Share of Agriculture in GDP | 3.2 | 13.4 | 8.4 | 14.4 | 0.1 | 11.1 | 35.2 | 46.0 | 56.8 | 20.9 | 13.1 |
| Share of Industry | 40.4 | 39.4 | 46.9 | 28.0 | 28.8 | 40.2 | 20.2 | 24.9 | 8.5 | 34.7 | 40.2 |
| Share of Manufacturing | — | 28.1 | 29.5 | 23.7 | 27.3 | 34.0 | 19.4 | 21.0 | 7.9 | 20.7 | 40.2 |
| Share of Services | 56.4 | 47.2 | 44.7 | 57.6 | 71.1 | 48.7 | 44.6 | 29.2 | 34.7 | 44.4 | 46.7 |
| **Trade Structure** | | | | | | | | | | | |
| Imports/GDP (%) | 19,198.56[d] | 27.0 | 100.0 | 51.0 | 141[c] | 66.0 | 76.0 | 42.0 | 46[b] | 74.0 | 31.0 |
| Exports/GDP (%) | 29.71[d] | 31.0 | 121.0 | 52.0 | 171[c] | 71.0 | 65.0 | 29.0 | 19[b] | 66.0 | 34.0 |
| Primary export/Merchandise exports (%) | 88.0 | 44.0 | 23.0 | 10.0 | 13.0 | 22.0 | 3.0 | — | 61[b] | 46.0 | 8.0 |
| Manufactured/Merchandise exports (%) | 12.0 | 56.0 | 76.0 | 55.0 | 84.0 | 75.0 | 97.0 | — | 39[b] | 53.0 | 91.0 |
| Hi-tech exports/Manufactured exports (%) | 5.0 | 16.0 | 55.0 | 64.0 | 59.0 | 30.0 | — | — | — | 6.0 | 30.0 |
| **Human Development Index** | | | | | | | | | | | |
| HDI value | 0.9 | 0.7 | 0.8 | 0.8 | 0.9 | 0.8 | 0.6 | 0.6 | 0.6 | 0.7 | 0.8 |
| Life expectancy at birth (years) | 76.6 | 67.2 | 73.4 | 70.7 | 78.9 | 70.3 | 56.5 | 55.1 | 60.5 | 70.8 | 71.9 |
| Adult literacy rate (%, 15 and above) | 92.7 | 90.4 | 88.7 | 92.6 | 92.5 | 92.6 | 73.6 | 68.7 | 89.9 | 90.3 | 90.9 |

| | | | | | | | | | | | |
|---|---|---|---|---|---|---|---|---|---|---|---|
| **Education** | | | | | | | | | | | |
| Education index | 0.9 | 0.8 | 0.8 | 0.9 | 0.9 | 0.9 | 0.7 | 0.7 | 0.8 | 0.8 | 0.8 |
| **Public Expenditure for Education** | | | | | | | | | | | |
| as % of GD (2002–2004) | 9.1c | 0.9 | 8.0 | 3.2 | — | 4.2 | 2.0 | 2.3 | — | — | — |
| as % of Total Government Expenditure (2002–2004) | 9.1c | 9.0 | 28.0 | 17.2 | — | 40.0 | 15.32 | 11.0 | — | — | — |
| Tertiary students in Math, Science & Engineering (% of all students, 1998–2004) | 8.0 | — | 40.0 | 25.0 | — | — | 19.0 | 11.0 | 42.0 | — | — |
| Combined gross enrolment ratio for primary, secondary and tertiary schools (2004, %) | 77.0 | 68.0 | 73.0 | 82.0 | 87.0 | 74.0 | 60.0 | 61.0 | 49.0 | 63.0 | 70.0 |
| **Research and Development** | | | | | | | | | | | |
| Expenditure/GDP; % (2000–2003) | — | — | 0.7 | — | 2.2 | 0.2 | — | — | — | — | 1.3 |
| Researchers/1 million people (1990–2003) | 274.0 | — | 299.0 | — | 4,745.0 | 286.0 | — | — | — | — | 663.0 |
| **Infrastructure** | | | | | | | | | | | |
| Telephone mainlines (per 100 inhabitants, 2005) | 25.57c | 5.7 | 16.8 | 4.2 | 43.5 | 11.0 | 0.3 | 1.3 | 0.79e | 18.8 | 26.6 |
| Cellular subscribers (per 100 inhabitants, 2005) | 56.3 | 21.1 | 75.2 | 39.5 | 103.4 | 43.0 | 7.6 | 10.8 | 0.17e | 11.4 | 29.9 |
| Internet users (per 100 inhabitants, 2005) | 15.3 | 7.2 | 42.4 | 5.3 | 57.9 | 11.0 | 0.3 | 0.4 | 0.12e | 12.7 | 8.4 |
| Electricity consumption per capita (kilowatt-hours, 2003) | 9,133.0 | 498.0 | 3,196.0 | 655.0 | 8,087.0 | 1,896.0 | 9.0 | 135.0 | 126.0 | 503.0 | 1,440.0 |

NOTES:  a.   All figures refer to the year 2004 unless otherwise specified.
b.   Data refer to 2002; From Lamberte, Arboleda, and Reyes (2006) and Central Statistical Organization, Myanmar Statistical Yearbook 2003; Manufactured exports of Myanmar includes category labelled as 'others'.
c.   Data refer to 2000–2002.
d.   Data refer to 2003.
e.   Data refer to 2004.

SOURCE: UNDP Human Development Report 2006. ADB Key Indicators 2006. UN Statistics Division Database. ITU Website.

threshold level of economic and social development to participate effectively in both the regional integration and globalization processes.

The analysis indicates that to be effective and meaningful, efforts at regional integration must be accompanied by or even preceded by domestic reforms. Section III gives an overview of the progress of economic integration and co-operation in ASEAN. The reforms that the Philippines has undertaken and still has to implement are then discussed in the Section IV.

## III. OVERVIEW OF TRADE, INVESTMENT, AND FINANCIAL INTEGRATION AND CO-OPERATION IN ASEAN

### III.1 Trade and Investment Integration

While ASEAN has been in existence since 1967, efforts to integrate the economies have not been seriously pursued until 1992, with the advent of the ASEAN Free Trade Area (AFTA). Prior to this, trade co-operation came in the form of a Preferential Trading Arrangement (PTA) and piecemeal approaches such as ASEAN Investment Projects (AIPs), ASEAN Industrial Complement-ation Programmes and ASEAN Industrial Joint Ventures (AIJVs) — programmes that failed to come up with a comprehensive approach to forging closer economic co-operation (Ariff 2000).

AFTA is considered to be the centrepiece of the ASEAN economic integration. It is implemented through the Common Effective Preferential Tariff (CEPT) Scheme, a comprehensive tariff listing that at present covers 65,529 tariff lines, 84 per cent of which is in the Inclusion List (Table 4). When AFTA was first introduced, most ASEAN countries took a defensive stance and enumerated a wide range of products in the exclusion list. However, as the CEPT scheme was implemented, exclusion listing has been substantially cut down. Even agricultural products, which were previously excluded, are now scheduled to be included in 2010.[2] Since most ASEAN members embraced this scheme freely, deadlines were even moved closer from 2008 to 2003 to achieve the 0–5 per cent tariff level for products covered. By January 2002, six years ahead of original schedule, the ASEAN-6 realized the target of 0–5 per cent tariff level, covering 95.7 per cent of tariff lines and 90 per cent of intra-ASEAN trade in goods.

As far as attracting FDI is concerned, ASEAN's performance is commendable. Upon signing of the Agreement in 1995, the share of FDI in the region grew from 26 per cent in 1995 to 51 per cent in 2001. While FDI fell by 50 per cent during the financial crisis period, it recovered right away in 1999, showing a 49 per cent increase in priority goods and services sectors (Austria 2004).

**TABLE 4**
**AFTA: Common Effective Preferential Tariff (CEPT) List for 2001**

| Country | Inclusion List | Temporary Exclusion List | General Exception List | Sensitive List | Total |
|---|---|---|---|---|---|
| Brunei | 6,284 | — | 202 | 6 | 6,492 |
| Indonesia | 7,190 | 21 | 68 | 4 | 7,283 |
| Malaysia | 9,654 | 218 | 53 | 83 | 10,008 |
| Philippines | 5,622 | 6 | 16 | 50 | 5,694 |
| Singapore | 5,821 | — | 38 | — | 5,859 |
| Thailand | 9,104 | — | — | 7 | 9,111 |
| **ASEAN-6 Total** | **43,675** | **245** | **377** | **150** | **44,447** |
| **Percentage** | **98.26** | **0.55** | **0.85** | **0.34** | **100** |
| Cambodia | 3,115 | 3,523 | 134 | 50 | 6,822 |
| Laos | 1,673 | 1,716 | 74 | 88 | 3,551 |
| Myanmar | 2,984 | 2,419 | 48 | 21 | 5,472 |
| Vietnam | 4,233 | 757 | 196 | 51 | 5,237 |
| New Members Total | 12,005 | 8,415 | 452 | 210 | 21,082 |
| Percentage | 57 | 40 | 2 | 1 | 100 |
| **ASEAN Total** | **55,680** | **8,660** | **829** | **360** | **65,529** |
| **Percentage** | **85** | **13** | **1** | **1** | **100** |

SOURCE: ASEAN Secretariat.

Another strategy crafted is the ASEAN Framework Agreement on Services (AFAS) for services liberalization. Signed on 15 December 2005, AFAS aims to enhance co-operation in services among member states, eliminate restrictions to trade in services and liberalize trade in services beyond each member's commitment under the General Agreement on Trade in Services (GATS) with the end goal of realizing a free trade area in services.[3] It complements AFTA and ASEAN Investment Area (AIA) by promoting free flow of services within the region, with heavy emphasis on business services, transportation, telecommunications, and finance. However, like most trade arrangements, welfare losses may arise, but these are estimated to be fairly small compared with potential gains. Furthermore, in most cases, the losses are not created by AFTA. Thus, AFTA can be aptly called a positive-sum game, because integrating the economies will help everyone emerge as winners, and no one will end up losing.

## III.2 Financial Co-operation

Interest in regional monetary and financial co-operation and integration increased in the aftermath of the 1997 Asian financial crisis. Regional financial and monetary co-operation can be justified by three phenomena that were highlighted during the 1997 debacle (Montiel 2003): (i) spillovers from exchange rate policies, which present a reason for exchange rate co-ordination; (ii) inadequate supplies of international liquidity; and (iii) common structural weaknesses in the financial sector and corporate governance, which can be addressed more effectively by cross-country co-operation. The European experience is also cited as a factor that has heightened interest in greater financial and monetary co-operation.

Meanwhile, it is acknowledged that trade liberalization brings pressure for financial liberalization, and that financial liberalization is as important, complex and arduous as trade liberalization. As trade becomes more open and free, so do financial flows. Money flowed in and out of Southeast Asia, increasing not only its volume but also its volatility (Estanislao 2000).

Financial reform programmes in the region were initially motivated by stabilizing currencies rather than co-ordinating macroeconomic policy or achieving overall financial stability. An important strategy is the Chiang Mai Initiative (CMI) of May 2000. CMI expanded the existing ASEAN swap arrangements to include all ASEAN countries and set up a network of bilateral currency swap and repurchase arrangements among ASEAN+3 countries. The initiative aims to provide additional short-term hard currency for countries facing possible liquidity shortfalls. It also seeks to achieve better monitoring of capital flows, regional surveillance and training of personnel. In the CMI, Japan and China play key roles as they are the only ones that can take the role of lender should the network be activated (Amyx 2005).

In 2002, ASEAN integrated its financial reforms aimed at targeting structural weaknesses in the financial systems of ASEAN member countries. One of the major problems identified is the presence of "double mismatch" in financial markets. Double mismatch is the mismatch between debt maturities (short-term borrowing for long-term investments) and the denomination of this debt (in foreign rather than local currencies). The presence of a double mismatch has the potential to bring about a currency crisis. The ASEAN Bond Market Initiative was introduced to address this issue. By establishing the option of longer-term capital procurement and investment in the region, bond markets potentially may be able to spur greater productivity in national markets across the region. ASEAN+3 Bond Market Initiative is at the heart of financial reforms and liberalization of ASEAN+3 countries.

Meanwhile, exchange rate co-ordination is one aspect of general macroeconomic policy co-ordination that has been gaining adherents. Countries can benefit from co-ordinating macroeconomic policy, for example, monetary policy among G8 countries, even if they do not co-ordinate their exchange rates. On the other hand, exchange rate co-ordination requires co-ordination in other macroeconomic policies, particularly monetary and fiscal policies. A typical list of preconditions for a successful regional basket peg regime reads as follows (Ito and Park 2003):

- Ability to manage (independent) monetary policy prudently when countering external and internal shocks, without nominal anchor (possibly with inflation targeting);
- fiscal policy prudence; and
- credibility in macroeconomic management.

These conditions guarantee the removal of factors that lead to fluctuations due to domestic macroeconomic stability. The criteria generally apply to any regional exchange rate co-ordination scheme. While the fiscal and monetary reforms implemented by the Philippine government are geared primarily towards domestic macroeconomic stability, they are also necessary conditions for successful exchange rate co-ordination.

At the heart of all these regional initiatives is the goal of narrowing the development gap in ASEAN and East Asia, in general, by enhancing economic institutions, creating accountable, transparent and pro-people governments that adhere to good governance practices, and helping address resource limitations of member countries, particularly institutional and human resource inadequacy. This is a huge task that requires focused assistance programmes with clear timelines from ASEAN, as well as clear commitments and supportive domestic policies from all ASEAN member states.

## IV. STATUS OF ECONOMIC REFORM IN THE PHILIPPINES IN AREAS IMPORTANT TO REGIONAL ECONOMIC INTEGRATION

### IV.1 Trade Reforms

The government introduced a comprehensive trade reform programme in the 1980s to liberalize trade unilaterally. The programme spanned more than a decade and was implemented in three phases up to the 1990s. The first phase was implemented from 1981 to 1985, and narrowed down the tariff structure from a range of 100–0 per cent to 50–10 per cent. This was accompanied by the Import Liberalization Programme (ILP), which sought to eliminate non-tariff import measures. Implementation of the programme, however, was stalled by the economic and political crises in the country in the mid-1980s (Clarete 2005).

The second phase of trade liberalization was implemented in 1991, which was aimed at lowering tariff rates over a five-year period. The programme clustered the commodities within a tariff range of 10–30 per cent. The following year in 1992, Executive Order 8 was issued to provide tariff protection measures to replace quantitative restrictions (QRs) on imports of 153 commodities (Clarete 2005, p. 248).

The third and final phase of the unilateral trade reform took place in 1994. It created a four-tier tariff structure with the end goal of achieving a low, uniform tariff by 2002. This aims to simplify the tariff structure and targeted achieving the following rates: 3 per cent for raw materials and capital equipment that are not available locally; 10 per cent for raw materials and capital equipment that can be sourced locally; 20 per cent for intermediate goods; and 30 per cent for finished goods. The third phase was implemented by four Executive Orders (Clarete 2005, p. 248):

- EO 189 issued on 1 January 1994 reduced tariff rates on capital equipment and machinery.
- EO 204 issued on 30 September 1994 lowered tariff rates on imported textiles, garments and chemical inputs.
- EO 264 issued on 22 July 1995 reduced tariffs on 4,142 lines of the Harmonized System (HS) in the manufacturing sector. This is considered to be the biggest reform in the tariff code.
- EO 288 introduced on 1 January 1996 complemented the reform in 1995 through reduction of tariffs on non-sensitive agricultural products.

With the country's accession to the WTO, it committed to eliminating all its quantitative import restrictions on agricultural products, except rice. The Congress passed Republic Act 8178 on 29 March 1996 to implement this, supplemented by Executive Order 313 which specified the tariff equivalent rates for each agricultural quantitative restrictions.

Further, the government expressed its intention to adopt a uniform 5 per cent tariff by the year 2004 to comply with the AFTA-CEPT Agreement where the tariffs on most products is to be reduced to a range between 0 and 5 per cent by 2002. This has been complied with as the average CEPT Tariff Rate in the Philippines at present is already at 3.75 per cent.

The series of reforms gradually lowered nominal and weighted average tariff rates and simplified the tariff structure. Temporary periods of reversals were implemented such as during the Asian financial crisis in 1998 and 1999 and another increase in tariff protection for certain industries in 2003, particularly for steel, sugar, and polymers, with specific schedules to lowering them gradually.

It is significant to note that under this tariff restructuring regime, aggregate exports expanded dramatically, overtaking aggregate imports, but growth occurred in only a few sectors, particularly in manufacturing, machinery and transportation equipment. Moreover, value added generated by these export sectors has been relatively low, a phenomenon that will be discussed in more detail later. In a number of sectors such as raw materials, and animal and vegetable oils, it has remained stagnant or even declined. Notably, per capita income has not changed, and there is mixed evidence as to whether the reforms really helped in alleviating poverty and improving income distribution in the country (Clarete 2005).

## IV.2 Financial Reforms[4]

Relative to other Asian countries, the Philippines was less adversely affected by the financial crisis of 1997. The resilience of the country's financial sector is largely attributable to policy and institutional reforms that the country undertook more than a decade before the crisis erupted. Most significant of these reforms were: institutional reforms and the rehabilitation of the financial system including the restructuring of the Central Bank, interest rate reforms and the liberalization of the foreign exchange market, and liberalization of bank entry (Bautista 1992; Lamberte 1993; Lamberte and Llanto 1993; Intal and Llanto 1998). These strengthened prudential regulations minimized pricing distortions in credit decisions by eliminating subsidy coming from the Central Bank and imposing a uniform and market-based rediscount rate. This facilitated the entry of foreign banks into the country's financial sector. With these reforms, the financial sector became more robust such that the country was able to withstand the impact of the crisis, particularly the depreciation of the peso, the rise in interest rates and the slowdown of the economy without any collapse in the financial institutions.

A major reform effort to resuscitate a poorly functioning financial sector was the strengthening of the Central Bank, which had suffered losses in the 1980s as a result of swap arrangements and interest rate losses. A series of enactments in 1993 made the Central Bank more independent and substantially boosted its capitalization. The problem assets of the old Central bank were transferred to a separate body for liquidation.

To complement these reforms, the foreign exchange market was liberalized, resulting in the elimination of the restrictions in the current account and reduction of regulations on inward and outward capital flows. At the same time, the Central Bank lifted the prohibition on off-floor foreign exchange trading. This transformed a highly regulated foreign exchange market with significant controls on capital flows to a highly deregulated one.

Lastly, an important policy change was the liberalization of entry of foreign banks in 1994 either as fully owned full service branched through equity purchase in an existing bank, or the establishment of a joint venture between foreign and local groups. With the liberalization of bank entry, banks were allowed to open branches anywhere as long as requirements on capital adequacy, liquidity, profitability, and soundness of management are met. This also paved the way for the entry of new commercial banks in the country.

While it posted relatively strong growth in 2003–2006, financial health of the banking sector remains fragile due to certain factors, particularly the high level of non-performing assets (NPAs) and non-performing loans (NPLs), which has resulted in a cutback in bank lending. NPL ratio as of 2004 stood at 13.9, and is one of the highest among Asian countries (see Table 5). Other countries have been able to reduce their NPL because of sufficient fiscal room for the creation of state-owned asset management companies (AMCs). Unfortunately, for the Philippines, the government was not capable of intervening in this manner because of its huge fiscal problem (Ladan 2005, p. 4).

Other identified problems in the banking sector are increasing interest rates (brought about by fiscal problems and not by an increased credit demand), high operating expenses (operating expenses eat up 89 per cent of the operating income in banks), corporate governance problems (as shown by few bank auditors, absence of domestic credit rating agencies, lack of transparency in sharing of information), and compliance with international standards.

**TABLE 5**
**Non-Performing Loans (NPLs) of Select Asian Countries**

|             | 2000 | 2004       |
|-------------|------|------------|
| China       | 22.4 | 17.9 ('03) |
| Japan       | 5.3  | 4.7        |
| Korea       | 8.9  | 2.4        |
| Indonesia   | 34.4 | 14.9       |
| Malaysia    | 15.4 | 12.6       |
| **Philippines** | **14.9** | **13.9** |
| Singapore   | 3.4  | 2.9        |
| Thailand    | 17.7 | 12.4       |

SOURCE: Global Financial Stability Report (2005).

Recently the Bangko Sentral ng Pilipinas (BSP) adopted the Basel II Framework, which aims to address the abovementioned issues. Basel II, which is to be fully implemented in 2007, is the revised set of standards issued by the Basel Committee on Banking Supervision (BCBS) in 2004.[5] Also known as the International Convergence of Capital Measurement and Capital Standards, Basel II promotes the adoption of stronger risk management practices by banks and is governed by three pillars: minimum capital requirements (that is, banks should have adequate capital for their risk-taking activities), stronger supervisory review process (banks should be able to properly assess their capital adequacy in relation to the risk they are taking, and supervisors should be able to evaluate the soundness of assessments), and market discipline (banks should be disclosing pertinent information necessary to enable market mechanisms to complement the supervisory oversight function) (Espenilla 2005).

The BSP is also working on adopting capital market reforms by developing the domestic capital market and to optimize the country's access to international capital. This reform effort is carried out by price stability measures such as inflation targeting and using of higher level of transparency requirements. It also aims to broaden the array of available capital market instruments such as tier 2 paper, LTNCDs (Long Term Negotiable Certificate of Deposit), documented repos, structures debt, collateralized debt obligations, and credit derivatives. On the demand side, the trust business is reformed with the conversion of the common trust funds into Unit Investment Trust Fund (UITF). It will also encourage the entry of more high quality rating agencies and institutionalize an independent securities custody system to improve investor protection, defeat market malpractices and reduce systemic risks (Tetangco 2005). Further, BSP pushes for amendment of its Charter to strengthen the institution and to make it on par with other well-performing central banks.

## IV.3 Fiscal Reforms

Beyond financial reforms, another key factor that helped the country withstand the crisis is fiscal consolidation done in the early 1990s. Efforts at strengthening the country's fiscal position resulted in surpluses of less than 1 per cent of GDP in 1994–97, a stark contrast from years of fiscal deficit in the 1980s up to the early 1990s (Manasan 2004).

However, while the Philippines did not suffer as much as other Asian countries, one visible mark left by the financial crisis is that it squandered fiscal gains achieved in the 1990s. Deficits persistently grew, from 1.9 per cent of GDP in 1998 to 4.1 per cent in 2000, and reached a peak of 5.4 per cent in 2002. The level subsequently fell in 2003, 2004, and 2005, with the deficit/GDP ratio recording 4.6, 3.9, and 2.7 per cent respectively

Meanwhile, the debt crisis in the country continued to worsen. As of 2005, the national government's debt was already equivalent to 79.3 per cent of GDP. Consolidated public sector debt accounted for more than 130 per cent of GDP (Pacific Economic Outlook, 2005–2006). The problem was aggravated by policy mistakes, government inaction in specific problem areas, and the government's heavy reliance on budgetary cuts instead of revenue generation for fiscal adjustment.

Studies conducted showed that the widening deficit is not the result of increased national government expenditures, as it remained stable at around 19.4 per cent of GDP from 1997 to 2003, but the consequence of poor revenue effort, which declined progressively from 19.4 per cent of GDP in 1997 to 15.6 per cent in 2000. In 2004, revenue effort fell to only 14.6 per cent of GDP before recovering to 15.1 per cent in 2005. As of November 2006, the government managed to pull together 86.7 billion peso in total revenues signifying a 19 per cent increase over a comparable period in 2005.[6] This puts revenue effort on track to reach 15.7 per cent in 2006.

Instead of addressing the problems squarely, the government relied on expenditure cuts to narrow the deficit. This took a heavy toll on public service as government agencies had to work with budgets so much smaller than what is needed to effectively deliver social service (see Table 6).

Moreover, Government and Controlled Corporations (GOCCs) exacerbated the country's fiscal position as many of these GOCCs suffer from poor cost recovery due to inadequate tariff adjustments, political interference in tariff setting, government intervention in pricing policy, liabilities that they had contracted through the years, poor revenue generation performance, and overstaffed structures with grossly overpaid staff.

Manasan (2004) showed that the fourteen GOCCs of the country are responsible for the huge deficit of the non-financial public sector, which had risen steeply since 1996 and had expanded from 75.4 per cent of GDP to 103 per cent of GDP in 2002. The most notable in terms of contribution to the deficit are: the National Power Corporation (NPC), the National Food Authority (NFA), the Light Rail Transit Authority (LRTA), the Metropolitan Waterworks and Sewerage System (MWSS), the National Irrigation Administration (NIA), and the Home Guaranty Corporation (HGC).

The government aims to balance the national government fiscal position by 2010. Thus, efforts towards improving the public sector's fiscal position include:

**TABLE 6**
**Real Per Capita National Government Expenditures on Social Services,**
**1996–2004**
**(2000 Prices)**

|  | 1996 | 1997 | 1998 | 1999 | 2000 | 2001 | 2002 | 2003 | 2004 |
|---|---|---|---|---|---|---|---|---|---|
| Total Social Services | 2,188 | 2,487 | 2,417 | 2,323 | 2,302 | 2,035 | 2,022 | 2,016 | 1,999 |
| Education | 1,534 | 1,789 | 1,761 | 1,675 | 1,608 | 1,516 | 1,505 | 1,455 | 1,412 |
| Health | 230 | 266 | 221 | 223 | 202 | 166 | 171 | 151 | 141 |
| Soc. Security, Welfare, and Employment | 317 | 392 | 387 | 364 | 376 | 331 | 327 | 392 | 418 |
| Housing and Community Devt. | 107 | 39 | 48 | 61 | 115 | 22 | 19 | 19 | 29 |

SOURCE: Manasan (2004).

- Operation RATE (Run After Tax Evaders), RATS (Run After the Smugglers) and RIPS (Revenue Integrity Protection Service): Operation RATE targets high-profile tax evaders, RATS targets smugglers, particularly high-profile oil importer and Bureau of Custom personnel, and RIPS targets erring government officials and employees.
- Tighter monitoring of the Bureau of Customs, particularly strengthening of the anti-smuggling campaign, auction of overstaying containers, tightening of post-entry audit, and expansion and speeding up of computerization programme.
- Programmes to improve collection efficiency of the Bureau of Internal Revenue through benchmarking revenues and deductions against industry standards and use of third-party information to check veracity of tax returns.

Legislative measures were also pushed by the government to reform the tax policy of the country. The Arroyo administration's eight-point approach to this end are:

- adoption of gross income taxation;
- indexation of excise tax on tobacco and liquor;
- excise tax on petroleum products;
- rationalization of fiscal incentives;
- general tax amnesty with submission of Statements of Liabilities;

- lateral attrition system;
- franchise tax on telecoms; and
- review of the Value Added Tax (VAT) System.

As of 2006, only three have been approved by the legislature. Raising of "sin taxes" or excise tax on tobacco and alcohol has been approved, although the original bill, which called for the indexation of the excise tax to inflation, has been revised and is no longer included in the final version. The increase in the "sin taxes" is expected to raise 15 billion peso. Another bill that was approved was the Lateral Attrition Law, passed in January 2005. The bill aims to provide incentives to revenue collecting agencies and is expected to increase collection by 10 billion peso. Finally, the more contentious bill revising the current VAT Law was also approved. The Expanded Value Added Tax (E-VAT) was passed on May 2005. It removed many of the exemptions listed in the old VAT law such as power generation and exemptions for oil companies. It also gave President Arroyo the power to raise VAT to 12 per cent from 10 per cent and raise corporate income tax to 35 per cent from 32 per cent starting from 2006, before cutting it to 30 per cent in 2009. The VAT changes are expected to raise an additional 28 to 31 billion peso in revenue.

Thus far, the Philippine experience showed that it is not enough that the government cut down on expenditures to improve fiscal performance. The government should focus its efforts on tax policy and tax administration reform to address the widening fiscal gap. It is also important that efforts towards curbing corruption, minimizing wastage in government resources, and addressing the fiscal problems of GOCCs are addressed.

## IV.4 Additional Domestic Reform Measures and Issues

Significant strides have been made in integrating the Philippines in the global economy as a result of economic reforms undertaken in the past decade. However, there are still much to be done in order for these reforms to translate into actual economic development. For example, even with policies that enhance market access through various means of trade liberalization (unilateral and negotiated), the Philippines remains to encounter problems with maximizing opportunities. This failure is primarily due to poor economic structures and lack of good governance mechanisms that affect the country's competitiveness and overall economic performance. Clarete (2005) emphasized high transaction costs and poor investment climate as the culprit in the country's failure to capture as much FDI as other ASEAN countries. In addition, major setbacks from political upheavals (particularly the attempted coup attempt in 1990) and the power crisis in 1992 (which was also a result of poor economic structure and lack of good governance mechanisms) have seriously stunted whatever momentum gained from the reforms at that time.

Trade and industrial reforms have been inadequate in fuelling faster GDP and employment growth and economic transformation in the Philippines as shown by data in Table 7. Compared with China, Indonesia, Korea, Malaysia, and Thailand, the share of manufacturing value added in the Philippines is lower in 2002. Moreover, the share actually fell between 1990 and 2002 in the Philippines while it increased in the other countries.

The structure of domestic manufacturing value added and manufactured exports is quite revealing. The Philippines has the highest share of medium-or-high technology products in manufactured exports among these countries in 2002. However, it also has the lowest share in terms of domestic manufacturing valued added  in the medium-or-high technology sectors. The variance indicates a dichotomy between the domestic manufacturing sector and export sector.

What are the major factors that have prevented the Philippines from maximizing its gains from globalization? A number of these factors can be traced to policy shortcomings, foremost of which are:

1. *Low investments in infrastructure.* According to World Bank estimates, a middle-income country in East Asia will need to spend at least 5 per cent of GDP on infrastructure to meet their needs in the next ten years. Infrastructure expenditure in the Philippines is far below this benchmark as it only accounts for 2.8 per cent of GDP. In addition, resources allotted for infrastructure development are spent inefficiently. Infrastructure upgrading is necessary to improve economic performance of the country as it would help attract more investments and reduce production costs. The lack of infrastructure programme is largely related to the fragile fiscal situation of the government.

2. *Lack of political will to implement a sustained and credible fiscal reform programme.* Weak fiscal institutions led to the creation of policies that increased the debt burden and inherently biased towards deficit-spending. They are also responsible for the fiscal blunders created such as politicized spending and delayed fiscal consolidation during crises. To be effective, fiscal reforms should aim at creating stronger fiscal institutions that adhere to rules and do not easily give in to populist demands. Reforms should also create accountable and more transparent institutions that will implement the revenue generation programmes and include capability enhancement measures

TABLE 7
Six Indicators of Industrial Performance, 1990 and 2002

| | Manufacturing value added (MVA) per capita (1995 US$) | | Manufactured exports per capita (US$) | | Share of manufacturing in total output (GDP) (%) | | Share of manufacturing in total exports (%) | | Share of medium-or-high-technology production in MVA (%) | | Share of medium-or-high-technology products in manufactured exports (%) | |
|---|---|---|---|---|---|---|---|---|---|---|---|---|
| | 1990 | 2002 | 1990 | 2002 | 1990 | 2002 | 1990 | 2002 | 1990 | 2002 | 1990 | 2002 |
| China | 100.7 | 359.4 | 41.6 | 234.5 | 33.1 | 34.5 | 76 | 91.6 | 51.6 | 57.3 | 34.4 | 45.6 |
| Hong Kong SAR | 2,042.8 | 1,133.0 | 4,842.9 | 3,211.6 | 16.3 | 8.7 | 95.3 | 94.9 | 41.8 | 58.5 | 40.6 | 36.8 |
| India | 49 | 77.6 | 16.8 | 38.5 | 16.6 | 15.8 | 79.6 | 85.8 | 55.3 | 58.4 | 17.9 | 19.7 |
| Indonesia | 162 | 278.7 | 82 | 224 | 20.7 | 27 | 58.6 | 76.9 | 30 | 43.4 | 10.5 | 31.3 |
| Japan | 9,696.9 | 9,850.9 | 2,263.9 | 3,595.2 | 26.5 | 25 | 97.5 | 93 | 66.5 | 68.1 | 83.9 | 86.3 |
| Korea, Republic of | 2,237.6 | 4,858.7 | 1,455.4 | 3,591.1 | 28.8 | 33.9 | 96.2 | 96.5 | 55.1 | 64.1 | 52.9 | 70.6 |
| Malaysia | 757.5 | 1,516.5 | 1,286.5 | 4,120.5 | 26.5 | 35.9 | 78 | 93.3 | 52.3 | 65.1 | 50.6 | 76.2 |
| Philippines | 252.4 | 269.5 | 69.8 | 482.4 | 24.8 | 24.2 | 52.7 | 96.2 | 31.2 | 38.3 | 30 | 81.8 |
| Singapore | 4,410.3 | 6,582.5 | 16,266.1 | 33,105.8 | 28.6 | 28.2 | 93.2 | 96.8 | 78.8 | 87.6 | 62.3 | 78.9 |
| Taiwan Province of China | 2,842.1 | 4,397.5 | 3,148.7 | 6,563.7 | 32.7 | 28.1 | 95.8 | 98.3 | 52.2 | 58.6 | 51.6 | 71.2 |
| Thailand | 520.9 | 999.6 | 338.6 | 869.6 | 27.2 | 33.6 | 80.6 | 87.4 | 23.7 | 42.6 | 33.3 | 60.3 |

SOURCE: UNIDO Industrial Development Report, 2005.

to reinforce technical capacity of these institutions to fully mobilize revenues for the country's needs (Canlas 2005).

3. *High transaction costs.* Transaction costs refer to market-related infrastructure, facilities and services needed to conduct business. It also includes costs in acquiring and exchanging information in transactions and contract enforcement. If transaction costs are high, these become a disincentive to the producers to participate in any market exchange. It has been argued that the relatively poor performance of Philippine exports may be explained by high transaction costs in the country rather than market access issues. Logistical cost disadvantages have hindered domestic industries from benefiting fully from the effects of trade liberalization and have discouraged foreign investors from considering the Philippines in their production and logistical networks.

4. *Lack of a coherent industrial policy.* This is an area that has been overlooked because of the controversy it generates. However, recent work has attempted to provide a pragmatic approach that eschews ideological prescriptions and instead looks more closely at historical experience (Rodrik 2004; Hausmann and Rodrik 2006). The basic argument is that industrial policy is as much about eliciting information from the private sector on significant externalities — primarily information and co-ordination externalities — and their remedies as it is about implementing appropriate policies. However, the capacity to apply industrial policy is also important, which leads to the importance of governance and institutions. Since 1972, Philippine economic managers followed a programme that largely mimicked the Washington Consensus and did not allow for strategic intervention on the part of the government.

5. *Low priority given to basic social services.* Effective delivery of basic social services is the most cost-effective way of combating poverty and inequity. At the World Summit for Social Development held in Copenhagen in 1995, the 20/20 Initiative was crafted. This Initiative proposed that in order to achieve universal coverage of basic social services, 20 per cent of budgetary expenditure in developing countries and 20 per cent of aid flows should on average be allocated to social services. Basic social services account for only 8.6 per cent of the Philippine national budget in contrast to the combined debt service and defence budget, which account for 40.6 per cent. Greater social spending also implies a higher level of education, which is necessary to encourage FDI and enhance the technological capability of the economy.

There were also gaps in the implementation of reforms, and this is related to failure to address issues in good governance. This focuses on anti-corruption initiatives and institutionalization of corporate governance practices. The Philippines has always been cited as a country whose potential for growth has been eroded by corrupt institutions. In 2005, it ranked 117th in the Transparency International Survey of countries with the least corrupt government. According to World Bank figures, 20 per cent of annual government budget is lost to corruption. On average, this is equivalent to 3.8 per cent of GNP.

It is of utmost importance that measures to curb corruption are undertaken. Anti-corruption strategy should be reinforced by a committed leadership and able management skills to implement the programmes and sustain the progress made. Continued re-engineering of the bureaucracy is necessary, with reforms focused not only on achieving efficiency and effectiveness, but also instilling a culture of adherence to rules (Balboa and Medalla 2006).

## V. STRATEGIES AT THE REGIONAL LEVEL: ADDRESSING DEVELOPMENT GAPS

ASEAN recognizes that for genuine economic co-operation to take place, it must first address the existing development gaps in member countries. Developmental gaps may be characterized by economic gaps (GDP, life expectancy, education, health, poverty incidence), resource limitations (institutional capacity), and governance issues (transparency, accountability, rule of law, efficient and effective institutions and participatory process). The Bali Concord II explicitly embedded this agenda to ASEAN. Adopted in the ASEAN Summit in 2003, the Concord specifies the modalities and extent to which co-operation can take place. It envisioned a three-pillared ASEAN community composed of the ASEAN Economic Community (AEC), ASEAN Security Community (ASC) and the ASEAN Socio-Cultural Com-munities (ASCC). This is expected to be fully realized in 2020.[7]

The Vientiane Plan of Action (VPA) launched in 2004 provides the framework to realize these goals. VPA builds on existing initiatives such as the Initiative for ASEAN Integration (IAI), the Roadmap for the Integration of ASEAN (RIA), the Hanoi Declaration on Narrowing Development Gap for Closer ASEAN Integration in 2001 and the Vientiane Declaration on Enhancing Economic and Integration among CLMV.[8] It seeks to ensure that the benefits of economic integration is maximized and equitably distributed across and within member countries. It also aims to deepen integration through intensified dialogue, making binding commitments, extending national and regional competencies, developing institutional frameworks, responses and human resources in a range of areas. Three types of development co-operation interventions are envisioned: regional policy initiatives, development of regional implementation and human-capacity building.[9]

The VPA Programme Areas and Measures include specific strategies for co-operation in trade and investments, trade facilitation, trade in services, industrial co-operation and enterprise development, intellectual property rights, tourism, institutional strengthening, infrastructure enhance-ment, economic integration activities and social development to complement the national poverty reduction programmes. It creates a comprehensive development agenda that encompasses economic reforms and political development. It sets out specific action points for political, economic and socio-cultural progress. This strategy highlighted the need to promote human rights and obligations and also strengthen domestic institutions and establish rule of law, functional legal structures, and good governance.

The Philippines was actively involved in the crafting of the VPA. It submitted the first draft Plan of Action at the Special SOM Brainstorming Session for the Vientiane Plan of Action in Laos on December 2003. In formulating the plan, consultations were held with the National Committee on Culture and Information (COCI). Concerned agencies and institutions involved in drafting regional programmes in social development were also consulted, making sure that the VPA is consistent and supportive of its various programmes.

Even in this context the VPA, in particular, or regional economic integration, in general, is not the primary motivator of the domestic reform efforts in the Philippines. Financial and fiscal reforms are geared primarily towards macroeconomic stability. Meanwhile, trade reforms were prompted by the general malaise of the economy in the late 1970s, IMF-World Bank conditionalities, and subsequent WTO commitments. Nevertheless these reforms can be considered as necessary conditions for effective and meaningful regional economic integration.

## VI. CONCLUSION

Regional integration in Southeast Asia is mainly characterized by "regionalization" or market-oriented integration, hence initiatives undertaken to promote closer co-operation used to be, for the most part, focused on trade liberalization strategies. However, despite aggressive trade liberalization initiatives, what has been shown is that economic openness did not necessarily translate to economic opportunities. Lessons from the Philippine experience established that even with trade liberalization and compliance to regional economic co-operation programmes, sustained economic development remained elusive. Despite economic reforms, the Philippines continue to post very high unemployment rate and relatively high poverty incidence. Moreover, a dichotomy between the domestic manufacturing sector and export sector has evolved.

Clearly, market integration through trade reforms is not sufficient to achieve development goals and address the economic divide in the region. For trade co-operation to be an agent of development, it should be accompanied by other fundamental macroeconomic strategies at the national level, particularly sustainable financial reforms, fiscal consolidation, and perhaps a coherent industrial policy. Moreover, reforms should be complemented by strategies to integrate good governance practices, strengthen support institutions, infrastructure and adequate social development programmes that will ensure that gains from these reforms result in concrete opportunities that will benefit the people.

## Notes

The authors acknowledge the excellent research assistance of Fatima Lourdes E. del Prado. The usual disclaimer applies.

1. The analysis of Venables (2003) focuses on the effect of the formation of a customs union. The arguments can readily be extended to the formation of an FTA.
2. Since some unprocessed agriculture products (UAPs) are classified as "sensitive" and "highly sensitive", special arrangements were made which was articulated in the 31st ASEAN Economic Ministers Meeting in 1999. The Protocol on the Special Arrangement for Sensitive and Highly Sensitive Products paved the way for the agreement to integrate sensitive products into the CEPT Scheme by 2010 with 0–5 per cent tariff rates without any QRs or NTBs. This does not cover rice, considered to be a highly sensitive product for the Philippines, Malaysia, and Indonesia, which is allowed an end tariff of over 5 per cent. A staple food in almost all ASEAN member countries, sufficiency in rice production has become an end goal for these countries. Rice is considered not just an economic commodity, but also political commodity, giving a human security dimension to the rice sufficiency issue.
3. ASEAN Framework Agreement on Services, p. 2.
4. This sub-section is mostly drawn from Intal and Llanto (1998).
5. Basel I was issued by the Basel Committee on Banking Supervision in 1988 and 1996, respectively.
6. Bureau of Treasury Fiscal Report. Press Release, 19 December 2006.
7. Mely Caballero-Anthony, "Understanding Development Gaps in ASEAN", IDSS Commentaries, 31 May 2005.

8. Vientiane Action Programe (VAP) 2004–2010.
9. Ibid., p. 12.

## References

Amyx, Jennifer. "What Motivates Regional Financial Cooperation in East Asia Today?". Analysis from the East West Center. No. 76, February 2005.

Austria, Myrna S. "The Pattern of Intra-ASEAN Trade in the Priority Goods Sectors". Downloaded from http://www.aadcp-repsf.org/docs/03-006e. Final Main Report August 2004.

Balboa, Jenny and Erlinda Medalla. "Anti-Corruption and Governance: The Philippine Experience". http://www.apec.org.au/docs/06ASCC_HCMC/06_9_1_Balboa. pdf. Paper presented in the APEC Senior Officials Meeting II at Ho Chi Minh City, Vietnam, 23 May 2006.

Bautista, E. "A Study on Philippine Monetary and Banking Policy". Working Paper Series No. 92-11, PIDS, August 1992.

Bureau of Treasury (BTr). Press release (online). http://www.treasury.gov.ph/news/ news/FiscalReport-121906.pdf. 2007.

Caballero-Anthony, Mely. "Bridging Development Gaps in Southeast Asia: Towards an ASEAN Community". UNISCI Discussion Papers, May 2006.

Canlas, Mark Emmanuel. "Rewriting Fiscal Institutions in the Philippines: The Case for Fiscal Rules with Numerical Limits. Senate Planning Office". Unpublished paper, 2005.

Clarete, Ramon. "Philippines: Ex-post Effects of Trade Liberalization". Paper presented at the conference on Adjusting to Trade Reforms: What are the Major Challenges for Developing Countries?, organized by the Trade Analysis Branch, United Nations Conference on Trade and Development in Geneva, Switzerland, 18–19 January 2005.

Espenilla, Nestor. Jr. "Impact of Basel II on the Philippine Banking Sector with Special Focus on Risk Management". Asian Institute of Management Quarterly Risk Management Forum, 7 September 2005.

Estanislao, Jesus. "Southeast Asia: Development, Finance and Trade". In *A New ASEAN in A New Millenium*, edited by Simon S.C. Tay, Jesus Estanislao and Hadi Soesastro. Jakarta: Center for Strategic and International Studies, 2000.

Fabella, Raul V. "The Soft State, the Market, and Governance". In *Studies in Governance and Regulation: The Philippines*, edited by D.B. Canlas and S. Fujisaki. Tokyo: Institute of Developing Economies, 1999.

Hausmann, Ricardo and Dani Rodrik. "Doomed to Choose: Industrial Policy as Predicament". September 2006. Downloaded from http://www.cid.harvard. edu/bluesky/papers/hausmann_doomed_0609.pdf.

Intal, Ponciano Jr. and Gilberto Llanto. "Financial Reform and Development in the Philippines, 1980–1997: Imperatives, Performance and Challenges". PIDS Discussion Paper Series No. 98-02. January 1998.

Ito, Takatoshi and Yung Chul Park. "Exchange Rates in East Asia". In *Monetary and Financial Integration in East Asia: The Way Ahead*, vols. 1 and 2. Manila: Asian Development Bank, 2003.

Krumm, Kathie and Homi Kharas. *East Asia Integrates*. Washington, D.C.: The International Bank for Reconstruction and Development/The World Bank, 2004.

Ladan, Laarni. "Banking on Banking: Issues and Challenges Facing the Banking Sector". Senate Economic Planning Office. *Policy Insights*, May 2005.

Laird, Sam et al. "Coping with Trade Reforms: A Developing Country Perspective on the WTO Industrial Tariff Negotiations". DITC/UNCTAD, 2005.

Lamberte, M. "Assessment of Financial Market Reforms in the Philippines, 1980–1992". *Journal of Philippine Development* XX, no. 2 (Second Semester 1993): 231–59.

————— and G. Llanto. "A Study of Financial Sector Policies: The Philippine Case". Paper presented at the Conference on Financial Sector Development in Asia, Manila, September 1993.

Lamberte, M.B., H.R. Arboleda, and C.M. Reyes. "ASEAN Baseline Report: Measurements to Monitor Progress Towards the ASEAN Community". March 2006.

Llanto, Gilberto M. and Eduardo T. Gonzalez. "Policy Reforms and Institutional Weaknesses: Closing the Gap". Paper presented at the conference on Microeconomic Foundations of Economic Performance in East Asia, hosted by the Australian National University and the Philippine Institute for Development Studies, Manila, 23–24 November 2006.

Manasan, Rosario. "Fiscal Reform Agenda: Getting Ready for the Bumpy Ride Ahead". PIDS Discussion Paper Series No. 2004-26, August 2004.

Montiel, Peter. "An Overview of Monetary and Financial Integration in East Asia". *Monetary and Financial Integration in East Asia: The Way Ahead*, vols. 1 and 2. Manila: Asian Development Bank, 2003.

Pacific Economic Outlook. "Economic Prospects for the Asia Pacific Region". Pacific Economic Cooperation Council, 2004–2005.

—————. "Economic Prospects for the Asia Pacific Region". Pacific Economic Cooperation Council, 2005–2006.

Rodrik, Dani. "Industrial Policy for the Twenty-First Century". Downloaded from http://ksghome.harvard.edu/~drodrik/UNIDOSep.pdf. September 2004.

"Southeast Asia Human Development Report". UNDP 2005.

Tay, S., J. Estanislao, and H. Soesastro. *A New ASEAN in a New Millenium*. Jakarta: Centre for Strategic and International Studies, 2000.

Tetangco, Amando. "Continuing Reforms in the Philippine Financial Sector". *ABA Journal* XXI, no. 1 (2006).

Teves, Margarito. "Building on Success, Committed to Further Reforms". Unpublished paper. Department of Finance, 5 September 2005.

Venables, Anthony, J. "Winners and Losers from Regional Integration Agreements". *Economic Journal* 113 (October 2003).

World Bank Group in the Philippines. "Meeting Infrastructure Challenges in the Philippines". Washington, D.C.: International Bank for Reconstruction and Development/The World Bank, 2005.

Yap, Josef. "Trade, Competitiveness and Finance in the Philippine Manufacturing Sector". In *Finance and Competitiveness in Developing Countries*, edited by Jose Maria Fanelli and Rohinton Medhora. London: Routledge, 2002.

———. "Economic Integration and Regional Cooperation in East Asia: A Pragmatic View". PIDS Discussion Paper Series No. 2005-32, December 2005.

# 8

# MACROECONOMIC SURVEILLANCE AND FINANCIAL CO-OPERATION

## Worapot Manupipatpong

### I. LESSONS FROM AND RESPONSES TO THE EAST ASIAN FINANCIAL CRISIS

The East Asian financial crisis of 1997–98 provides several valuable lessons for all parties concerned, including governments, the private sector, and international financial institutions that came to the region's rescue. It highlights how vulnerable a small, open (capital account) economy is to an adverse shift of capital flows. It also demonstrates how quickly investors' confidence can erode and how their panic can spread contagion to neighbouring countries. The international financial rescue of 1997–98 came in slightly too late, and its initial liquidity support was too small to provide a sufficient cushion for the magnitude of capital outflows. The rescue consequently failed to calm the market, resulting in continued outflows of capital and depreciating exchange rates. Policy prescriptions also failed to recognize the negative effects of austerity measures imposed on the already worsening economies and the welfare of their people, plunging crisis-affected countries deeper into a recession.[1] As noted by Bird and Rajan (2001), there exists a trade-off between the severity of adjustment in the short run and the availability of international liquidity in the event of a crisis. In particular, the shortage of liquidity led to a quicker and more intensive economic adjustment that resulted in much larger output losses compared with previous crises.

In August 1997, Japan, together with several ASEAN countries, proposed the idea of an Asian Monetary Fund (AMF) to provide financial support for Thailand. It aimed to raise US$50 billion to US$60 billion from six ASEAN countries, Korea, China, Hong Kong, and Taiwan, and another US$50 billion from Japan. It was designed to be independent and would take up some IMF activities, such as regional surveillance.[2] However, the AMF proposal never got off the ground due to strong opposition from the United States and the International Monetary Fund (IMF). It was argued that such an arrangement would both create a problem of moral hazard and, in competing with the IMF, a double standard.[3]

## II. THE MANILA FRAMEWORK

A similar idea but significantly toned down — and with recognition of the IMF's central role in the international monetary system — emerged a few months later when ministry of finance and central bank deputies of fourteen Asia-Pacific economies met on 18–19 November 1997 in Manila to discuss a concerted approach to restoring financial stability in the region.[4] They came up with new initiatives under the so-called Manila Framework, that included regional surveillance and a regional financing arrangement. In particular, the Framework called for:

1. a mechanism for regional surveillance to complement the global surveillance of the IMF;
2. enhanced economic and technical co-operation, particularly in strengthening domestic financial systems and regulatory capacities;
3. measures to strengthen the IMF's capacity to respond to financial crises; and
4. a co-operative financing arrangement that would supplement IMF resources.

The announcement made on 19 November 1997, which is an agreed summary discussion of the meeting, highlighted the need for the IMF to quickly mobilize its financial assistance on "a scale sufficient to restore market confidence".[5] In that context, the deputies also agreed to explore ways to supplement IMF and other international financial institution resources through a co-operative financing arrangement in the region.

## III. THE ASEAN SURVEILLANCE PROCESS

At their special meeting in Kuala Lumpur a few weeks later, the ASEAN finance ministers concurred with the proposals of the Manila Framework and decided to implement it. The first initiative of the Framework — a mechanism for regional surveillance — was deliberated further at the Second ASEAN Finance Ministers Meeting (AFMM) on 28 February 1998 in Jakarta, where it was agreed that the ASEAN surveillance mechanism should be established immediately, within the general framework of the IMF and with the assistance of the Asian Development Bank (ADB).

Since then, the details of the mechanism have been worked out by the senior ASEAN finance and central bank officials, in consultation with representatives from the ADB. A Terms of Understanding (ToU) for the ASEAN Surveillance Process (ASP) was finalized together with the indicative implementation activities in August 1998 in Kuala Lumpur, and was subsequently endorsed by the Special ASEAN Finance Ministers Meeting in Washington, D.C. on 5 December 1998.

Under the ToU on the ASP, the ASEAN finance ministers wanted the ASP to be informal, simple, based on the peer review process, and complementary to the global surveillance exercise undertaken by the IMF. Recognizing the need for closer economic review and policy dialogues, they agreed to share a set of baseline data, as provided to the IMF during the Article IV consultation mission, and decided to meet more frequently — at least twice a year — to discuss surveillance matters. The ADB also agreed to provide technical assistance to the development and operation of ASP mainly through capacity-building of ASEAN finance and central bank officers, national surveillance units in some ASEAN countries, and the ASEAN Secretariat.[6]

To co-ordinate the ASP, a small unit called the ASEAN Surveillance Co-ordinating Unit (ASCU) was set up at the ASEAN Secretariat as well as in the ten ASEAN economies, to monitor global economic and financial developments, and to co-ordinate all surveillance related activities, including preparing semi-annual ASEAN Surveillance Reports (ASRs). The ASR analyses the most recent developments in major international economies and the ten ASEAN countries, identifies any emerging or increasing vulnerability, and raises important and relevant policy issues for the consideration of the ASEAN finance ministers during their peer review.

## IV. REGIONAL SURVEILLANCE OF ECONOMIC RECOVERY AND REFORMS

The ASP became operational in early March 1999, when the ASEAN finance ministers conducted their first peer review in Hanoi. At their peer review, the ministers pledged to persevere with structural reforms even though financial stability had been largely restored. The discussion was also focused on policies that support revival of domestic demand and economic activities (accommodative monetary and fiscal policies), and reform of the international financial architecture.[7] On the latter, they agreed on an ASEAN position on the international financial architecture, including among others:

1. a call for a global effort to resolve the crisis and to recognize the diverse circumstances and priorities of individual economies at different stages of development;
2. a call for due priority to be accorded to measures to protect the poor and most vulnerable segments of society in international reform efforts; and
3. a call for closer and more co-ordinated monitoring of short-term capital flows, including disclosure and information-sharing among national and international regulators.

During subsequent peer reviews, which have been conducted twice a year, the ASEAN finance ministers exchanged views on recent economic developments with an emphasis on recovery and structural reform efforts and progress. At their second peer review in November 1999 in Manila, they agreed to press on with structural reforms, including the implementation of measures in the financial sector, further progress in corporate and debt restructuring, improvement of legal structures, and implementation of social safety net programmes. Progress on these reforms, the status of economic recovery, external challenges, and measures to sustain economic recovery were closely monitored and remained the main issues for the subsequent peer review discussions.[8]

## How Effective is the ASP?

Since the ASP was designed to complement IMF surveillance, we could measure its effectiveness to the extent to which it fills a gap in the IMF surveillance process, and specifically in its ability to forewarn — and thus prevent — a financial crisis. The shortcoming, noted by Crow, Arriazu, and Thygesen (1999), is not the (poor) quality of policy advice, but rather the reluctance of the recipient government to implement the Fund's recommendations, particularly on exchange rate policy, which is a highly political issue. It was further observed in the same report that "the policy advice did not come early enough in the case of Thailand where in other cases the advice, early or not, was not nearly as strong".[9]

As mentioned above, one of the key aspects of the ASP is the peer review process, which recognizes the potential benefits of peer pressure in encouraging a member government to implement politically difficult policy adjustments that are needed to address increasing vulnerability in its economy.[10] The effectiveness of the peer review in this regard would, therefore, depend on: the ability to detect early signs of emerging or increasing vulnerability that might lead to a crisis if not timely and properly addressed; the ability to identify appropriate policy responses; and the ability to engage officials concerned in a frank discussion on these policy issues.

## How Does the ASP Spot Emerging Weaknesses or Vulnerability?

ASCU has been monitoring closely the developments of prudential indicators in six key sectors: real,[11] monetary, fiscal, external, corporate, and social sectors. In doing so, it relies on the submission of surveillance indicators by the authorities (ministries of finance or central banks), as well as relevant indicators that can be obtained from public sources (member countries' websites, publications, relevant publications of international financial institutions such as the IMF, World Bank and ADB). Any adverse developments, or lack of progress in structural reforms, are brought to the attention of relevant authorities (such as the ASEAN finance and central bank deputies and the ASEAN finance ministers), together with policy recommendations, normally through the ASR.[12] Complementing the submission of surveillance data, country reports have usually been prepared by surveillance officials of the ASEAN countries and provided to ASCU. The Regional Economic Monitoring Unit of the ADB also prepares an independent report on the "ASEAN Economic Outlook" and presents it to the ASEAN finance and central bank deputies meetings.

Recognizing the limited resources, both at the ASEAN Secretariat and some member states, the ADB and United Nations Development Programme (UNDP) provided technical assistance to ASCU, which allowed it to outsource technical studies on important policy issues, such as financial and corporate restructuring, fiscal sustainability, and the development of an ASEAN bond market.[13] Policy recommendations from these studies were then discussed among the ASEAN finance and central bank officials and incorporated into the ASR for further discussion at the peer review. The ADB also provided technical assistance for surveillance training of the ASEAN finance and central bank officials and ASCU staff, and capacity-building for ASCU and national surveillance units in Cambodia, Laos, Indonesia, the Philippines, Thailand, and Vietnam.

Technical assistance from the ADB, UNDP, Economic and Social Commission for Asia and the Pacific (ESCAP), and Organization for Economic Co-operation and Development (OECD) has also been provided to improve on the availability and timeliness of key surveillance indicators in some countries. At present, the quality of surveillance data that member countries submit to ASCU is uneven. While this mainly reflects the different stage of development in member countries' data collection and reporting systems, it is sometimes caused by the authority's reluctance to provide some data. Poor quality of data, particularly on the availability and timeliness of some key indicators in some countries, contributes to the inability to conduct cross-country analysis in some sectors, and it limits the ability to monitor closely developments in those sectors where only annual data are available (and sometimes with considerable lags).

## Does ASP Provide Value Added to the Existing Surveillance Mechanisms?

Despite the above shortcomings, there are a few areas where the ASP may be able to provide value added as an early warning mechanism. While recognizing the comparatively high quality of the IMF surveillance and policy advice, Crow, Arriazu, and Thygesen (1999) noted that its surveillance team needs more financial sector expertise, more policy-making experience, and a greater involvement of outside experts given its expanded coverage and past criticism of not paying due attention to the country's current — including political — situation and differences among countries. It was further recognized that "Fund advice often focuses on identifying the first-best general policy. But when policy-makers, quite reasonably, respond that they live in a second-best world, staff are apparently not as good at suggesting how the first-best might actually be implemented in practice, or at developing and analysing alternative, specific, policies."[14] Therefore, one main advantage of the ASP is its surveillance network, comprising a group of regional experts and ASCU staff. Being familiar with the region on a day-to-day basis enables regional economists to better appreciate the impact a particular policy adjustment would have on the regional economies, or the influence that political situations can have over government policy decision-making.

Another gap that the ASP can potentially fill has to do with the current efforts to encourage countries to adopt internationally agreed standards and codes in order to enhance the effective operation of market forces and the resilience of financial systems. These standards and codes include the IMF code of good practices on transparency in monetary and financial policies, the IMF code of good practices on fiscal transparency, and the OECD principles of corporate governance. Observance of these codes and principles, once agreed, can be monitored and their progress discussed as a continuing agenda under the ASP.

## How Does the ASEAN Surveillance Peer Review Work?

Policy issues are identified through the ASP and discussed first among ASEAN senior finance and central bank officials (during the ASEAN Finance and Central Bank Deputies Meeting, or AFDM), when they consider the ASEAN Surveillance Report prepared by ASCU.[15] Agreed policy issues are then brought up for discussion by the ASEAN finance ministers during their peer reviews. The setting for the peer review session is usually less formal to encourage ministers to engage in an open and frank discussion of one another's economic situations and policies, particularly where they may have contagious effects on other economies in the region. This was indeed the main concept agreed to by a group of finance ministers who pushed for the ASP in 1998. In this regard, the peer review is at least as effective as the executive board review of the staff's surveillance report since important economic developments and policy advice are discussed among countries that are likely to have to share — or bear — the consequences of a particular development, situation, or policy.

The peer review is considered to be a departure from the "ASEAN way" of non-interference in other member countries' domestic affairs. As mentioned above, ASCU watches closely for any emerging or increasing vulnerability, either external or national, and brings it to the attention of the ASEAN finance and central bank deputies and finance ministers for policy discussion. If nothing has yet been done to address such a vulnerability, a recommendation will be put forward for their consideration. If policy measures have already been announced and implemented, its progress would be monitored, assessed, and reported. As such, the forum provides both peer pressure by encouraging timely and proper policy actions, and peer support by providing assistance and sharing of relevant experiences and practices, from within the region and internationally. The peer review focuses on important economic and financial issues (and not political issues — unless they could have serious adverse economic and financial implications) that need to be addressed to promote financial stability and sustained economic growth in the region (or to prevent contagion), which encourages the officials concerned to willingly share their views and openly discuss the policy issues being tabled for their consideration.

However, the peer review could be made more effective if the heads of central banks/monetary authorities also joined their respective finance ministers at the peer review, as it would allow for a more fruitful discussion over a wider range of economic and financial issues. At present, the central bank forum is held separately, even though senior central bank officials participate and provide inputs on monetary policies and situations at the AFDM. Recognizing the benefits of their involvement, but mindful of different practices regarding the independence of the central banks or monetary authorities, the ministers agreed that the participation by (the heads of) the central banks or monetary authorities at their meetings would be voluntary. Greater involvement by ASCU in the IMF's Article IV consultation missions to ASEAN countries would also be required to minimize overlapping activities.[16]

## V. FROM REGIONAL SURVEILLANCE TO REGIONAL FINANCING ARRANGEMENT

Over the past few years, regional co-operation has not only intensified but also expanded to include neighbouring countries in Northeast Asia, particularly China, Japan, and South Korea. The widened forum has been officially named "ASEAN Plus Three". ASEAN financial co-operation with China, Japan, and South Korea (ASEAN Plus Three) has gathered pace since March 1999 when the first ASEAN Plus Three Finance and Central Bank Deputies Meeting was held in Hanoi, followed by the ASEAN Plus Three Finance Ministers Meeting in Manila a month later. At the ASEAN Plus Three Summit in Manila in late November that same year, the ASEAN Plus Three leaders, in their joint declaration on East Asia co-operation, agreed to "enhance this dialogue process and strengthen co-operation with a view to advancing East Asian collaboration in priority areas of shared interest and concern even as they look to future challenges". Particularly in monetary and financial co-operation, they agreed to "strengthen policy dialogue, co-ordination and collaboration on the financial, monetary and fiscal issues of common interest, focusing initially on issues related to macroeconomic risk management, enhancing corporate governance, monitoring regional capital flows, strengthening banking and financial systems, reforming the international financial architecture, and enhancing self-help and support mechanisms in East Asia through the ASEAN Plus Three Framework, including the ongoing dialogue and co-operation mechanism of the ASEAN Plus Three finance and central bank leaders and officials".[17]

Priorities for regional co-operation activities among the ASEAN Plus Three countries include enhancing self-help and support mechanisms, monitoring capital flows, and establishing mechanisms for closer and more effective economic review and policy dialogue.

## VI. THE CHIANG MAI INITIATIVE

At the ASEAN Plus Three Finance Ministers Meeting in Chiang Mai in May 2000, one of the main topics of discussion was how to develop a regional financing arrangement that could be utilized to maintain financial stability in the East Asian region. At that time, the discussion on the expansion of the ASEAN swap arrangement (ASA) to include all ASEAN countries and increase its size to US$1 billion by the ASEAN central banks was near its final stage. The ASEAN Plus Three countries decided to combine the expanded ASA with a network of bilateral swap arrangements (BSAs) among the ASEAN Plus Three countries to establish the first regional financing arrangement called the "Chiang Mai Initiative" (CMI).

The expanded ASA, while relatively small in size compared with other international financing facilities, is unconditional and designed for quick activation and disbursement. It became effective in November 2000 and allows member banks to swap their local currencies with major international currencies — such as the U.S. dollar, Euro, and yen — for a period of up to six months, and for an amount up to twice their committed amount under the ASA.[18] In line with its role as a rapid disbursement facility, a member's swap request for temporary liquidity or balance of payments assistance will be confirmed through the Agent Bank,[19] which will inform and consult with the rest of the members to assess and process the request as expeditiously as possible.

To facilitate the bilateral negotiations on the BSAs, the ASEAN Plus Three countries agreed on the basic framework and main principles that include, among others, linkages to the IMF, maturity, and interest rate structure. Recognizing that the problems leading to balance of payments imbalances may be structural in nature, one of the main conditions is that members who request liquidity support through this network should also look to the

IMF for assistance, except for the first 10 per cent of the BSA facility. This does not mean, however, that negotiation with the IMF needs to be finalized before the member can draw upon the BSA, as that would defeat its main objective of quick disbursement. What it does require, as a minimum, is that the swap requesting member takes necessary steps to seek additional support from the IMF, unless it is already in the IMF programme or eligible for the Contingent Credit Line (CCL).

As agreed under the main principles of the BSA, the swap will be for a period of ninety days, renewable up to a maximum of seven times, at an interest rate equivalent to the London Interbank Offered Rate (LIBOR), plus 150 basis points for the first drawing and first renewal. Thereafter, the premium increases by 50 basis points every two renewals, subject to a maximum of 300 basis points. Negotiations on the swap arrangements are to be conducted bilaterally based on the agreed main principles. Details of the final agreement can differ, including the size and some covenants, taking into account specific needs and legal structures of the recipient countries.

The interest rate structure was designed to address partially the concerns on moral hazard associated with cheap financing. The predeter-mined rates may be considered higher than what some ASEAN countries can obtain in good times, but not unrealistically high, given that this facility is likely to be activated in an event potentially leading to a crisis. Compared with the historical movements of sovereign spreads during past crises, these rates are reasonably well below the rates that the private market would require in the event of the crisis (if at all). The progressive rate structure is also designed to discourage the continued use of this facility as medium-term financing.

The linkage to the IMF also helps prevent moral hazard, given the current lack of a surveillance mechanism for the ASEAN Plus Three countries. In its current form, the linkage to the Fund should not be cause for concern, that it would jeopardize the quick disbursing ability of the BSAs, or that member countries would end up with too strict conditionality. For one thing, while the IMF has been criticized in its past rescue packages for its textbook type of policy advice and programme conditionality, which tend to be too strict — as well as disregarding differences among countries, and paying little attention to social consequences — its stance of late seems to show a willingness to balance the trade-off between its imposition of swift reforms and austerity measures, and the general welfare of the recipient's economy. For another, the IMF has also improved its financing facility to deal better with capital account crises, and recognized the need for a quick disbursing facility and introduced the Supplemental Reserve Facility (SRF) at the end of 1997. The SRF has no predetermined limits, but carries higher and progressive interest charges. It was further complemented by the introduction of the CCL in 1999, which aims to provide precautionary credit lines to countries with demonstrably sound policies, but wish to secure an additional facility that they could draw upon in time of crisis.

The CMI can be considered as the region's first line of defence, complementing the Fund's SRF and CCL, while at the same time providing member countries some leverage in negotiating with the IMF for additional financing (and reasonable conditionality), that would turn their economies around, without severe output losses or excessive financial volatility. To date, six BSAs have been successfully concluded with a combined total size of US$14 billion, while several others are under negotiation. The concluded BSAs are summarized in Table 1.

To complement the CMI, the ASEAN Plus Three countries agreed to strengthen their economic review and policy dialogues. In this regard, an ASEAN Plus Three Study Group was established to explore possible arrangements for a more effective economic review and policy dialogues among the ASEAN Plus Three countries. At present, senior finance and central bank officials exchange views on economic and financial developments — through country presentations and discussion on issues of mutual interest — whenever they meet, which is usually twice a year.

A separate but related development to further strengthen regional co-operation on surveillance is regional efforts to exchange information on short-term capital flows among ASEAN Plus Three countries. Currently, the exchange of information on short-term capital flows is conducted bilaterally between interested member countries. To facilitate this, Japan has been providing technical assistance to some member countries to improve

### TABLE 1
### Current Status of BSA Network

| BSA[a] | Currencies | Status | Size |
|---|---|---|---|
| Japan–Korea | U.S. dollar/won | Concluded/4 July 2001 | US$2 billion |
| Japan–Thailand | U.S. dollar/baht | Concluded/30 July 2001 | US$3 billion |
| Japan–Philippines | U.S. dollar/peso | Concluded/27 August 2001 | US$3 billion |
| Japan–Malaysia | U.S. dollar/ringgit | Concluded/5 October 2001 | US$1 billion |
| China–Thailand | U.S. dollar/baht | Concluded/6 December 2001 | US$2 billion |
| Japan–China[b] | yen/renminbi | Concluded/28 March 2002 | US$3 billion |

NOTES

a.  These are in addition to the bilateral swaps that Japan is providing to Korea and Malaysia, under the New Miyazawa Initiative.

b.  The BSA between Japan and China is a two-way swap.

their monitoring, collection, and reporting systems on capital flows, with an emphasis on short-term flows.

## VII. BEYOND THE CMI: AN EAST ASIAN MONETARY FUND

Given the recent developments on the CMI and ASEAN Plus Three economic review and policy dialogue, is the ASEAN Plus Three region moving towards putting in place a regional self-help and support mechanism reminiscent of the Asian Monetary Fund? Compared with the IMF's three main operational aspects — financing, sur-veillance, and policy adjustment programmes — the ASEAN Plus Three countries are gradually developing a regional self-help and support mechanism that partly resembles a regional monetary fund, through its establishment of the CMI and ongoing efforts to strengthen its regional surveillance mechanism. Putting these two initiatives together gives us a regional support mechanism that may eventually lead to the establishment of an East Asian Monetary Fund (EAMF).

The establishment of the CMI reflects, or in fact implements, the fourth initiative of the Manila Framework that calls for a co-operative financing arrangement that would supplement IMF resources. While the CMI alone is unlikely to be sufficient in providing the needed liquidity in times of crisis, it streamlines the financing process by formalizing the regional support arrangement (or bilateral donors' support), so that it can be quickly activated, thereby providing timely (though partial) financial support without which the resulting policy adjustment might have to be unnecessarily large and painful. Under the present CMI arrangement, the IMF still plays a key role as the lender of last resort.

With closer co-operation and integration of the thirteen economies over time, the BSAs between China, Japan, and Korea and the ASEAN countries are likely to graduate into two-way swaps first, and ultimately, a multilateral swaps facility similar to the ASA as (political) trust builds up, along with intensifying co-operation activities. Considering the ASEAN Plus Three estimated combined foreign exchange reserves of US$800 billion, the size of BSAs can also be easily increased when they are to be reviewed, depending on the needs and development of the regional financing arrangement over the next two years. The CMI (the ASA and BSAs) could, therefore, gradually become the region's first line of defence against a balance of payment crisis.

With the CMI being gradually established, the attention of the ASEAN Plus Three countries now turns to the other component that is at least as important as the financing facility: the regional surveillance mechanism. As mentioned above, current surveillance among the ASEAN Plus Three countries is conducted through the voluntary exchange of views and self-reporting, with no standard format or template. With an increasing number of BSAs being concluded, a more formal mechanism for surveillance is required to monitor more closely and effectively economic and financial developments, at least in countries that are parties to the BSAs. This type of surveillance is needed not only for early warning purposes, but also to enable swap providing countries to gain a better appreciation of the situations and liquidity needs of countries that request an activation of the BSAs.

## How Could the Current Economic Review and Policy Dialogue among ASEAN Plus Three Countries be Strengthened?

While possible modalities are currently being considered by the ASEAN Plus Three study group, certain alternatives are worth mentioning. The first and probably the most obvious is to build upon the existing process, the ASP. With its coverage of the ten ASEAN economies, the ASP could be expanded to cover China, Japan, and Korea, with appropriate capacity-building to address the weaknesses mentioned earlier. However, it would require member countries to regularly (at least quarterly) make available selected indicators based on an agreed template. The ASEAN Plus Three finance and central bank deputies and finance ministers would also have to include peer review sessions to discuss policy issues raised by the "ASEAN Plus Three Surveillance Process". Despite being a larger group than ASEAN, it might work more effectively since it is tied to possible financing in times of balance of payment difficulties.[20] Being within an ASEAN Plus Three framework, it is also easier for the ASEAN countries to break away from their tradition of non-interference.

A weaker (but easier to implement) arrangement would be to follow the modality adopted in the exchange of information on capital flows, which is agreed to be voluntary and bilateral in nature.[21] To facilitate the comparability of country presentation and make it more focused, an agreed format and data template could be designed and adopted. Countries that are already parties to the BSAs could start first, while others could join in when they become members of the BSA network.

An ideal structure for the most effective regional surveillance would be to establish an independent institution to conduct surveillance and provide policy advice. To optimize the utilization of resources and to avoid duplication of activities, co-operation and co-ordination with the IMF should be sought as much as possible. For example, the Article IV mission staff report could be made available to the ASEAN Plus Three surveillance team on a confidential basis, subject to the member countries' consent. The size and the focus of this surveillance unit would, therefore, depend on how IMF resources would be shared.

Given the current stage of regional co-operation among the ASEAN Plus Three countries, the most likely scenario may be voluntary participation to get the regional (East Asian) surveillance off the ground, similar to the modality for the exchange of information on short-term capital flows, while a more formal structure continues to be explored. The exact modality should, however, become clearer within the next few months when the ASEAN Plus Three study group concludes its deliberation on the issue. Whatever modality of regional surveillance is chosen, it should build on what the IMF is already doing on exchange rate system surveillance, and try to fill in any remaining gaps. For example, the ASEAN Plus Three surveillance mechanism should be in a better position to identify the "second best" policy measures that are more appropriate for the crisis-affected countries in the region, taking into account specific conditions of member economies, and the most likely outcome of the implementation of such measures including financial contagion.

Regional surveillance and peer review when conducted effectively can serve as early warning and early action systems that would significantly improve the crisis prevention capacity of the new international financial system. Surveillance can also help identify the appropriate liquidity needs of a country where a crisis is looming. This is one of the two major roles proposed by Bergsten (1998) when he introduced the idea of an Asia-Pacific Monetary Fund (APMF) that builds on the Manila Framework. Regional peer pressure, he noted, is probably the most promising route to induce anticipatory policy measures. The other role that the APMF is expected to play is as a provider of bridge financing through a quick disbursing mechanism. The establishment of the CMI, which shares the same financing role as the APMF, and current efforts to put an effective regional surveillance in place, however, is contrary to Bergsten's view that "no Asian country could effectively lead the effort".

How much would the (East Asian) region need to provide proper protection against a future crisis? While it may be impossible to predict what a future crisis will look like, or where it might happen, a review of rescue packages for past crises could still give us a useful clue as to the amount a country may need should a financial crisis arise. For the 1997–98 East Asian financial crisis, the combined costs of bailing out Indonesia, Thailand, and Korea was US$118 billion, almost half of which was for Korea. About 30 per cent of the financing came from the IMF, 20 per cent from the ADB and the World Bank, and the remaining half from bilateral donors who were mostly from the region (except in the case of Korea). Further, assuming that: (1) the

EAMF acts as a first line of defence by providing quick short-term financing to counter any possible speculative attack and to stabilize the impacts of sudden capital outflows; and (2) financing is unlikely to be provided to several countries at the same time but to the first country that is most vulnerable, US$60 billion would seem sufficient.[22] This amount represents about 7 per cent of the region's combined international reserves.[23]

Finally, should the EAMF operate independently of the IMF? Given the size of the CMI at present, it is unlikely that it alone can sufficiently provide the amount of liquidity needed to address a financial crisis. Therefore, even with an established regional surveillance capability, it would still have to complement the IMF. Even when the EAMF can be established with sizeable contributions — that is, US$60 billion — it would still be desirable to achieve a certain degree of co-operation with the IMF. In this regard, East Asian countries may wish to follow the good example set by the ADB and the World Bank. They recently entered into a co-operative agreement that aims to strengthen co-operation between the two organizations, minimizing overlapping activities and helping them to focus on areas where each has a comparative advantage.

With the completion of the network of BSAs under the CMI and the establishment of a regional surveillance mechanism in East Asia probably within the next few years, an East Asian Monetary Fund is gradually becoming a reality. Its development will influence the ways in which East Asian countries will work together, as well as with international financial institutions (particularly the IMF and, to a lesser extent, the ADB and the World Bank) in promoting greater financial stability in the region. There will definitely be closer co-ordination as well as more regional elements in surveillance, no matter what modality for East Asian surveillance is pursued. Countries in the region will rely more on one another in their efforts to prevent, as well as respond to, future crises. In that connection, the EAMF and other similar regional organizations will become an integral part of the new international financial architecture, playing an increasingly substantial role in safeguarding the region's financial systems, while the IMF will continue its key role in maintaining global financial order as well as providing medium to long-term financing to crisis-affected countries.

## Notes

The views expressed in this article are those of the author and do not necessarily reflect those of the ASEAN Secretariat, ASEAN, ASEAN Plus Three, or any of their members.

1. Thailand is a good example, where its IMF financial support package seemed like a copy of those previously designed for Latin American countries, which experienced external imbalances with massive public debt, hyperinflation, and low savings rate, none of which was applicable to Thailand. Amid falling private spending, the IMF programme further contracted public spending by requiring a budget surplus of 1 per cent of GDP. Closure of domestic finance companies without proper support measures also eroded investors' confidence and precipitated the crisis.

2. IMF surveillance under the Article IV consultation is bilateral in nature. The outcome of its mission has never been discussed in a regional setting, even though its Executive Board may consist of some executive directors from the Asian region.

3. One main concern for a competing facility is that the recipient country would tend to opt for the facility with less stringent conditions, if conditions being imposed are different, thereby creating a double standard.

4. The fourteen economies were: Australia, Brunei Darussalam, Canada, People's Republic of China, Hong Kong SAR of China, Indonesia, Japan, Korea, Malaysia, New Zealand, the Philippines, Singapore, Thailand, and the United States.

5. Paragraph 7 of the Agreed Summary of Discussions, Meeting of Asian Finance and Central Bank Deputies, Manila, Philippines, 18–19 November 1997.

6. The ToU on the ASP is available on the ASEAN Secretariat's website at <www. aseansec.org>.

7. This is in addition to the "Bold Measures" announced by the ASEAN leaders at their Sixth ASEAN Summit in Hanoi on 16 December 1998, in an effort to attract foreign direct investment into the region. The Bold Measures included, among others, (1) acceleration of the ASEAN Free Trade Area by one year, from 2003 to 2002; and (2) tax breaks, 100 per cent foreign equity ownership, duty free imports, and other incentives for investments during 1999–2000.

8. The outcome of the peer review is usually made public, and included in the joint ministerial statements issued after the AFMM. They are also available on the ASEAN Secretariat website at <www.aseansec.org>. The ASEAN Surveillance Reports, on which the peer review is based, are treated as confidential documents.

9. Crow, Arriazu, and Thygesen (1999, p. 52).

10. It has been noted by Fisher (2001), though indirectly, that Thailand had been warned of the looming crisis, but apparently no policy action was taken by the Thai government at that time.

11. Mainly through the development of gross domestic product (GDP) and its components (by sectors and by expenditures).

12. No early warning model is used at present, though the ADB is working on an early warning system prototype that each member state can adapt to fit its current economic structure and stage of development.

13. ASCU is currently staffed with two economists and two research assistants

(technical officers). The unit also co-ordinates other finance co-operation activities in ASEAN and ASEAN Plus Three, in addition to the ASP.

14. Crow, Arriazu, and Thygesen (1999).
15. The ASEAN central banks/monetary authorities have their own exclusive forum called the ASEAN Central Bank Forum, where the deputy governors share views on economic and financial situations and discuss monetary policies. They usually meet "back to back" with the AFDM, and brief the AFDM on the outcome of its discussion. Deputy governors also attend the AFDM.
16. ASCU was not allowed to participate, even though the Fund has pledged support for the ASP, in past surveillance missions either as a member or an observer of the IMF surveillance team or the member country's team. The main purpose of ASCU involvement in the Article IV mission is to minimize duplication of surveillance activities. The IMF cited its confidentiality agreement with member countries, but suggested that ASCU could participate as a member of the government team, while the government would prefer that ASCU be a part of the Fund's mission. As a result, no participation by ASCU in Article IV missions has been made to date.
17. Joint Statement on East Asia Co-operation, Third Informal ASEAN Summit, Manila, 28 November 1999. Available at <www.aseansec.org>.
18. The first Memorandum of Understanding on the ASA was signed on 5 August 1977 among the original five ASEAN central banks/monetary authorities of Indonesia, Malaysia, the Philippines, Thailand, and Singapore, with a total facility amount of US$100 million. This was subsequently increased to US$200 million in 1978.
19. In order to co-ordinate the implementation of the ASA, an Agent Bank shall be appointed on a rotating basis, based on alphabetical order, for a term of two years.
20. As Crow, Arriazu, and Thygesen (1999) noted in their report, the IMF's advice carries more weight (compared with others that do not lend) when it is attached to a financial programme, or because it might be called upon to extend financing.
21. This loose form of surveillance may be acceptable as a starting point, but will not be as effective as formal surveillance, since member countries will generally tend to be optimistic on their economic prospects and may try to avoid sensitive issues.
22. This amount represents the value of all contributions in a network of bilateral swaps or multilateral swap arrangements, while the amount available to each member would depend on the bilateral swaps that it has in effect, or some predetermined multiple of its contribution in the case of a multilateral swap arrangement.
23. Japan's foreign exchange reserves at the end of 2001 stood at about US$400 billion, while China had US$200 billion. ASEAN and Korea made up the balance with about US$100 billion each.

# References

Bergsten, Fred C. "Reviving the Asian Monetary Fund". Policy Brief No. 98-8, Institute for International Economics, 1998.

Bird, Graham and Ramkishen Rajan. "Regional Arrangements for Providing Liquidity in a Financial Crisis: Developments in Asia". Discussion Paper No. 0127, Centre for International Economic Studies, 2001.

Boorman, Jack, Timothy Lane, Marianne Schulze-Ghattas, Ales Bulir, Atish R. Ghosh, Javier Hamann, Alexandros Mourmouras, and Steven Phillips. "Managing Financial Crisis: The Experience in East Asia". IMF Working Paper 00/107, Washington, D.C., June 2000.

Crow, John, Ricardo Arriazu, and Niels Thygesen. *External Evaluation of IMF Surveillance*. Washington, D.C.: IMF, 1999.

Eichengreen, Barry. "Toward a New International Financial Architecture: A Practical Post-Asia Agenda". Institute for International Economics, February 1999.

Fisher, Stanley. "Asia and the IMF". Speech delivered at the Institute of Policy Studies, Singapore, June 2001.

Larsen, Flemming. "The Challenges of the New Financial Economy: the Efforts of the IMF to Reduce the Risk of Financial Crisis". Statement at the Joint Meeting of the Commission des Finances of the French National Assembly and the Haut Conseil de la Co-operation Internationale, Paris, November 2001.

Manzano, George. "Is There Any Value-Added in the ASEAN Surveillance Process". Discussion Paper No. 0105, Centre for International Economic Studies, February 2001.

Masson, Paul R. and Michael Mussa. "The Role of the IMF: Financing and Its Interactions with Adjustment and Surveillance". IMF Pamphlet Series No. 50. Washington, D.C., 1995.

Rana, Pradumna. "Monetary and Financial Co-operation in East Asia: the Chiang Mai Initiative and Beyond". Presentation at the KIEP/NEAEF Conference on Strengthening Economic Co-operation in Northeast Asia, Honolulu, August 2001.

Rose, Andrew. "Is There a Case for an Asian Monetary Fund". FRBSF Economic Letter No. 99-37, 17 December 1999.

Wade, Robert. "The Resources Lie Within". *Economist*, 5 November 1998.

Yoshitomi, Masaru and Sayuri Shirai, "Technical Background Paper for Policy Recommendations for Preventing Another Capital Account Crisis". ADB Institute, Tokyo, July 2000.

# INDEX

www.ingramcontent.com/pod-product-compliance
Lightning Source LLC
Chambersburg PA
CBHW020353270326
41926CB00007B/419